LIBRARY SERVICES FOR ADULTS IN THE 21ST CENTURY

D0760192

LIBRARY SERVICES FOR ADULTS IN THE 21ST CENTURY

Elsie A. Rogers Halliday Okobi

LIBRARIES UNLIMITED

AN IMPRINT OF ABC-CLIO, LLC
Santa Barbara, California • Denver, Colorado • Oxford, England

Copyright 2014 by Elsie A. Rogers Halliday Okobi

All rights reserved. No part of this publication may be reproduced, stored in a retrieval system, or transmitted, in any form or by any means, electronic, mechanical, photocopying, recording, or otherwise, except for the inclusion of brief quotations in a review, without prior permission in writing from the publisher.

Library of Congress Cataloging-in-Publication Data

Okobi, Elsie A. Rogers Halliday.
  Library services for adults in the 21st century / Elsie A. Rogers Halliday Okobi.
    pages cm
  Includes bibliographical references and index.
    ISBN 978–1–59158–705–7 (pbk.) — ISBN 978–1–61069–618–0 (ebook)   1. Adult services in public libraries—United States. 2. Public services (Libraries)—United States. 3. Libraries and adult education—United States. 4. Libraries and community—United States. I. Title.
  Z711.92.A32O38   2014
  027.6—dc23   2013030621

ISBN: 978–1–59158–705–7
EISBN: 978–1–61069–618–0

18 17 16 15 14   1 2 3 4 5

This book is also available on the World Wide Web as an eBook.
Visit www.abc-clio.com for details.

Libraries Unlimited
An Imprint of ABC-CLIO, LLC

ABC-CLIO, LLC
130 Cremona Drive, P.O. Box 1911
Santa Barbara, California 93116-1911

This book is printed on acid-free paper ∞

Manufactured in the United States of America

This book is dedicated to my wonderful and patient children Obidimma (Obi), Chukwnweze (Chukky), Olisemeka (Emmy), and Ndidi (Didi), with whom I started this journey of life as a single parent 28 years ago. We made it, and I thank you for being good and loving kids.

CONTENTS

Contents

PREFACE

The twenty-first-century adult has more leisure time and can look forward to a longer, more active social, and more intellectual life than their twentieth-century counterparts. The twenty-first-century public adult librarian needs to develop and implement adult services that address the composition, diversity, and needs of today's adult population. This book begins (in Part I) with a survey of the history and development of services to adults and the status of adult services today. It will also introduce the reader to adult learning and leisure theory and how it applies to adult services in the public library. Part II covers tools for planning and assessing adult services. Part III focuses on various specific adult services. Part IV discusses core competencies for the adult services librarian in terms of initial professional training and continuing professional development.

The last text devoted to the topic of adult services was published in 1990: *Adult Services: An Enduring Focus for Public Libraries* (Heim and Wallace). Other more recent texts mention some aspects of adult services such as readers' advisory services, genealogy, or services for minorities. However, there does not seem to be any single current text that can be used for training adult services librarians to work with today's adults.

Library Services for Adults in the 21st Century grew out of the need for a textbook that could be used to teach a course in materials and services for adults in the Library and Information Program at Southern Connecticut State University in New Haven, Connecticut. The primary role of public libraries has remained the same since the inception of public libraries three centuries ago—to provide education and free access to information for the masses. Public libraries have been called the people's university. Public libraries have been trying to respond to the shifting needs of adults. The services remain the same, but the patron population has been changing as it has become more diverse. Therefore, it requires services tailored to the information needs of ethnic populations, baby boomers, and other special populations. Public libraries have embraced the use of technology in the delivery of services. In writing this book, I tried to provide a framework for providing instruction for adult services in public libraries. Each library will have to adapt the framework to suit the needs of the patrons that it serves.

The book is divided into four sections. Part I deals with the historical definition of adults and adult services. Chapter 1 addresses the question of who adults are and what adult services are. The chapter provides a definition of the term "adults" and the characteristics of the different categories of adults. It tries to provide answers about what constitutes adult services and the different library functions and services that define the concept. Chapter 2 addresses the history and development of adult services and traces its evolution from adult education to adult services. It also discusses the role of the American Library Association and its various divisions and committees. Chapter 3 discusses the state of adult services at the turn of the century. This chapter reviews the types of services public libraries provided adults in the twentieth century. It also looks at tools provided by the American Library Association and the Public Library Association that public libraries can use to plan and implement service responses.

Part II addresses planning for adult services. It recognizes patrons' changing expectations and the shifting nature of services to anytime, anywhere service models, implementing technology to deliver library services, and tools and techniques needed for planning adult services in the twenty-first century. Chapter 4 discusses the steps involved in planning and the importance of conducting community analysis as the first step. It presents the tools and methods needed to conduct community analysis including demographic information from census data and resources such as the American Community Survey (ACS), Geographical Information Systems (GIS), and other data collection tools. Chapter 5 addresses assessment of adult services (this chapter was contributed by Dr. Mary E. Brown). It discusses the important role assessment plays in any activity. It provides step-by-step instructions on how to assess adult services. It also provides ways of looking at adult services as well as checklists and materials for conducting assessments.

Part III addresses types of service responses. Chapter 6 discusses readers' services and examines its history in public libraries. Fiction and nonfiction readers' advisory techniques and tools are discussed, as are required competencies and training. Chapter 7 covers services for the business community. It reviews current library services provided to the business community, explores the relevant service models, and identifies the types of responses that the business community needs in the twenty-first century. Chapter 8 examines the concept of lifelong learning as it relates to libraries serving adults. The lifelong learning needs of different categories of adults and the role of demographic, social, and technological changes on lifelong learning are also discussed. Leisure learning is also explored. Chapter 9 addresses services provided to diverse populations. This group is set apart on the basis of ethnic, cultural, linguistic, and sexual orientation. Chapter 10 defines some special populations and reviews services provided to specific populations. Services for people with disabilities and the role of assistive technologies are discussed, as are services for people who are homeless, poor, and older. The role of cultural awareness and cultural competence in planning and implementing services for diverse populations is outlined. Chapter 11 lists competencies and promotes professional development for adult services librarians. It looks at reference services as well as other American Library Association core professional competencies related to service responses. The role of the library and information science curriculum in the provision of needed competencies is discussed, as is the importance of continuing education and professional development for adult services librarians and librarians in general.

I wish to thank Blanche Woolls—my editor, mentor, and friend—who approached me about writing this book to fill a gap in the literature. She has been an able guide and editor throughout the journey. And what a journey it has been from the day I pulled a fresh lined tablet of paper in front of me, picked up a pen, and began putting my thoughts into written words. I owe her a great debt of gratitude for all her help and patience through the process of writing this book. She encouraged and pushed me to finish the book, and for that I am very grateful.

It is my hope this resource accomplishes all that Blanche imagined and I intended, and that it helps to inform current librarians and future librarians about the needs of adults. I also hope it gives them the knowledge, skills, and inspiration to address future service challenges and opportunities we cannot imagine today.

Elsie Rogers Halliday Okobi
New Haven, Connecticut

ACKNOWLEDGMENTS

The fact that this book has been completed is a testament to the support and assistance that my friend and colleague Dr. Mary Brown provided throughout the writing of this book. She is the reason the book was completed, as several times I was ready to give up, and she insisted that the task be completed. She provided pep talks when I needed them—which was quite often—and extensive editorial support. She also contributed a chapter. I cannot thank her enough for all the emotional support and encouragement at times when it seemed that I could not go on. I also want to thank the reference librarians in Buley Library, especially Rebecca Hedreen and Alba Rynaga, for all their assistance as they helped track down reference and useful web resources. I want to thank Blanche Woolls, my editor and mentor, whose idea it was to write the book. She encouraged and supported me through the process and ensured that the book would become a reality. I also want to thank the other people who contributed to the completion of this book that I may have forgotten to name—you know who you are, and you know that without your help this book would still be a work in progress.

PART I

Introduction

"Study the past if you would define the future."

—Confucius

CHAPTER 1

The Need for Adult Services

Society has benefitted from public libraries since the fourth century BCE (Krasner-Khalt, 2001). In its design, the library has long offered services of specialized interest, from the Roman complexes that combined baths and libraries to the Carnegie Library and Music Hall in Carnegie, Pennsylvania, to quiet reading and games rooms and gardens in the Bibliothèque Nationale de France (National Library of France, BnF) in Paris. Society, however, is made up of a broad spectrum of individuals with diverse interests and needs. One quality that helps to predict some interests and needs is age.

Public libraries plan their services based on three distinct developmental stages: services for children ages birth–12, services for young adults ages 12–17, and services to adults ages 18 and over. This compartmentalization of services allows libraries to define their scope of services in the context of the human life cycle.

WHO ARE THE ADULTS?

The way adults are distinguished from nonadults depends on the context. Legal adults have reached the age of majority as defined by law, which can vary by state; for example, by age 18 or 19 or 21, or by educational status such as graduation from high school, or by which of these two comes first or later. Biological adults are generally considered to have reached physical maturity.

Library adults, however, have been defined as "those who have completed compulsory secondary schooling or have passed the age of compulsory school attendance" (Wente, 1979, p. 231). In many states, the legal dropout age is 16, and a few states have exceptions that can lower this to 15. Some states even permit withdrawal once a child has met requirements for sixth-grade educational levels (Compulsory School Age Requirements, 2010). Wente's definition, therefore, means that library adults at the lower age limits can be below legal age and possibly not fully grown (i.e., not yet a biological adult).

The American Library Association (ALA) has designated a special category that includes the teen years, the young adult, as being between the ages of 13 and 18 (YALSA, n.d.). Given the professional divisions that focus on service for children (birth to 12) and young adults, we might feel confident in defining the library adult as over age 18. Yet, for those who have completed compulsory education and may have taken on responsibilities of an adult while not yet 18 years of age, the designation defined by birthday may seem arbitrary and ill-fitting. For the purposes of this book, we accept Wente's definition of the library adult as citizens who have completed compulsory secondary schooling or have passed the age of compulsory school attendance. This means that the library adult needs to be defined locally, thereby better matching the needs that a particular library serves. For the purposes of discussion and to facilitate discussion of numbers of adults, we will use the age of 18, as the various perspectives and considerations seem to fix on the notion that by 18 one is an adult.

Adults in your library come from a cross section of the community and represent different conditions (including economic, social, moral) and phases of life (postsecondary education students, new persons in the workforce, parents, older adults) as well as involvement (including community activists, volunteers, business owners, public servants), all of whom require different types of library services to satisfy their unique information needs (Wente, 1979).

Public librarians generally plan their services by three distinct developmental stages designated as services for children ages birth–12, services for young adults ages 13–18, and services to adults ages 18 and over. This compartmentalization of services allows librarians to define the scope of library services in the context of the human life cycle. This book focuses on adults. Adults as defined by age (18 and over) constitute a disproportionate heterogeneous share of society, a group that is affected by an array of societal factors that make for shifting and ever-changing needs. The array of factors and changing needs impact the nature of services provided to adults in public libraries. Adults' needs continually change, and sometimes an adult will need basic personal information relevant to the individual's status at that point in life (Martin, 1984). Adults need information for the following reasons as well: personal fulfillment, concern for personal survival, and to help make decisions (Martin, 1984). Information services provided to adults also must be sensitive to the generations into which we separate American society.

Generations of Adults

A generation within a family is represented by the number of years between a parent's birth and the birth of his or her first child (Martin, 2006). In society, however, a generation includes those born within a given time span, generally about 30–35 years in length, who share attitudes and attributes generally associated with historical events that help to define the generation. Library patrons, therefore, are made up of generations of individuals who have attributes that impact their interactions with others and with information. Members of the same generation have shared experiences of their youth that may have led them to develop similar skills and values (Martin, 2006). Understanding societal generations allows libraries to better serve their communities' information needs.

Five generations currently make up U.S. society: traditionalists, baby boomers, Generation X, the millennials, and the global generation. The traditionalists' generation is made up of people born prior to the end of World War II. This generation's experience was shaped for the most part by the Great Depression and World War II. They tend to be loyal and hard workers, and they have a great deal of faith in institutions such as the church and state (Lancaster & Stillman, 2002, p. 4). It has been said that the traditionalists, persevering through wars and depression, created the U.S. society of today (Bradley, Cameron, & Trogdon, 2004). At the upper age of this generation are those who experienced World War II as adults, sometimes called the GI generation or veterans, and at the younger end are those who experienced World War II as children, also called the silent generation.

Baby boomers are those who were born following World War II, between approximately 1945 and 1964 (Bradley, Cameron, & Trogdon, 2004). Lancaster and Stillman (2002) describe baby boomers as an idealistic, educated, and highly competitive generation that seeks rewards for achievement and is much more self-focused. Baby boomers tend to be more affluent than the traditionalists and have more time and money to spend on leisure activities.

Generation X refers to those born between 1965 and 1981 (Ulrich & Harris, 2003). They are said to be independent, skeptical, and uncomfortable with change. This generation grew up in an era shaped by technological advances, especially the Internet. Generation X is said to process information differently from earlier generations (Zemke, Raines, & Filipczak, 2000). Gen Xers process information through a "parallel processing" or multitasking mode similar to computers; that is, they often carry out two or more tasks at the same time (Zemke, Raines, & Filipczak, 2000).

Millennials are those born between 1982 and 2003. This group grew up with computers and is influenced by the ubiquitous technology in every aspect of life. The millennial generation spans a wide range of library

Summary of the Generations in Current Society

Generation	Alternate Names	Shaping Events	Characteristics
Traditionalists (born during or after World War I and before the end of World War II)	Silent generation, veterans, GI generation, greatest generation	Stock market crash of 1929; Great Depression; World War II; Lindbergh's first transatlantic flight; New Deal; establishment of the Social Security system	Tend to be loyal and have a great deal of faith in institutions; frugal and risk adverse
Baby boomers (born between the end of World War II and the mid-1960s)	Boomers	Civil rights movement; Civil Rights Act; birth control pills; Woodstock; first man walked on the moon; Cultural Revolution in China and other foreign countries; Vietnam conflict; first time society doted on children	Idealistic, educated, and highly competitive; understand need to work together for a united workforce; seek rewards for their achievement and are highly focused on themselves; believe in growth and expansion; challenge authority
Generation X (born between the mid-1960s and the beginning of the 1980s)	Generation Jones; 13th generation; baby busters; MTV generation; boomerang generation	Divorce rates exploded and single-parent households greatly increased; latchkey kids; milk cartons with photographs of missing children; AIDS epidemic; O.J. Simpson trial; terrorist bombings; oil tanker spills; Internet, cell phones, pagers, cable TV	Independent, skeptical, and uncomfortable with change; grew up in an era shaped by technological advances, especially the Internet; highly motivated; tend to rely on themselves and are practical in their approach to work

Generation	Also known as	Defining experiences/events	Characteristics
Millennials (born between the beginning of the 1980s and the beginning of the twenty-first century)	Generation Y; Echo Boom; iGeneration; Generation Next, Nexters	Dawn of the twenty-first century; War on Terror; rise of the Information Age; Iraq War; taught to go the extra mile; return of "family values"	Grew up with computers; influenced by the ubiquitous technology in every aspect of their life; optimistic outlook; self-assurance; strong morals; focused on achievement; aware of diversity; service to community; sense of loyalty; crave meaning in all they do; collaboration and co-operation
Global Generation (born after the turn of the century/millennium)		Digital globalization	
Cuspers (born during the two- to three-year period around the shift in generations)		Share experiences with more than one generation	Display a combination of characteristics of the generations with which they are associated; serve as a catalyst between the different generations

services. At the upper age of the millennial generation are adult users (who are just turning 30 at this writing) and at the younger end are school-aged children (the very youngest, at this writing). Only the newest generation, the global generation, falls outside of adult services.

If librarians are to provide access to information for decision making to all members of the community, librarians need to be cognizant of the generational diversity of their patrons. They should create programs to accommodate the needs, wants, and information behavior styles of the different generations of their patrons. These are shown in the chart on pages 6–7.

Demographic Changes in Generations in the Twenty-First Century

Panz (1989) identified two major shifts in trends in the U.S. population in the twenty-first century: (1) an aging population, and (2) changes in the workforce. The aging population can be attributed to decreasing birthrates and longer life expectancy due to medical and other technological advances. The 1990 census showed that 12.5 percent of the population of the United States was over the age of 65 (Meyer, 2001). In the first decade of this century, the 65-and-over population also grew at a faster rate than the population of those under age 45 (Howden & Meyer, 2011, p. 2). It is projected that between 2010 and 2050, the U.S. population 65 and older will more than double (Vincent & Velkoff, 2010), with 20.7 percent of the population in 2050 expected to be 65 years or older (Holder & Clark, 2008). This will have a profound impact on the delivery of library services to this group of patrons, though the percentages of people in this age group will not be equal in all areas of the country. Differences by geography can be profound. For example, in 2010 the Northeast had a higher percentage of those 65 and older than did the West. Florida and West Virginia had the highest percentages of residents 65 and older (17.3 and 16.0 percent, respectively), and Alaska had the lowest (7.7 percent) (Howden & Meyer, 2011).

The second trend, the change in the workforce, includes a projected reduction in the number of workers by just over 9 percent by 2030. Further, the move from an industrial to a knowledge society will change the work environment. Jobs in the twenty-first century require higher educational qualifications. Consequently, only those with the requisite skills will be able to fill the high-paying jobs created by advances in computers and technology, a situation that may serve to widen the gap between the haves and have-nots. Baby boomers will benefit from this environment, as they tend to be more educated and more affluent (Bouvier & Gardner, 1986). They therefore have more leisure time and are apt to use libraries more as long as the library can provide services to meet their needs. Adults will engage in learning to improve their earning capacity, so librarians must continue to provide educational opportunities as well as lifelong learning programs. However, in 2006, 15 percent of people over the traditional retirement age of 65 were still in the labor force, a situation attributed to financial and other economic conditions (Holder & Clark, 2008). If the proportion of those past the age of 65 who stay in the workforce remains constant or increases, this will impact the types of resources and services needed by both those over 65 and those under 65.

The increasing number of women entering the workforce is a trend predicted in the twentieth century that has been realized in the twenty-first century. In 1970, the number of women with preschool children who were in the workforce was less than 30 percent, and this figure increased to 50 percent in the 1980s (Robey, 1985). In 2010, 58.6 percent of women age 16 and over in the United States were working or looking for work (U.S. Department of Labor, 2010). The higher the level of education attainment, the more likely a woman is to be a labor force participant (i.e., working or looking for work). Looking at women 25 and over, 33.5 percent of those with less than a high school diploma are in the workforce compared to 52.4 percent with a high school diploma, 62.3 percent with some college, 70.6 percent with an associate's degree, and 72.4 percent with a bachelor's degree or higher (U.S. Department of Labor, 2010). Women in the workforce have also affected the economic and social balance within the family and thereby on decisions related to how resources (income and time) are spent. In a lighthearted exposé, Dvorak (2010) highlights accomplishments and contradictions in the modern working women's lifestyle, observations that could be key to consider when planning adult services in a given community.

Diversity in Adult Populations

The U.S. Census Bureau (2010) reports that those who are foreign born make up 12.9 percent of the U.S. population, with over half (53 percent) from Latin America (with over half [55 percent] from Mexico), 28 percent from Asia, 12 percent from Europe, 4 percent from Africa, 2 percent from North America, and less than 1 percent from Oceania. Over half of the foreign-born people in the United States reside in four states: California, New York, Texas, and Florida (Grieco et al., 2012). Population diversity in the United States will continue to expand in the twenty-first century, and increasing numbers of non-native English-speaking adults will impact the types of services libraries need to provide. In particular, librarians need to consider rising rates of Spanish-speaking adults. The Hispanic population in the United States increased from 13 percent of the total population in 2000 to 16 percent in 2010 (Ennis, Rios-Vargas, & Albert, 2011).

The Census Bureau (2012) predicts that by the year 2030, the Hispanic population will comprise 23 percent of the U.S. population, and 30 percent by 2050. This growth has implications for adult services in public libraries because services for Spanish-speaking people will constitute a large component of services to adults in the twenty-first century, especially in the urban areas with large concentrations of Spanish-speaking adults.

Robey (1985) points out that one of the top trends affecting U.S. society is internal migration from metropolitan areas to nonmetropolitan or rural areas. Falcigno and Guynup (1984) also articulated the impact of this migration on library services, citing statistics and noting that the migration will increase service demands on rural libraries. Not everyone agrees that libraries should be aware of changes in service demands. Ballard (1988) observed that there was no way to serve rural populations adequately and that library managers need not be overly concerned about creating special services for rural residents. The shift of more people to less populated areas places a great demand on rural librarians to provide technological services because people in these areas have access to a wide variety of digital devices at home and want to have access to eBooks from their library.

Changes in Family Structure

Traditional husband-wife families (with or without children) have been declining as a percentage of the total population, from 55.2 percent in 1990 to 51.7 percent in 2000 to 48.4 percent in 2010. A traditional husband-wife couple with children made up 20.2 percent of the total households in the United States in 2010 (Lofquist et al., 2012). Two-adult households (husband-wife, unmarried opposite-sex partners, and same-sex partners), with and without children, together account for 54.6 percent of the households in the United States, based on the 2010 Census. Families with a single head of the household (no spouse present) represent 18.1 percent of the population. Since 2000, there has been an 18 percent increase in households headed by a female and a 31.5 percent increase in those headed by a male. Households comprised of a single adult and children make up 9.6 percent of all households. Changes in family makeup have implications for public libraries—we must take into account the makeup of families and households when considering services provided directly to adults and also those services designed for children and youth. These considerations include the economic and social consequences of changing household makeup. Librarians need to be attuned to the family structures represented in their communities and need to plan services to address some of the opportunities and challenges these structures create.

What Are Adult Services?

The year 2008 marked the beginning of a nationwide housing crisis, and San Diego County Library (in California) helped the community face the challenges by arranging free clinics and expert panelists to help residents find relief. In the fall of 2011, the Las Vegas–Clark County Library District worked with the Nevada Justice Association to offer classes on bankruptcy and foreclosure prevention (Koray, 2013). Public libraries provide adult literacy programs and services to promote computer literacy (Deane, 2004; Forsyth, 2012; Notar, 2008; Pearson, 2013; Thompson, 2012). Games are beginning to be explored as part of lifelong learning opportunities within libraries (Forsyth, 2012). Public libraries provide programming that promotes civic engagement and community development (Coleman & Hadley, 2012; Reid, 2012; Smith, 2012). Public libraries offer summer reading programs for adults (Bostwick, 2012; Hibner & Kelly, 2008). Libraries are becoming a source of guidance for adults seeking jobs and information on skills needed for today's labor market (Gutsche, 2011).

Adults in any society are a heterogeneous group of individuals with continually changing information needs, both as individuals and as groups (Wente, 1979). As we can see from the few examples in the previous paragraph, these changing needs affect the form of services needed in the public library.

Differences in chronological age (see Cooke, 2010), individual characteristics and circumstances, and information needs of adults as a group make it difficult to have a unified concept of "adult services." Today, adult services still comprise "all those services provided to the adult clientele of the library to fill their educational, informational, cultural and recreational library needs" (Wente, 1979, p. 231). That is, "Adult Services is an inclusive term designating all services provided to adults in the public library" (McCook, 1991, p. 386). The basic, or traditional, adult services as outlined by McCook (1991) still continue and now include selection of resources (including newer and emerging media) for the library's collection; providing access (including remote access) to the collection; providing instruction, readers' advisory, and guidance; providing reference and information services; and encouraging use of the library's resources by individuals as well as by community groups. Changing demographics, technology, and local and national conditions impact the scope of special interests the library covers as well as the way services can be delivered.

Adult services in the literature is discussed in terms of the types of services provided. Wente (1979) found, however, that adult services are difficult to categorize because they serve a population that "[b]e they patrons, parents, senior citizens, students or community activists ... will require different library services to fill their unique needs" (p. 232). Every librarian needs to determine the nature of his or her adult services based on community needs. The basic functions of adult services are information, guidance, instruction, and stimulation (Schlachter, 1982). Underlying these basic functions of adult services is the provision of assistance to users. This assistance is the basis of modern reference service as defined in Samuel Green's 1876 paper, "Personal Relations between Librarians and Readers." The basic elements of reference, information, instruction, and guidance are found in various discussions of adult services in the literature (Wente, 1979; Rolstad, 1993).

Today's adult services librarian job descriptions paint a rich picture of the public library as the community's post–compulsory education information and learning center. A review of job announcements provides a list of a number of skill areas, such as the ability to provide reference services, both in person and virtually, and content development such as subject guides, user manuals, and tutorials. Librarians should be able to provide instruction and make presentations. They should be able to organize programs for all library patrons, be involved in community activities, and interface with community organizations. They need to provide readers' advisory services, and they must be innovative and proactive in the use of technology to implement services. They also have to keep up with trends and emerging technology for library applications.

Monroe and McCook (1991) remind us that library staff determines the nature of their library's adult services. To assist with this planning, the ALA and the Public Library Association (PLA) have provided guidelines and standards for implementation of adult and other services in public libraries in a number of publications, including *Planning & Role Setting for Public Libraries* (McClure et al., 1987); *Adult Programming: A Manual for Librarians* (RUSA Occasional Papers, No. 21, 1997); *5-Star Programming and Services for Your 55+ Library Customers* (ALA Programming Guides, 2003); and *50+ Library Services; Innovation in Action* (Schull, 2013). Other useful publications include *Something to Talk About: Creative Booktalking for Adults* (Cyr & Gillespie, 2006) and *Adult Learners Welcome Here: A Handbook for Librarians and Literacy Teachers* (Weibel, 2007).

Consider again the previously mentioned job descriptions for adult services librarians. The concept of the public library as the post–compulsory education information and learning center of the community is rooted in the eight major roles of libraries in their communities (McClure et al., 1987) as a community center for (1) community activities, meetings, and services, and (2) collection, classification, and distribution of current information on community organization, issues, and services; as support centers for (3) formal education and (4) independent learning; collections of (5) popular material, (6) reference, and (7) research; and as (8) a point of access to learning for preschool-aged children. In contrast, McClure and colleagues (1987) labeled the eight library roles as: (1) community activities center, (2) community information center, (3) formal education support center, (4) independent learning center, (5) popular materials library, (6) preschoolers' door to learning, (7) reference library, and (8) research center.

Many librarians design their adult services based on established library roles. These roles help libraries make decisions about what services to offer. A study of the roles outlined by the PLA found that the most important role of the library is that of supporting the educational needs of the community (D'Elia & Rodger, 1995). In this study, D'Elia found that the roles receiving the largest percentages of "very important" responses were library as an educational support center for students of all ages (88 percent), a learning center for adult independent learners (85 percent), a discovery and learning center for preschool children (83 percent), a research center for scholars and researchers (68 percent), and a center for community information (68 percent).

In 1998, *Planning for Results: A Public Library Transformation Process* (Himmel et al.) listed 13 "service responses" that provide a framework for librarians to link community needs with specific library services and programs. A service response is "what a library does or offers to the public in an effort to meet a set of well defined community needs . . . Service responses are very distinct ways that libraries serve the public" (Nelson, 2001, p. 146). The 13 service responses are:

- Basic literacy
- Business and career information
- Commons
- Community referral
- Consumer information
- Cultural awareness
- Current topics and titles
- Formal learning support
- General information
- Government information
- Information literacy
- Lifelong learning
- Local history and genealogy

The planning process uses these service points to focus on the importance of connecting community needs with the development of library services. In 2001, *The New Planning for Results* used the same 13 service points to define broad categories of service that give a general description of what a library should offer. The service points refer to services designed to respond to an identified community need. The assumption is that by using the service points for planning adult services, the librarian will be able to match library services to community needs.

Structure of Adult Services

The service points and roles of the adult services librarian fit into the structure of adult services as defined earlier in 1986 by Heim and Monroe. Their structure has two elements, (1) user orientation, and (2) major service functions, with four major service functions that were defined by Dresang in an earlier article and discussed below (1982).

User Orientation focuses on a study of community needs and the information-seeking behavior of the adults. An understanding of the needs and interest of the community is said to be "a prime element in the structure of Adult Services" (Heim & Monroe, 1986). User orientation has been the hallmark of adult services in public libraries. The ALA Library Community Project in the 1950s and 1960s pioneered community analysis as a basis for adult service programs in public libraries. One of the major outcomes of community analysis is the focus on "special publics" as a basis of planning adult services. Some of the special publics identified over the years include foreign-born patrons, new adult readers, and those unemployed or under employed during the economic downturns. This also resulted in the development of outreach programs to older adults, ethnic minorities, people with disabilities, and others.

Four Functions of Adult Services

In an essay called "The Public Service Paradigm," Dresang (1982) outlined her model for public service as consisting of four functions: (1) information, (2) instruction, (3) guidance, and (4) stimulation. These functions are the basis of the implementation of reference services in libraries and exist in an ever-changing relationship, varying based on the aim of the service. The four functions are used to implement public services, including adult services, with each function varying in emphasis depending on the objectives and identified needs of the community.

In answer to the question "What are adult services in public libraries?" Rolstad (1993) said that adult services are "... the programmatic and organizational expression of the public library's role as an educational institution in its community. Although it is closely related to reference services, it emphasizes an active stance through services such [as] adult education programs including literacy programs, readers' advisory services, and a variety of community and cultural programs. Adult services is the modern expression of the 19th-century vision of the public library as the 'people's university'" (p. 34).

Each library should provide services in response to needs identified in the community it serves. In any particular community, this might include support services for parents (Gourley & DeSalvo, 1980) or reading rooms and other services for the homeless and low-income library users (DeCandido, 1989; Milone, 2011). Another library might provide an innovative twist to a social phenomenon (Speed Dating, 2006) or adapt a successful children's program to create an adult summer reading program (Hibner & Kelly, 2008). Yet another library could provide learning centers and professional training to create a culture of lifelong learning (Butcher & Street, 2009) or reference services specifically for older adults (Prasad, 2009).

The public library has a role to fill in helping to build its community. It does this through (1) facilitating access to information and learning,

(2) facilitating inclusion and equity in that access, and (3) fostering civic engagement through creating a bridge to resources that facilitates community involvement and promotes economic vitality (Scott, 2011). Specially trained adult services librarians are needed to answer a long-standing call for aggressive action by libraries to "move from passivity to activism" to meet the information and service needs of society's adults (Nyren, 1981, p. 2219).

REFERENCES

American community survey. (2011). Retrieved July 22, 2013, from http://fact-finder2.census.gov/faces/tableservices/jsf/pages/productview.xhtml?pid=AC-S_11_1YR_S1101&prodType=table

Andrew Carnegie Free Library and Music Hall. http://www.carnegiecarnegie.org/

Ballard, T. (1988). *The best reading for the largest number at the least cost.* Paper presented at the Conference on the Future of Public Libraries, Dublin, OH.

Bibliothèque nationale de France. http://www.bnf.fr/fr/acc/x.accueil.html

Bostwick, D. S. (2012, Fall). Can you read one book this summer? *Florida Libraries*, 55(2), 11–12.

Bouvier, L., & Gardner, R. (1986). *Immigration to the U.S.: The unfinished story.* Washington, D.C.: Population Reference Bureau.

Bradley, D. B., Cameron, M., & Trogdon, M. (2004). Generational diversity in small business. Retrieved July 22, 2013, from http://www.sbaer.uca.edu/research/asbe/2004/PDFS/07.pdf

Butcher, W., & Street, P-A. (2009). Lifelong learning with older adults. *APLIS*, 22(2), 64–70.

Coleman, C., & Hadley, K. (2012, Winter). Working together to close the civic engagement gap: The Saint Paul story. *National Civic Review*, 101(4), 15–17.

Compulsory school age requirements. (2010, June). Denver, CO: Education Commission of the States. Retrieved July 22, 2013, from http://www.ncsl.org/documents/educ/ECSCompulsoryAge.pdf

Cooke, N. A. (2010, November). Becoming an andragogical librarian: Using library instruction as a tool to combat library anxiety and empower adult learners. *New Review of Academic Librarianship*, 16(2), 208–227.

DeCandido, G. A. (1989, January 1). Multnomah [OR] provides reading room for homeless. *Library Journal*, 114(1), 23.

D'Elia, G., & Rodger, E. J. (1995). The roles of the public library in the community: The results of a Gallup poll of community opinion leaders. *Public Libraries*, 34, 94–101.

Deane, P. (2004, September 1). Literacy, redefined. *Library Journal*, 129(14), 49–50.

Dresang, E. T. (1982). Service paradigm: An introduction. In G. Schlacter (Ed.), *The service imperative for libraries: Essays in honor of Margaret E. Monroe* (pp. 13–20). Littleton, CO: Libraries Unlimited.

Dvorak, P. (2010, January 19). Bringing home more bacon, still cleaning the pan. *Washington Post*. Retrieved July 22, 2013, from http://articles.washington post.com/2010-01-19/opinions/36924076_1_marriages-husbands-women

Ennis, S. R., Rios-Vargas, M., & Albert, N. G. (2011, May). The Hispanic population: 2010. *2010 Census Briefs*. Retrieved July 22, 2013, from http://www.census.gov/prod/cen2010/briefs/c2010br-04.pdf

Exeter, T. (1987). How many Hispanics? *American Demographics, 9*, 36–39.

Falcigno, K., & Guyup, P. (1984). U.S. population characteristics: Implications for libraries. *Wilson Library Bulletin, 59*, 23–26.

Forsyth, E. (2012, December). Learning through play: Games and crowdsourcing for adult education. *APLIS, 25*(4), 166–173.

Gourley, J., & DeSalvo, N. (1980, April). Parent support services in Glastonbury & Farmington [CT]. *School Library Journal, 26*(8), 26.

Gutsche, B. (2011, September 1). A boon to the workforce. *Library Journal, 136*(4), 28–31.

Hibner, H., & Kelly, M. (2008, July/August). Not just for kids. *Public Libraries, 47*(4), 7–9.

Himmel, E. E., Wilson, W. J., & Revision Committee of the Public Library Association. (1998). *Planning for results: A public library transformation process*. Chicago: American Library Association.

Holder, K. A., & Clark, S. L. (2008). *Working beyond retirement age*. U.S. Census Bureau, Housing and Household Economics Labor Force Statistics Branch. Presented at the American Sociological Association Annual Conference, Boston, August 2, 2008. Retrieved July 22, 2013, from http://www.census.gov/hhes/www/laborfor/Working-Beyond-Retirement-Age.pdf

Howden, L. M., & Meyer, J. A. (2011). Age and sex composition: 2010. *2010 Census Briefs*. Retrieved July 22, 2013, from http://www.census.gov/prod/cen2010/briefs/c2010br-03.pdf

Kong, L. (2013, January/February). Failing to read well. *Public Libraries, 52*(1), 40–44.

Koray, D. (2013, January/February). Libraries help homeowners flight foreclosure. *American Libraries, 44*(1/2), 56–59.

Krasner-Khalt, B. (2001, October/November). Survivor: The history of the library. *History*. Retrieved July 22, 2013, from from http://www.history-magazine.com/libraries.html

Lancaster, L. C., & Stillman, D. (2002). *When generations collide: Who they are, why they clash, how to solve the generational puzzle at work*. New York: HarperCollins.

Lofquist, D., Lugaila, T., O'Connell, M., & Feliz, S. (2012, April). Households and families: 2010. *2010 Census Briefs*. Retrieved July 22, 2013, from http://www.census.gov/prod/cen2010/briefs/c2010br-14.pdf

Martin, G. (1984). *Library services for adults*. Chicago: American Library Association.

Martin, J. (2006). I have shoes older than you: Generational diversity in the library. *Southeastern Librarian, 54*(3), 4–5, 11.

Mather, M. (2010, May). U.S. children in single-mother families. Data Brief, Population Reference Bureau. Retrieved July 22, 2013, from http://pdfcast.org/pdf/u-s-children-in-single-mother-families

McClure, C. R., Owen, A., Zweizig, D., Lynch, M. J., & Van House, Nancy A. (1987). *Planning and role setting for public libraries: A manual of options and procedures.* Chicago: American Library Association.

McCook, K. de la Peña. (1991). Adult services within the American Library Association: A historical examination of the move to synthesis. Adapted from adult services. American Library Association. 1990. *RQ, 30,* 386–394.

McCook, K. de la Peña. (2011). *Adult services.* In *Introduction to public librarianship* (3rd ed.). New York: Neal-Schuman.

Merriam Webster's Dictionary Online (2007). Retrieved from http://www.m-w.com/dictionary/Adult

Meyer, J. (2001). Age: 2000. *Census 2000 Brief* No. C2KBR/01-12. Washington, D.C.: U.S. Department of Commerce, U.S. Census Bureau. Retrieved from http://www.census.gov

Milone, N. (2011, November/December). Public libraries and the homeless. *Public Libraries, 50*(6), 13–22.

Monroe, M. E., & Heim, K. M. (1991). *Partners for lifelong learning: Public libraries & adult education.* Washington, D.C.: Office of Library Programs, U.S. Department of Education, Office of Educational Research and Improvement.

Nelson, S. S., & Public Library Association. (2001). *The new planning for results: A streamlined approach.* Chicago: American Library Association.

Notar, T. A. (2008, Fall). Teaching responsibility through example. *Adult Basic Education & Literacy, 2*(3), 179–181.

Nyren, D. (1981, November 15). Adult services overview [Review of *Public Libraries and New Directions for Adult Services, an institute in honor of Rose Vainstein, Margaret Mann Professor of Library Science*, edited by Joan C. Durrance and Rose Vainstein]. *Library Journal, 106*(20), 2219.

O'Connell, V., & Hilsenrath, J. E. (2001, May 15). Advertisers are cautious as household makeup shifts. *Wall Street Journal*, pp. B1 and B4.

Outlook '88. (1987, November/December). *Futurist, 21*(6), 53–60.

Panz, R. (1989). Library services to special population groups in the 21st century. *Journal of Library Administration, 11*(1/2), 151–171.

Passel, J., & Cohn, D. (2008, October). *Trends in unauthorized immigration: Undocumented inflow now trail legal inflow.* Washington, D.C.: Pew Hispanic Center.

Passel, J., & Cohn, D'V. (2008). U.S. population projections 2005–2050. Retrieved July 22, 2013, from http://www.pewhispanic.org/2008/02/11/us-population-projections-2005-2050/

Pearson, P. (2013, January/February). A new beginning. *Public Libraries, 52*(1), 25–26.

Prasad, P. (2009). Reference services to senior groups in the San Antonio Public Library. *Reference Librarian, 50*(10), 99–108.

Reid, R. H. (2012, Winter). Community libraries: Let us praise the last great civic place. *National Civic Review, 101*(4), 35–40.

Robey, B. (1985). *The American people.* New York: E. Dutton.

Rolstad, G. O. (1993). Adult services. In R. Wedgeworth (Ed.), *ALA encyclopedia of library and information services* (3rd ed., p. 34). Chicago: American Library Association.

Schlachter, G. (Ed.). (1982). *The service imperative: Essays in honor of Margaret E. Monroe.* Littleton, CO: Libraries Unlimited.

Scott, R. (2011). The role of public libraries in community building. *Public Library Quarterly, 30*(3), 191–227.

Smith, M. (2012, July/August). Making a difference. *Public Libraries, 52*(4), 34–39.

Speed dating with a bookish twist. (2006, November/December). *Public Libraries, 45*(6), 16.

Thompson, S. (2012, December). Public libraries: Central to adult learning and literacy. *APLIS, 25*(4), 190–191.

Ulrich, J., & Harris, A. (Eds.). (2003). *Generation X: A (sub) cultural genealogy.* Madison: University of Wisconsin Press.

U.S. Census Bureau. (2012, June 22). Who's Hispanic in America? Retrieved July 22, 2013, from: http://www.census.gov/newsroom/cspan/hispanic/2012.06.22_cspan_hispanics.pdf

U.S. Census Bureau (2012, November 13). Families and living arrangements. Retrieved July 22, 2013, from http://www.census.gov/hhes/families/

U.S. Census Bureau News (2010). 2010 Census shows nations Hispanic populations grew four times faster than total U.S. population. Retrieved August 30, 2012, from: http://www.census.gov/2010census/news/releases/operations/cb11-cn146.html

U.S. Department of Commerce, Bureau of Census. (2002). Number of foreign-born up 57 percent since 1990, according to census 2000. *Census Bureau News, CB02-CN.117.* Retrieved from http://census.gov

U.S. Department of Labor. (2010). Women in the labor force in 2010. Retrieved July 22, 2013, from http://www.dol.gov/wb/factsheets/Qf-laborforce-10.htm

Vincent G. K., & Velkoff, V. A. (2010). The next four decades, the older population in the United States: 2010 to 2050. *Current Population Reports,* P25-1138. Washington, D.C.: U.S. Census Bureau.

Wente, J. (1979). What are "adult services"? *RQ, 18*(3), 231–234.

Zemke, R., Raines, C., & Filipczak, B. (2000). *Generations at work.* New York, NY: American Management Association.

Zionts, N. D., Apter, J., Kuchta, J., & Greenhouse, P. K. (2010). Promoting consumer health literacy: Creation of a Health Information Librarian Fellowship. *Reference & User Services Quarterly, 49*(4), 350–359.

CHAPTER 2

History and Development of Adult Services

Libraries have existed since 3000 BC, when the Babylonians and Assyrians maintained libraries of clay tablets written in Cuneiform. These ancient libraries, as well as European renaissance libraries and pre-revolutionary American libraries, were designed to be used exclusively by adults. In America, pre-revolutionary libraries began as social clubs, such as Benjamin Franklin's Junto that in 1731 became the Library Company of Philadelphia, reserved for the select few who could afford to pay (Yu, 2002). These were the "social and subscription" libraries from which the present-day public library is recognized as the institutional descendant.

In 1833, the first tax-based library was commissioned in the town of Peterborough, New Hampshire. In 1852, the trustees of the Boston Public Library, founded in 1848, articulated a statement about the "ideal conception of public library service." As a result of this statement, the Boston Public Library was opened to the public in 1854 as the first large free municipal library in the United States. In the 1890s, following James Duff Brown's 1891 "A Plea for Library Readers to Help Themselves," open-shelf access was developed in public libraries along with lending policies and reading rooms. These libraries were set up to serve only adults. In 1889, the first children's room in a public library began as a book truck at the end of a corridor in the new Minneapolis Public Library. The early justification for public libraries was the "utmost importance as the means of completing the system of public education" (Boston Public Library, 1893, p. 1).

EARLY EDUCATIONAL OBJECTIVES OF PUBLIC LIBRARIES

When Samuel Swett Green wrote his paper about providing personal assistance to users in public libraries (1876), he acknowledged the role of librarians in activating collections for use. The educational objectives of public libraries were highlighted by the leaders of the American Library Association (ALA), which was founded that same year. One of these leaders, Charles Francis Adams, declared that the basic purpose of the library was to help patrons continue their self-education (Adams, 1877). Another leader, Henry Munson Utley, who was the librarian at the Detroit Public Library, said the public library was to be "purely and wholly education, truly the people's university" (Utley, 1851).

By 1910, reference services were separated from other services, and the first reference reading room was opened at the Boston Public Library. Full-time reference staff was appointed to serve students and business users (Heim & Monroe, 1986). In the early nineteenth century, public libraries started providing information and bibliographic services. Reference tools such as Poole's Index and other references came into existence.

John Cotton Dana, in the first draft of *A Library Primer* (observed that the educational role of the library should be achieved by the individual library user through implementation of self-administered education (Dana, 1899) and supported by reading guidance. This reading guidance for the casual reader was exemplified by the appointment of a "library hostess," who served as the reader's assistant. The assistant in the District of Columbia was to guess the wants of the vague reader and guide the reading selections of the aimless reader, thereby working to improve the quality of reading in the public library of the District of Columbia (Steinbarger, 1939). A similar service was implemented at the St. Louis Public Library—a librarian was designated to develop the advisory service to adult readers as part of the library's adult education responsibilities. Margaret Doud was in charge of the readers' advisers with help from others such as Jennie Flexner and Mabel Bolton, and they developed an informal network of communication for exchanging ideas on readers' advisory service (Rubin, 1982). This informal network provides the link between reader services and adult education in public libraries.

Librarians accepted these educational objectives of the public library and started providing recreational reading materials for adults. By 1920 the movement to provide recreational reading was institutionalized in public libraries (Lee, 1966). Other services, including children's and young adult services, were developed in the 1920s in major metropolitan libraries in conjunction with reference services. By the 1920s, services in public libraries consisted of: reference services, services to children, services to young adults, and the rest of the services, which were lumped under the rubric of "circulation services" (Flexner & Edge, 1927). Services to adults such as educational, cultural, and recreational services were carried out under the auspices of circulation services until the concept of adult services was crystallized. In their book *Circulation Work in Public Libraries*, Flexner and Edge (1927) listed circulation services as "the ultimate usefulness of any library depends on the ability of the staff and the public to find books on the shelves with ease and assurance" (p. 233).

Public libraries' educational objectives have been widely discussed in the literature, and they continue to be discussed in a variety of contexts. In the early twentieth century, these objectives focused on adult education and extension services.

ADULT EDUCATION AND EXTENSION SERVICES

Services to adults in the 1920s focused on providing information to support educational, cultural, and recreational activities with an opportunity to support adult education. Knowles (1977) identified 1924 as a "distinct turning point in the library's role as an adult educational institution." The ALA struggled to identify the relationship between public libraries and adult education, and in 1924, the Commission on Library and Adult Education was established with a grant from the Carnegie Corporation to investigate the role of the public library in adult education. The commission published its findings in 1926 in a report entitled *Libraries and Adult Education* (RUSA, n.d.). The report identified two categories of public library adult education services:

- Organized readers' advisory and adult education department.
- Programs of book distribution and library visits adapted to the needs of special groups such as workers, university extension students, immigrants, people who are blind, and patients of hospitals and prison inmates.

The commission's findings "enunciated a philosophy and set forth a set of directional guidelines which exerted a powerful influence on the development of the library as an educational institution" in the 1920s, 1930s, and 1940s in the context of adult education (RUSA, n.d.). The techniques and rationale for each service provided the foundation for the framework needed to develop public library adult services and became part of public libraries' educational objectives.

ADULT EDUCATION

Adult education in public libraries has a number of definitions. One definition is "self-education" (Chancellor, 1939). Rubin (1982) contends that, "Basically, library adult education refers to programs of a broadly educational nature as well as services for special individuals or groups." Asheim (1955) provides yet another definition, "those library activities for adult individuals and groups which form a part of the total educational process and which are derived from analysis of interests." These definitions include reference to all aspects of adult education activities in public libraries.

Services that make up adult education functions include provision of information about other community resources; circulation of resources to support formal and informal educational endeavors; community exhibits and displays; program planning for community groups; files and directories of community organizations; calendars of adult education activities; bibliographies and booklists; sponsorship of group programs, including book discussion groups, lectures, and classes; and film viewing (Rubin, 1982).

In the 1920s, public libraries focused their adult education services on individuals through readers' advisory services, and the emphasis changed from providing services to individuals to providing services to groups. Monroe (1979) identified three steps in the evolution of adult education in public libraries: (1) planned reading programs and the readers' advisory service, (2) library services to community organizations and agencies, and (3) library-sponsored group programs.

During this period, librarians started to develop services for groups within their communities. Cannons (1927) created the category of "Library Work for Special Classes of Readers" that included such subgroups as the "blind," "working class," "foreign populations," "clubs," and "reading circles." Services were tailored to fit the needs of these special groups.

Brenda Weeks Coleman (2008) completed a dissertation, "Keeping the Faith: The Public Library's Commitment to Adult Education, 1950–2006," in which she draws upon many of the sources found in this chapter (and in other portions of this book) as well as others. For those wishing a more detailed summary of the history of the public library and adult education, collected together into one volume, we recommended consulting Coleman. She begins with a review of the writings of C. W. Stone, M. E. Monroe, and R. E. Lee. Additional chapters look at the role of philanthropy, the federal government, the ALA, and research in adult education between 1950 and 1979 and also 1980 through 2006.

ADULT EDUCATION TO ADULT SERVICES

The ALA was established in 1876, which marked the beginning of the recognition of the library profession. ALA became the driving force behind the evolution of adult education services in public libraries in the 1920s. As reported earlier in this chapter, in 1924 the Commission on Library and

Adult Education was established, and it published a report in 1926. The commission established a subcommittee on readable books to encourage the production of books of educational value that would encourage reading among library patrons.

The ALA Board on Library and Adult Education was established in 1926 to take over the commission's functions. The board published a quarterly bulletin, *Adult Education and the Library*, and articles on techniques for providing services to adults, results of studies on reading, and other topics relevant to adult services. The board established programs such as the Reading with a Purpose Project, a consulting service to help promote readers' advisory, and other readers' services. This period saw the development of library extension services that addressed the fourth function of adult services, "stimulation" (Dresang, 1982). This function involves creating awareness of the existence of library resources relevant to patrons' specific needs and interests. Stimulation is said to have inspired library outreach programs in the 1970s (Weibel, 1982). Other programs such as Career Information Service as well as Information & Referral (I&R) were introduced under the rubric of outreach at the Brooklyn Public Library and the Onondaga County Public Library in the 1980s.

In 1934, the ALA Adult Education Board was combined with Library Extension in the Public Library Association (PLA). The new division's aim was to extend public library services to rural areas, and its members collaborated with the American Association for Adult Education and other like-minded organizations to plan extension programs. A number of publications came out of the interaction between these organizations, including *Reading with a Purpose: Journal of Adult Education and the Library* (1924–1930), Jennings's *Voluntary Education and the Library*, and Hoists Books of General Interest for Today's Readers (Weibel, 1982). In 1934 in its effort to continue the advancement of adult education in public libraries, ALA appointed John Chancellor to initiate a 10-year assessment of the development of adult education in public libraries. Alvin Johnson's study *The Public Library: A People's University* (1939) reiterated that the public library continued to be the source of knowledge for all users.

Librarians began to use the term "adult services" synonymously with "adult education." ALA continued to sponsor adult education projects. The term "adult services" came into the vocabulary of the profession in the mid-1940s when Heim (1990) observed, "adult education was increasingly being recognized as a philosophy rather than a specific set of services" and when "the services it had generated were recognized as generic to librarianship" (p. 11).

The first Office of Adult Services was established at the New York Public Library in 1946, and librarians were used to staff the office. Other libraries followed suit, and adult services came to be administered through an office with that name. The creation of an office of adult services provided public librarians with a way to include funding for adult services in their budgets. In 1946, the Adult Education Section was created within the PLA. Adult education projects were undertaken, such as the American Heritage Project (1951–1954), which was funded by the Ford Foundation under the Funds for Education (FAE). The project supported discussion groups on political and economic problems (Lee, 1966; Weibel, 1983).

The ALA Office of Adult Education was created in 1952 with funding from the Ford Foundation. The office was given $1.5 million to award grants to stimulate and promote adult education activities (1951–1961). Some of the outcomes of this funding included the Great Books Discussion Groups, which were designed to impart democratic values and political education.

Helen Lyman conducted a national survey of public libraries in 1954. This study was the first effort to describe the scope of adult services in public libraries in the United States. Her findings were reported in *Adult Education Activities in Public Libraries*. Adult services became such a large part of the services provided in public libraries that the ALA created a separate Adult Services Division (ASD) in 1957 with the goal of advancing all aspects of adult services in all libraries. ASD was "responsible for those library services designed to provide continuing educational, recreational services, and cultural development for adults" (RUSA, n.d.).

The ASD articulated the scope of its charge as providing:

- Indirect guidance (displays, reading lists)
- Advisory services (informed and planned reading)
- Services to organizations and groups (exhibits, reading lists, book talks, program planning support)
- Programs in the library (films, discussion groups, rebroadcasts of radio and television programming)
- Community advisory services

In 1964, the ASD published the *ASD Bulletin,* which absorbed the *Library Services to Labor* newsletter into the newer publication. The ASD carried out a number of bibliographic projects, including Notable Books projects, the Library Community Project, Reading for Change, and Working with New Adult Readers (McCook, 1990; Phinney 1967). Services for adults became fully accepted as a formal set of activities, and a column called "Adult Services" became a regular feature in the *ALA Bulletin* beginning in 1958. ASD focused on adults' cultural interests and the use of library services for leisure as well as formal education (ALA Bulletin, 1958). Group services expanded to include services to the individual. In 1966 a draft of "Guidelines for Library Services to Adults" was prepared by the Special Committee on Standards for Adult Services. In 1970, a fuller version of the statement emerged as "The Library Rights of Adults: A Call for Action" and was adopted by both the Adult Services Division and the Readers' Services Division of the American Library Association.

ADULT SERVICES

After the establishment of the ASD, services to adults flourished and expanded between 1960 and 1970. Libraries in the southern part of the United States and in urban areas focused on outreach (Josey, 1986; Weibel, 1983). The Office for Library Services to the Disadvantaged was established at ALA for three reasons: (1) to promote the provision of services to urban and rural poor of all ages and to those who are discriminated against because they belong to a minority group; (2) to encourage the development of user-oriented informational and educational library services to meet the needs of urban and rural poor, ethnic minorities, the underemployed, school dropouts, individuals who are semiliterate and illiterate, and those isolated by cultural differences; and (3) to ensure that libraries and other organizations have information about, access to, and technical assistance related to continuing education opportunities to assist them in developing effective outreach programs (McCook, 2001).

Adult services in public libraries grew in the 1960s, and the extent of that growth was documented by Margaret Monroe in the first issue of her *Newsletter from the President of ASD*. In "Signs of Growth of Adult Services in State and Public Libraries," Monroe confirmed that Adult Services had become a part of Readers' Services with the establishment of the Office of Adult Services at New York Public library. After almost 50 years (the 1920s through the 1970s) of attentiveness to the special library needs of adults, recognition of the library rights of adults emerged as a concern.

REFERENCE AND ADULT SERVICES: FURTHER DEVELOPMENT OF ALA SERVICE DIVISIONS

The Reference Services Division (RSD) was responsible for provision of information and bibliographic services as well as collections development to service adults as well as other library patrons. ASD and RSD collaborated on projects and instituted a policy called Library Rights of Adults: A Call for Action. This policy stated that each adult had the right to a library seeking to understand adults' needs and wants as well as searching for every way to satisfy those needs and wants. Because the two divisions had common goals, they were merged in 1972 to form the Reference and Adult Services Division (RASD). ASD ceased to exist, as did the *ASD Bulletin*. The journal of RASD, *RQ*, started publishing a section on adult services.

In 1985, the planning committee of RASD noted various aspects of adult services, including "development of services to adult user groups through techniques of planning, measurement and evaluation, publications development of standards and guidelines; programs and surveys" (Monroe, 2012, p. 11). In 1996, the RASD became the Reference and User Services Association (RUSA), as it became clear that adult service is a reference service. Adult service became subsumed in reference services, and RUSA established guidelines for information services as well as for services for different "special publics" (Monroe, 2012) such as older adults and people with disabilities. A new office—the Office for Literacy and Outreach Services (OLAS)—was created at ALA to take over the extension services of the 1960s as well as services to ethnic minorities and other underserved populations.

ADULT SERVICES, 1980–1990

In 1983, the Services to Adults Committee of the RASD conducted a national survey that was an extension of a similar survey conducted by Helen Lyman in 1950. The survey, "Adult Services in the Eighties (ASE) Project," was funded by an ALA Goal Award. The results were published in 1990 as *Adult Services: An Enduring Focus in Public Libraries* (Heim & Wallace, 1990), and they identified key services such as lifelong learning; services for minorities, job seekers, laborers, parents, people with disabilities, and genealogists; support for economic development; and public access to computers. Librarians developed these services using recommended planning processes with recommended "roles" and some responses to community needs identified through community assessment and analysis.

Adult services developed from readers' services and adult education activities. The nature of the services differ from community to community, and the objectives are the same—to provide access and guidance to adults using the public library's resources. The four functions of adult services—identified as the "service paradigm," (1) "information," (2) "instruction," (3) "guidance," and (4)"stimulation" (Dresang, 1982)—are the framework for implementing adult services in public libraries today. Adult services in the twenty-first century should be using identified community needs to plan. There have been and will continue to be demographic and societal changes as well as advances in information technology that will impact the nature and delivery of adult services in public libraries in the twenty-first century.

ADDITIONAL READING

Coleman, B. W. (2008). *Keeping the faith: The public library's commitment to adult education, 1950–2006.* (Doctoral dissertation). Retrieved from UMI Microform. (3326698)

Lee, R. E. (1966). *Continuing education for adults through the American public library, 1833–1964.* Chicago: American Library Association.
Schlachter, G. (Ed.). (1982). *The service imperative: Essays in honor of Margaret E. Monroe.* Littleton, CO: Libraries Unlimited.

REFERENCES

Adams, C. F. (1877). The public libraries and the public schools. *Library Journal, 1*, 1.
Asheim, L. (1955). *Training needs of librarians doing adult education work.* Chicago: American Library Association.
Boston Public Library. (1893). *Bulletin of the Public Library of the City of Boston,* Vol. XII. Boston, MA: Trustees of Boston Public Library.
Cannons, H. G. (1927). *Bibliography of library economy 1876–1920.* Chicago: American Library Association.
Chancellor, J. (1939). *Helping adults to learn.* Chicago: American Library Association.
Coleman, B. W. (2008). *Keeping the faith: The public library's commitment to adult education, 1950–2006.* (Doctoral dissertation). Retrieved from UMI Microform. (3326698)
Dana, J. C. (1899). *A library primer.* Chicago: Library Bureau.
Dresang, E. (1982). Service paradigm: An introduction. In G. Schlachter (Ed.), *The service imperative for libraries: Essays in honor of Margaret E. Monroe* (pp. 13–20). Littleton, CO: Libraries Unlimited.
Flexner, J., & Edge, S. (1927). *A readers' advisory service.* New York: American Association for Adult Education.
Green, S. S. (1876). Personal relations between librarians and readers. *Library Journal, 1*, 74–81.
Heim, K., & Monroe, M. (1986). Adult services. In R. Wedgeworth (Ed.), *ALA encyclopedia of library and information services* (2nd ed.). Chicago: American Library Association.
Heim, K. M., & Wallace, D. P. (1990). *Adult services: An enduring focus for public libraries.* Chicago: American Library Association.
Johnson, A. (1939). *The public library: A people's university.* Paper presented at the American Association for Adult Education: Conference on the Library in Adult Education, Princeton, New Jersey.
Josey, E. J. (1986). *Libraries, Coalition and the Homeless.* Paper presented at the American Library Association, New York.
Knowles, M. S. (1977). *A history of the adult education movement in the United States.* New York: Robert E. Krieger.
Lee, R. E. (1966). *Continuing education for adults through the American Public Library, 1833–1964.* Chicago: American Library Association.
McCook, K. de la Peña. (2001). Poverty, democracy, and public libraries. *Libraries & democracy American Lib. Assn.* (pp. 28–46). United States.
McCook, K. de la Peña. (2011). *Introduction to public librarianship* (2nd ed.). New York: Neal Schuman.

Monroe, M. E. (2006). *Margaret Monroe: Memoirs of a public librarian.* University of Wisconsin–Madison Libraries: Parallel Press.

Monroe, M. E. (2012 Literary Licensing, LLC; 1963 Scarecrow). *Library adult education: Biography of an idea.* New York: Scarecrow.

RASD. (Fall, 1970). Library rights of adults: A call for action. *ASD Newsletter,* 8, 2.

Reference and User Services Association (RUSA). (n.d.) Serving those who serve the public. Retrieved from http://www.ala.org/rusa/about/history

Rubin, R. J. (1982). Guidance. In G. Schlachter (Ed.), *The service imperative for libraries: Essays in honor of Margaret E. Monroe* (pp. 94–119). Littleton, CO: Libraries Unlimited.

Schlachter, G. (Ed.). (1982). *The service imperative: Essays in honor of Margaret E. Monroe.* Littleton, CO: Libraries Unlimited.

Steinbarger, H. (1939). The readers' advisory corps in a large divisional library. In J. Chancellor (Ed.), *Helping adults to learn: The library in action.* Chicago: American Library Association.

Utley. (1851). A public library. *Massachusetts Teacher,* 4(8), 2.

Weibel, K. (1982). The evolution of outreach 1960–1975 and its effect on reader services: Some considerations. *Occasional Paper No 156.* Urbana–Champaign: University of Illinois, Graduate School of Library and Information Science.

Yu, L. (2002). Role of the public library in the 21st century. *Journal of Educational Media & Library Sciences,* 37(3), 256–264.

CHAPTER 3

Adult Services in the Twentieth and Twenty-First Centuries

Adult services in public libraries, as described in Chapter 2, evolved from adult education services in public libraries. Adult education provided the impetus for the development of different models of adult services such as reading guidance, programming services to community organizations, and library-sponsored discussion programs (Heim, 1986). The terms "adult services" and "adult education" have been used synonymously in library jargon; however, the 1943 *A.L.A. Glossary of Library Terms* had no entry for "adult services," only "adult education" (Wente, 1979). The latest edition, *ALA Glossary of Library and Information Science* (2013), had both, defining "adult services" as "The provision of library materials, services, and programs to meet the specific interests and needs of adults by a public library" and "adult education" as "The education of adults beyond school age through regularly organized programs which have as their purpose the development of skills, knowledge, habits, or attitudes" (p. 5). According to these definitions, adult education is a function within adult services.

The service models listed in the preceding paragraph became the framework for the development and implementation of all adult services in public libraries. However, as stated in Chapter 2, the basic function of adult services is the provision of assistance to users, and it is the basis of modern reference service as defined in Samuel Green's 1876 paper "Personal Relations between Librarians and Readers." How to assist users with reference, information, instruction, and guidance is described in the literature about adult services (Wente, 1979; Heim, 1986; Dresang, 1982). The services are provided to adults to fulfill needs at different points in their lives. At times, these needs may be for survival concerns such as how to prepare for a job interview or a test. At other times, adults may come to the library for personal fulfillment such as to enjoy music or to find a recipe, or they may come for information to answer a specific question, for example, "What is the population of Connecticut?"

Adult services has been defined as providing four basic functions: information, instruction, guidance, and stimulation (Schlachter, 1982). Let's look at examples of each of these four functions from libraries today.

INFORMATION

The Greendale (Wisconsin) Public Library is proud of their wide range of adult services, in particular those that provide information to their patrons. These services, which are often listed under intriguing and inviting labels, include Ask Away (a service provided by a nationwide library consortium that allows patrons to log in to chat anytime night or day if they need help with information needs when the library is closed), WATTS UP? Power Analyzer and Watt Meter (a state-of-the-art digital microprocessor that monitors electricity, both voltage and current measurements for true power of any 120-VAC appliance; the meter can be checked out for one week), OverDrive Downloadable Media Collection (allows patrons to select and download audiobooks, films, and music to play directly on their home computer, play on an MP3 or iPod player, or burn to a CD), and VideoEye Power Magnification System (a video magnifier for public use; the system enlarges any item onto the 27-inch screen in black and white or color, allowing patrons to see whatever they bring in more clearly, e.g., newspapers, mail, prescription bottles) (Greendale Public Library, n.d.).

Zionts and colleagues (2010) found, through a market survey, that the public library is the first place many people turn to when seeking health information. But as Norman and Skinner (2006) observed, these resources provide little value if the patron lacks the skills to effectively use them. Thus, the patron needs to have consumer health literacy, and librarians may become the first point of contact as the patron seeks to use health information. In March 2010, the Medical Library Association Board of Directors approved a statement that "health librarians, because of their knowledge and training in the identification, selection, organization and dissemination of evidence-based information, play an important role in both consumer health information services and patient education" (CAPHIS, 2011, par. 1). The Delaware Academy of Medicine and the Delaware Division of Libraries extended this to cover the public librarian when they jointly issued *Consumer Health Information Service: Best Practices in Public Libraries* (http://libraries.delaware.gov/planning/pdfs/Consumer HealthBestracticesPublicLibraries.pdf). Examples of public libraries with consumer health services include the Lewes (Delaware) Public Library

(Lewes Public Library, n.d.); Crandall (New York) Public Library (http://crandalllibrary.org/programs/programs-consumerhealth.php); and the Iowa City (Iowa) Public Library (Smith, Logsden, & Clark, 2005).

INSTRUCTION

The public library endures as a center for adult education. Today, technology is a skill that can separate generations. The Livonia (Michigan) Public Library offers tutorials "for people who have never used a computer or mouse before," one-on-one computer instruction with teen volunteers who schedule one-hour blocks of instruction/assistance, basic computer classes with the adult services librarian, and eBook classes with the automation services librarian, who offers classes on using the eReader to check out books from the library (there are even separate sessions that focus on the Nook, Kindle, iPad, and Android-based devices) (Livonia Public Library, n.d.). The Lafayette (Louisiana) Public Library offers free computer classes that include using spreadsheets and integrating spreadsheets and word processing. Special programs range from presentations in honor of National Quilting Day, to a concert by a classical guitarist, to classes on buying and keeping a home and speakers as part of a community legal education series. There are also seasonal craft workshops (Lafayette Public Library, n.d.).

GUIDANCE

Job centers are available at many public libraries, such as the Job Center@Delaware Libraries, which offers free one-on-one help and workshops for Delaware's job seekers and career changers. It also offers training, career counseling, and resources to help patrons plan careers, focus job searches, apply for jobs online, create resumes and cover letters, and prepare for interviews. The Hartford (Connecticut) Public Library makes available self-assessment and personality tests, company research, networking through discussion lists and local groups, occupational training programs and test preparation, and over 500 continuing education courses, including those in office skills and business (Hartford Public Library, n.d.).

STIMULATION

The Nyack (New York) Public Library offers museum passes to the Guggenheim Museum, the Museum of the City of New York, and the Neuberger Museum of Art (at SUNY Purchase College) (Nyack Public Library, n.d.). The Chelmsford (Massachusetts) Library has a museum passes program that includes more than 12 museums, including the Massachusetts State Parks, the Museum of Fine Arts, the Museum of Science, the New

England Aquarium, the Roger Williams Park Zoo, and the John F. Kennedy Library and Museum (Chelmsford Public Library, n.d.). Maker Space at Westport (Connecticut) Public Library, based on the Maker movement, is a place for people to connect, invent, and create. According to Westport staff, "the concept originated from the realization that libraries, in this era of hands-on learning and interaction, should provide experiences that take people from imagining to actually producing" (Westport Public Library, n.d.). Services may also be designed for group activities to promote social interaction; or they may be created for special populations within the community such as the unemployed, homeless, or other targeted groups (Panz, 1989). This is an ongoing community need that public libraries continue to service.

A January 2011 report on the nation's homeless population suggests that "the poor and homeless are . . . a severely underserved community. It is time that each of our libraries steps up to the plate and develops a plan of service for these patrons" (Milone, 2011, par. 2). Milone further suggests that each public library should have a representative on the community homeless task force or coalition as well as one staff member tasked with tracking homelessness in the community and planning library-supported services appropriate to that population.

Older adults are a growing population that is beginning to raise concern. By 2030, it is expected that one in four people in the United States will be over the age of 65. Increased health care facilitates longer lives and also a growing need for consumer health literacy and access to consumer health information. Libraries will be called upon to provide additional services to the older adult population and additional accommodations for older adults with disabilities. The baby boomer generation (those born between 1945 and 1964) is now beginning to enter retirement years, and this group of older adults is different from previous generations of older citizens in that they are healthier, more active, and "view retirement not as an end, but as a new chapter in which to begin new activities and to set new goals" (Hildreth, 2006, p. 6). The baby boomers are diverse in terms of race and ethnicity, educational attainment, and family status, a situation that will create challenges as well as opportunities for libraries as they reassess services for older patrons.

The roles of the public library in addressing the service paradigms were identified by the Public Library Association (PLA). Four roles were described as centers, community activities (for a variety of activities that include meetings and services), a community information center (a clearinghouse for current information to help patrons find organizations, understand issues, and understand other services available to them), and a formal education support center for individuals of all ages who have educational objectives they may have developed when they were in a formal course of study. The next three included a current high-demand, high-interest collection of popular materials for everyone; a preschool door to learning to help children become ready to read; and the provision of information for parents and their children. The latter two referred to libraries with information for the community and a research center that would help scholars and researchers in the community find materials for in-depth studies as well as to help them with research on specific areas of knowledge. Although this was prepared in 1987, the authors had already tasked the librarian in particular and the library in general with helping patrons create new knowledge, and this is today's expanded role. Public librarians can assist their users both in locating the information they need and in helping them find the complete answers to their problems.

The role of the library must be identified before the staff can generate a list from which to select services appropriate for their library. The roles are broad categories of services that give general descriptions of what can be done or is being offered at the library. Librarians select which roles to implement depending on the needs of the community in which the library exists. At the end of the last century, Himmel and colleagues (1998) expanded the concept of library roles to 13 service responses (which were discussed in Chapter 1). Himmel provides details of the service responses, which are defined as "what a library does offer to the public in an effort to meet a set of well-defined community needs" (p. 54). These service responses are specifically designed to respond to identified community needs. It is the responsibility of the library staff to assess the needs and develop services to fit those needs.

CATEGORIES OF ADULT SERVICES

McCook (2011) reorganized the 13 service points into four categories that she says reflect a "larger vision" of the public library's importance to its communities. The four categories are:

- Public sphere
- Cultural heritage
- Education
- Information

Each category is subdivided into areas that address some of the service points in activities that best address the needs of the adult in the twenty-first century.

Public Sphere

The category related to the public sphere is divided into three components: commons, community information and referral, and current topics and titles. To confirm its role as a public sphere, the public library has been a meeting place for its patrons from the inception of public libraries; it serves as a storehouse of information as well as a meeting place. A Clarion University study found that 36 percent of respondents thought that the library helped them overcome loneliness (Vavrek, 1995). According to McCook (2011), "the public library is an important part of the public sphere and functions as a commons where community voices come together" (p. 207). *Strategic Planning for Results* discusses the following enhancements of the public sphere: being a citizen who is informed about local, national, and world affairs; knowing your community (community resources and services); and visiting a comfortable place (physical and virtual spaces) (Nelson & Public Library Association, 2008). The facets of the public sphere—the commons, community information and referral, and current topics and titles—are discussed in the following sections.

The Commons

The commons is explained by the Public Library Association (PLA) as "A library that provides a common environment that helps address the needs of people to meet and interact with others in their community and to participate in public discourse about community issues" (Nelson, 2001, p. 65). The commons provides a way to encourage dialog. The idea that a public library functions as a commons is not new; a number of books have addressed the role of public libraries in connection with society, among them *A Place at the Table: Participating in Community Building* (McCook, 2000) and *Civic Space/Cyperspace* (Molz & Dain, 1999).

The library has been identified as the starting point for community projects (Christensen & Levison, 2003). Through its Public Programs Office (PPO), ALA fosters programming that emphasizes the role of the public library as a commons that sponsors such programs as the American Heritage Project 1950. Other programs in the same vein include One Community, One Book and Long Gone: The Literature and Culture of African American Migration.

Community Information and Referral

Information and Referral (I&R) services link individuals with services to meet a specific need or solve a particular problem. I&R has long been a part of adult services in public libraries. Information about community agencies and organizations is made available through public libraries. There are three basic processes involved in maintaining an I&R service: (1) creating a resource file, (2) distributing the information, and (3) updating the file (Poe, 2006). I&R service is similar to the library's reference service in that (1) information is gathered in anticipation of the user's needs, (2) the librarian helps the patron find the needed information, and (3) the librarian advises the user, such as by providing an assessment of the resource (Poe, 2006).

At the national level, the proper role of libraries in I&R was defined in the National Commission on Libraries and Information Science (NCLIS) report of 1983. The report recommended that social service agencies act with libraries to provide I&R services. The Community Information Section (CIS) of the PLA formalized the activity by developing *Guidelines for Establishing Information and Referral Services in Public Libraries* in 1979. The guidelines have undergone four revisions, with the latest version having been published in 1997. The Internet and other technologies have impacted the delivery of I&R in libraries.

The Detroit Public Library led the way with its program The Information Place (TIP) in the 1970s and provided the model for I&R in public libraries. TIP is a free community information and referral service that helps people find answers to problems of everyday living. Librarians link individuals to agencies and local nonprofit organizations that offer services such as emergency food, health care, support groups, and parenting education. Among the resources on which the TIP librarians rely is the TIP database, a library-maintained resource file of detailed information on human services and social services provided to residents of southeast Michigan by over 2,000 agencies and organizations. Many local human services agencies also use the TIP database via subscription agreements that help defray data maintenance expenses (Detroit Public Library, n.d.).

The following libraries provide Community Information and Referral services:

- Memphis (Tennessee) Public Library: http://www.memphislibrary .org/linc/comminfo.htm
- Cabell County (West Virginia) Public Library: http://cabell.lib.wv .us/pages/aa-inforeferral.html
- Calhoun County (Florida) Public Library: http://fchr.state.fl.us/fchr/ outreach/community_resource_map/district_1/calhoun__1/information _and_referral_centers/calhoun_county_public_library
- Arlington County (Virginia) Public Library: http://www.virginia navigator.org/vn/information-referral-community-services/arlington -county-public-library/program-74705.aspx

Current Titles and Topics

Adult services include the selection and collection of library resources. Reading help and readers' advisory (RA) services are considered a hallmark of adult services in public libraries. RA services have grown to be one of the most offered components of services for adults in public libraries. A number of publications in the early literature address the topic, for example, *Fiction in Public Libraries, 1876–1900* (Carrier, 1985); *Fiction in Libraries, 1900–1950* (Carrier, 1965); and *The Geography of Reading* (Wilson, 1938).

More recently, *Genreflecting* (Herald, 1982) has been published in five editions since 1982 (Herald & Wiegand, 2006). The 1990s saw a resurgence of interest in RA services, and technology has enabled the development of electronic resources to support RA. Librarians are also able to deliver remote support for this service.

With RA services has come research in the role of reading in the lives of library patrons, that is, the study of why people read and what they read. RA has also become an element in providing lifelong learning services to adults. Efforts are continually being made to encourage reading among library patrons. The development of nonfiction RA has also become a big part of RA in the twenty-first century. "The power of reading to change lives through cultivation of the public sphere in libraries is mighty" (McCook, 2001, p. 193)

The rising popularity of eBooks has been touted in newspapers, in magazine articles, and on websites as bringing a range of consequences, from bringing the end to print publishing, to being an alternative vehicle of choice for content, to being a convenient companion to the printed book, not unlike a cellphone is to an office landline or a tablet is to a large flat-panel television. The rising popularity of the eBook has led to the exploration of lending eBooks through libraries; this has been met with varying levels of acceptance and success.

Publishers and libraries need "to work together in the eBook era just as they have done for many decades in the print era" (Clark, 2013, par. 4). "Throughout the course of the last year, ALA leaders met with Big Six publishers ... to discuss library ebook lending and to make the case why library lending is beneficial for publishers and society" (Clark, 2013, par. 5). With nearly a quarter of Americans having read at least one eBook in the past year (Brudno, 2013), RA can expect that "[a]ny time a new format is introduced in libraries, we need to look at how that format affects the readers' approach to the material" (Dunneback, 2011, p. 325).

Cultural Heritage

The second category in McCook's list of adult services—cultural heritage—combines three service points from Nelson's *The New Planning for Results: A Streamlined Approach* (Nelson, 2001). Librarians, particularly those in genealogy libraries or genealogy sections of libraries, have a long history of integrating cultural activities as well as collecting and preserving artifacts and other icons relevant to their patrons' historical and cultural heritage. Librarians use discussion groups, lectures, exhibits, and celebrations of different cultural events to promote cultural awareness. National entities such as the National Endowment for the Humanities (NEH) and the Center for the Book at the Library of Congress promote the exploration of culture and humanities by supporting and funding exhibitions, reading groups, lectures, catalogs, discussion series, and films. The Public Programs

Office (PPO) of the ALA collaborates with the NEH and Library of Congress to promote cultural programs. The Institute of Museums and Library Services (IMLS), established in 1996, is a federal grant-making entity. IMLS funds innovative cultural and library activities, and it encourages collaboration between libraries and museums in the implementation of cultural and informative programs.

This second category describes the resources being collected and maintained in today's public libraries. To make people aware of these resources and to meet the needs of patrons with different ethnic backgrounds requires cultural awareness.

The ongoing demographic changes in U.S. society that are resulting in the large increase in the number of foreign-born individuals and non–English speakers make understanding and appreciating other peoples' cultures imperative. Librarians from different ethnic backgrounds have organized their own organizations within ALA to help identify and articulate services appropriate for different ethnic groups. These organizations include the American Indian Library Association (AILA), the Black Caucus of the American Library Association (BCALA), the Chinese Library Association (CLA), the Asian Pacific American Library Association (APALA), and REFORMA (the national association to promote library and information services to Latinos).

Cultural heritage events supported by adult services programming provide learning opportunities for adults in public libraries. These also fit under the education category and include cultural heritage (preserving tangible and intangible living and remains of cultures), cultural awareness (understanding how an individual's culture may inform his or her values, behavior, beliefs, and basic assumptions), and cultural competence (ability to interact effectively with individuals of different cultures, beginning with understanding one's own culture). As local communities become more global in composition, cultural awareness and competence become increasingly needed basic skills. Libraries, along with archives and museums, are cultural heritage organizations that are "keystones sustaining communities' sense of place and cultural identity" (http://www.imls.gov/about/cultural_heritage.aspx, par. 1) within the broader society while helping to preserve the cultural heritage of the community and of society.

The NEH and the ALA have joined together to create a planned series of *Bridging Cultures* "Bookshelves" that will "provide free books, films and on-line resources to enhance libraries' collections and enable them to create new programs for their communities" (http://www.neh.gov/divisions/bridging-cultures/featured-project/neh-announces-bridging-cultures-programs-libraries). The *Bridging Cultures* initiative is intended to highlight "the importance of civility in American life and embrace the role of libraries in fostering community conversations that bring the humanities to the public in new ways" (NEH, par. 2).

San Diego Public Library (SDPL) "is San Diego's largest provider of free cultural programming, with more than 5,000 cultural and educational events each year" (http://www.supportmylibrary.org/projects/culturalprogramming, par. 1) with about half of the branch libraries hosting musical performances. The library partners with the community by encouraging patrons to attend a concert and make a contribution at the event, thereby encouraging individuals and groups to underwrite an individual concert or a concert series. The Central Library's musical performances date back to the mid-1950s. SDPL also presents museum-quality art exhibitions at the libraries and hosts artists' lectures, a television program, and other art-related activities (par. 5).

A 1999 report by the Center for Arts and Cultural Policy Studies at Princeton University, stated that 86 percent of public libraries serving populations of over 5,000 offer some form of cultural programming for adults (https://www.princeton.edu/~artspol/quickfacts/artsorgs/cppl98.html, par, 1). The most common forms of cultural programs include book discussions (61 percent), author readings and presentations (59 percent), lecture series (44 percent), musical performances (42 percent), dramatic performances (23 percent), film series (20 percent), and dance performances (14 percent). A newer trend incorporates intangible cultural heritage into library programming through establishing a local storyteller laureate or storyteller-in-residence program (Urbaniak, 2012).

In 2009, the ALA launched a cultural programming site (http://www .programminglibrarian.org/) to assist libraries of all types and sizes in creating cultural and community programs. The website includes a resource library, live learning opportunities, and a blog to keep librarians informed of library programming events and to provide inspiration for new library programs through access to programming tools, online learning, and resources. Resources (http:// www.programminglibrarian.org/library/events-celebrations) include National Hispanic Heritage Month (http://www.programminglibrarian.org/library/ events-celebrations/national-hispanic-heritage-month), African American History Month (http://www.programminglibrarian.org/library/events-celebrations/african-american-history-month), National Women's History Month (http://www.programminglibrarian.org/library/events-celebrations/ national-womens-history-month), Asian/Pacific American Heritage Month (http://www.programminglibrarian.org/library/events-celebrations/asian pacific-american-heritage-month), Jewish American Heritage Month (http:// www.programminglibrarian.org/library/events-celebrations/jewish-american -heritage-month), National Poetry Month (http://www.programminglibrarian .org/library/events-celebrations/national-poetry-month), Native American Heritage Month (http://www.programminglibrarian.org/library/events-celebrations/ native-american-heritage-month), Learn a Foreign Language Month (http:// www.programminglibrarian.org/library/events-celebrations/learn-a-foreign -language-month), and Jazz Appreciation Month (http://www.programm inglibrarian.org/library/events-celebrations/jazz-appreciation-month).

The National Initiative for a Networked Cultural Heritage (NINCH) published the *Guide to Good Practice in the Digital Representation & Management of Cultural Heritage Materials* (2002). This report, described as "a resource that will become a touchstone for new practitioners for years to come" is designed for those in all sectors of the cultural community who are digitizing and networking cultural resources. The report can be found at http://www.ninch.org/programs/practice. The International Federation of Library Associations and Institutions (IFLA) publishes a professional report on trends in cultural collaboration and cooperation, including best practices (Yarrow, Clubb, & Draper, 2008).

Education

McCook's third category is education. While the public library was originally promoted as the people's college, public librarians are also responsible for encouraging their patrons to become lifelong learners. "Lifelong learning is essential to help Americans adjust to the changing demands of the job market throughout their lives. Flexible educational arrangements—including part-time, anytime, anywhere opportunities—are essential" (U.S. Department of Education, 2000, p. 27). Lifelong learning is a conscious, voluntary, self-motivated process of acquiring knowledge for personal development or career advancement through formal or informal education throughout an individual's life span. Learning opportunities are provided to different categories of adults in libraries; people with various educational needs are supported with different types of library resources, information services, and programming as well as outreach services.

Van Fleet (1995) tells us that library services have had "essentially the same goals for all patrons, to enrich leisure, to gather and disseminate information for effective living, and to provide for continued growth and learning throughout life. The specific manner in which these goals are fulfilled will vary according to community need and demand" (p. 4).

The PLA supports librarians through the Adult Continuing and Independent Learning Service Committee. The committee is responsible for developing guidelines for adult education services as well as helping to assemble independent learning resources. The PLA states that a library that provides a lifelong learning service response "helps address the desire for self-directed personal growth and development opportunities" (Nelson, 2001, p. 211). The provision of Internet access also supports lifelong learning activities.

The EveryoneOn Connect2Compete campaign is a public awareness effort designed to help all Americans access free digital literacy training in their libraries and community centers. "Eighty-three percent of [libraries] offer informal training in digital literacy, helping people learn how to use computers, navigate the web, and find the best and most useful information. And 44 percent offer formal classes" (Hildreth, 2013, par. 4).

The Information Policy and Access Center (iPAC) within the College of Information Studies (iSchool) at the University of Maryland–College Park maintains the Public Libraries and the Internet website (http://www.plinter

netsurvey.org/), which helps users to learn more about technology access either in their libraries or their states. They are also able to participate in surveys about library funding and technology access.

The Hamburg Declaration, which was adopted during the 1997 UNESCO/CONFINTEA meeting in Hamburg, stated that "UNESCO should strengthen libraries, museums, heritage and cultural institutions as learning places and partners in the lifelong learning process and modern citizenship" (Häggström, 2004, p. 1). As we become a society of lifelong learners, public libraries will play a fundamental and critical role as they become "nodes connecting the local learning setting—whether it is of a formal or informal kind—with the global resources of information and knowledge" (Häggström, 2004, p. 3).

Information

Information covers four of the "service responses" from *New Planning for Results* (Nelson, 2001). These categories are:

- General information
- Business and career information
- Consumer information
- Government information

General Information

General information is provided through reference services that may take different forms. They may include direct individual assistance, group instruction, or signage and the development of guides to library resources. The services may be delivered in person or remotely to support distance learners. The framework for delivery of information services is provided by RUSA and articulates six categories: services, resources, access, personnel, evaluation, and ethics. Each is briefly described in the following paragraphs.

Services offered should be accurate and accessible and include instruction, publicity, and country information. They should add value to information and referral. To meet the guideline for *resources*, librarians should collect information resources using collection development policies and should support the information needs of all users in all formats. The contents of the collections should be accurate and current. *Access* refers to the need to organize these resources to address the needs of all people, including people with disabilities, which is a responsibility for facilities planners. State-of-the-art technologies should be used to provide access for all.

To meet the *personnel* guideline, libraries must have qualified personnel who can communicate effectively with all components of the community regardless of the patron's age, gender, sexual preference, ethnicity, disability, or language proficiency. Library staff should be provided with opportunities to expand their cultural awareness and competencies, their awareness of and skill in working with special populations, and their skill in communicating with non-native speakers. In a survey of public, academic, and special librarians, Crary (1982) found that 38 percent needed foreign language for their work, and two-thirds indicated that foreign language knowledge was needed by librarians in other positions in the library. Increasingly, librarians need to consider gaining at least basic communication skills in the primary foreign language spoken in their community.

The guideline for *evaluation* mandates that library staff continually evaluate services and make necessary adjustments. Evaluation should be conducted in a number of areas: the overall adult services department or area, reference and information services, physical collections, digital collections, programming (overall and individual events), and staff. The evaluation of all who work in the library, including any volunteers, should always be done in an *ethical* manner and governed by the ALA code of ethics which is the last category.

Business and Career Information

Public libraries provide access to information for economic development in the community in which they exist. Librarians provide information for individuals as well as businesses. They collaborate with chambers of commerce as well as other government agencies such as the Small Business Administration (SBA) to provide information for economic development. Through the Business Reference and Service Section (BRASS), RUSA provides resources for supporting business information services for the community. BRASS members set up committees that focus on service to public libraries. BRASS also provides publications such as *Public Libraries Briefcase,* which can be found at http://www.ala.org/rusa/sections/brass/brasspubs/publibbrief/publiclibraries, and *Guidelines for Medical, Legal and Business Responses*, at http://www.ala.org/rusa/resources/guidelines/guidelinesmedical.

The PLA further provides ways for librarians to help provide public library service to the business community and to patrons through the PLA Career and Business Services Committee. Librarians must support job seekers in their community with career services. These services are especially critical in times of economic downturn as they provide resources such as books, online job searching tools, computers, and resume writing support. To reach a wide audience, librarians work diligently to make their career services known to the entire community. These services are essential to help poorer members of any community who would otherwise lack the resources to afford this information to prepare them to compete in the job market.

As we have discussed elsewhere in this book, public libraries can be centers to help individuals gain job skills, gain job search skills, and access resources to find job opportunities. One example was mentioned earlier, Job Center@Delaware Libraries (http://lib.de.us/jobcenter/). This is a free service for job seekers and career changers. The center offers training, career counseling, and resources to help people find jobs and enhance job skills. Patrons can plan a career, focus a job search, create a resume and cover letter, apply for jobs online, and prepare for job interviews. The Yonkers (New York) Public Library (http://www.ypl.org/job-info-center) offers free sessions with a career counselor and drop-in sessions with a job coach. The Tacoma (Washington) Public Library (http://www.tacomapubliclibrary.org/Page.aspx?nid=216) offers free classes with leading career coaches in the region; GED preparation materials and practice tests; practice placement and entrance exams (e.g., ACT, SAT, GRE); interactive online practice tests for preparatory exams, including certification, licensing, and civil service tests; and free computer classes.

Consumer Information

Libraries also provide access to consumer information such as health information, consumer reports, and other types of information that create public awareness on consumer issues. This includes referrals to other agencies in the community so that patrons can find the government offices—national, state, and local—they need to help them take care of their needs.

Best practices in public libraries for consumer information services include:

- Forming strategic partnerships that include public libraries, relevant special libraries or collections, and relevant community organizations and agencies
- Assessing community needs and planning the scope of services
- Providing consumer information at the time of need and at the point of services
- Offering current, reliable, and accurate sources of information
- Promoting and marketing the services widely
- Developing plans to sustain and/or expand the service

(Adapted from http://libraries.delaware.gov/For_Libraries/Planning/documents/Consumer_Health_Best_Practices_-_Public_Libraries.pdf)

Some examples of consumer information services are:

- Consumer Information, Madison (Wisconsin) Public Library (http://www.madisonpubliclibrary.org/consumer-information)
- Consumer Reports & Information, Seattle (Washington) Public Library (http://www.spl.org/library-collection/articles-and-research/consumer-reports-and-information)

- Consumer Information, Kansas City (Kansas) Public Library (http://www.kclibrary.org/consumer-information)
- Consumer Information, Palatine (Illinois) Public Library District (http://www.palatinelibrary.org/research-resources/consumer-information)

Government Information

Government information is an important component of adult services in public libraries. Libraries have offered access to government laws and regulations and to state and municipal documents. Developments in information technology have made it possible for federal, state, and municipal information to be available electronically, and the Internet has become a major source of government information. Depository libraries provide access to federal documents and sometimes documents of international agencies such as the World Bank or United Nations. Because these documents are usually free, they are an excellent resource for patrons. However, many patrons are not able to carry out the type of research needed to find relevant information, and the librarian can help patrons sort through these laws and regulations. Librarians who need help in understanding what government documents can offer can access the ALA's roundtable that points out new documents.

Members of the Government Documents Roundtable (GODORT) of ALA oversee government document issues and appoint task forces to deal with problems related to delivery of or access to government documents. GODORT's mission is to (1) provide a forum for discussion of problems and concerns, and for exchange of ideas by librarians working with government documents; (2) provide a force for initiating and supporting programs to increase availability, use, and bibliographic control of documents; (3) increase communication between documents librarians and other librarians; and (4) contribute to the extension and improvement of education and training of documents librarians (http://www.ala.org/godort/). Membership in GODORT is open to individuals and institutions with an interest in government information and offers opportunities for discussion, continuing education, and participation.

This last of McCook's categories, information, points to public libraries as holding essential resources—book, media, and electronic. In this provision of resources, the librarian's role is to help patrons sort through the vast amounts of information at their fingertips. The suggestion that electronic resources provide all that is needed and that libraries are irrelevant does not address the fact that not all adults have access to electronic resources. Nor do they have the ability to sift through the information to discover what is relevant and accurate. Teaching patrons how to sift through the ocean of information is one role of the librarian in the provision of information.

Public librarians endeavor to provide services to all members of the community and, according to McCook (2000), "the services should be configured to community needs and must take into consideration the needs of the individual adults and the challenges to provide access for everyone in the community" (p. 201). Public librarians are striving, with the help of ALA, PLA, and government agencies, to provide service for all adults in their community no matter their physical or socioeconomic situation. Guides are set up for services for older adults, people with disabilities, and non-English speakers.

IMPACT OF TECHNOLOGY

Librarians have been in the forefront of applying technology to library functions. They were first adopters of computers, beginning with the use mainframes for library management. Circulation systems and online catalogs greatly increased access, and while many patrons lamented the loss of their beloved card catalogs, almost all libraries—academic, public, school, and special—have online public access catalogs. A complete history of the early impact of librarians on library automation in all types of libraries can be found in Brown-Syed's *Parents of Invention* (2011). A shorter version of this history is provided here.

Black (2007) documented the first use of punch cards in 1934 at the Boston Public Library for circulation, purchases, and membership transactions. The University of Texas used punch cards in 1936 for circulation control. Two punch card machines were installed at the Montclair Public Library in New Jersey for recording charging transactions.

As new technologies such as mainframe computers, minicomputers, photocopiers, audio-visual materials, and satellites were introduced, librarians implemented the technologies. The major area of computer application in libraries was cataloging. In 1968, machine readable cataloging (MARC) was introduced by the Library of Congress in conjunction with the Ohio College Library Center (OCLC). Bibliographic data became available initially in batch mode. In 1970, the batch system was replaced with online systems (Martin, 1978). In the beginning, the application of computers in libraries was in "back–room," or technical, services. With the introduction of online systems came the use of computers in public services such as circulation. The online catalog was introduced, and OCLC expanded it, which led to the development of bibliographic networks for shared cataloging and resource sharing. Online public access catalogs (OPACS) became part of the mechanism for providing access to the holdings of libraries and library networks.

In the early 1970s, Lockheed Information Systems and Systems Development Corporation (SDC) began to distribute online databases. By the end of 1977, a large number of databases were accessible online, especially in special and academic libraries. Many of these systems ran on mainframe or minicomputers. In the early 1980s, microcomputers were introduced, which made it possible for public libraries to provide increased access to information sources by implementing microcomputers in all aspects of public services (Davis, Lambson, & Whitney, 1987). Five major distinct areas were identified as being impacted by evolving technologies:

- In-house public computer laboratories for use in educational, informational, and recreational activities
- Ongoing computer literacy classes
- Online information retrieval services
- Online reference services
- Career counseling and microcomputer services

With the addition of computer technology public libraries have become a main source of Internet access as well as a place to come to use a computer and to receive training in technology literacy. A survey by the National Center for Education and Statistics (NCES) showed that 92 percent of large public libraries serving communities of over 100,000 people reported that they provided Internet access for adults for independent use, while 84 percent of medium libraries (serving communities of 25,000–100,000) and small libraries (serving communities of under 25,000) provide Internet access for adult patrons. In addition to providing Internet access, public libraries use the Internet, via the library's website, to provide access to the library's catalog holdings and digital holdings such as eBooks and full-text journal articles. Library websites may also provide links to community information. (Lewis & Farris, 2002). With new technologies, librarians are now providing remote services to patrons, including chat reference and 24/7 content delivery services. With the advent of Web 2.0, participatory services are available using blogs, instant messaging (IM), wikis, podcasts, and RSS feeds.

Public librarians have developed new models of service delivery because of these emerging technologies. Librarians also need to teach their patrons to use the new technologies, and they also need to show patrons how to evaluate the resources they find using the Internet. Public libraries now offer access to information in all its formats. In some cases, they have to deliver information to the patron's doorstep. The need to serve patrons wherever they are was reiterated in 2006 by McDonough and Cohen.

ASSISTIVE TECHNOLOGIES

The ability to provide services to patrons with disabilities has improved with advances in technology. Passage of the Americans with Disabilities Act (ADA) in 1990 made equal access to the public library a major issue for librarians who try to deliver services via assistive technology (AT) to patrons with disabilities. The Technology-Related Assistance to Individuals with Disabilities Act of 1988 defines AT as "any item, piece of equipment or product system whether acquired commercially, modified or customized that is used to increase, maintain or improve the functional capabilities of individual with disabilities" (http://michcy.org/laws/ata).

The Technology-Related Assistance for Individuals with Disabilities Act was renewed in 1998 in the Assistive Technology Act (ATA). The Act references computers with speech output, screen magnifiers, Braille readouts, electronic magnifiers and pointers, and other similar devices. Librarians not only need to provide AT resources, but they also need to provide increased awareness about their existence in the library. Public libraries in the twenty-first century are heavily dependent on new and emerging technologies to provide equal access to all library resources in all formats to their patrons no matter where they may be, whether at home, school, or work.

Public libraries should also inform patrons with disabilities about resources available through the Library of Congress. Taped newspapers and books have been replaced by electronic resources.

Librarians develop service models by using the "service responses" and guidelines from various professional organizations. The implementation of technology in the development and delivery of adult services has made it possible for services to be provided remotely to adults who otherwise cannot come to the library. Services for adults in the twenty-first century have been relying and will rely very strongly on information and telecommunications technology.

REFERENCES

Black, A. (2007). Mechanization in libraries and information retrieval: Punched cards and microfilm before the widespread adoption of computer technology in libraries. *Library History*, 23(4), 291–299.

Brown-Syed, C. (2011). *Pioneers of invention*. Santa Barbara, CA: Libraries Unlimited.

Brudno, S. (2013, February). Ebooks: Reading, libraries, and connectedness. *Information Today*, 30(20), 13.

Carrier, E. J. (1965). *Fiction in public libraries, 1876–1900*. Lanham, MD: Scarecrow.

Chelmsford Public Library. (n.d.). http://www.chelmsfordlibrary.org/library_info/museum_passes.html

Clark, L. (2013, March 27). Penguin revisits library pilot terms. American Libraries, E-content blog, http://americanlibrariesmagazine.org/e-content/penguin-revisits-library-pilot-terms

Consumer and Patient Health Information Section (CAPHIS). (2011). The librarian's role in the provision of consumer health information and patient education. Retrieved March 30, 2013, from http://caphis.mlanet.org/chis/librarian.html

Crary, R. L. (1982, Fall). Foreign languages and the librarian. *Journal of Education for Librarianship, 23*(2), 110–124.

Davis, D. M., Lambson, N., & Whitney, S. L. (1987). Public access microcomputer services in public libraries. *Library Journal, 112*(18), 56.

Delaware Public Library. (n.d.). http://libraries.delaware.gov/planning/pdfs/ConsumerHealthBestracticesPublicLibraries.pdf

Detroit Public Library. (n.d.). http://www.detroitpubliclibrary.org/specialservice/tip/

Dunneback, K. (2011). E-books and readers' advisory. *Reference & User Services Quarterly, 50*(4), 325–329.

Greendale Public Library. (n.d.). http://greendalepubliclibrary.org/Services_Facilities/Adult_Services/Adult_Services.htm

Häggström, B. M. (Ed.). (2004). The role of libraries in lifelong learning: Final report of the IFLA program under the Section for Public Libraries. http://archive.ifla.org/VII/s8/proj/Lifelong-LearningReport.pdf

Hartford Public Library. (n.d.). http://www.hplct.org/library-services/job-career/

Heim, K. (1986). Adult services as a reflective of the changing role of the public library. *RQ, 27*(2), 180–187.

Herald, D. T., & Wiegand, W. A. (2006). *Genreflecting: A guide to popular reading interests* (6th ed.). Westport, CT: Libraries Unlimited.

Hildreth, S. (2006, November/December). Public libraries and baby boomers. *Public Libraries, 45*(6), 6–7.

Hildreth, S. H. (2013, March 21). Everyone on! Libraries play essential role in Connect2Compete campaign. UpNext (the official blog of the Institute of Museum and Library Services). http://blog.imls.gov/?p=3078

Himmel, E. E., Wilson, W. J., & Revision Committee of the Public Library Association (1998). *Planning for results: A public library transformation process.* Chicago: American Library Association.

Johnson, D. W. (1999). *Cultural programs for adults in public libraries: A survey report.* Chicago: American Library Association.

Lafayette Public Library. (n.d.). Retrieved August 11, 2013, from http://lafayettepubliclibrary.org/?page_id=1241

Lewes Public Library. (n.d.). Retrieved August 11, 2013, from http://www.leweslibrary.org/information/consumer_health_services.htm

Lewis, L., & Farris, E. (2002, November). *Programs for adults in public library outlets* (NCES 2003-010). Washington, D.C.: U.S. Department of Education, Office of Educational Research and Improvement. http://nces.ed.gov/pubs2003/2003010.pdf

Livonia Public Library. (n.d.). http://livonia.lib.mi.us/adultservices

Martin, G. (1984). *Library services for adults.* Chicago: American Library Association.

Martin, S. K. (1978). The impact of technology on libraries and librarians: A literature review. Preface and introduction by E. J. Josey (Ed.), foreword by Clara Stanton Jones, *The information society: Issues and answers/[sponsored by] American Library Association's Presidential Commission for the 1977 Detroit annual conference* (pp. 20–25). Phoenix, AZ: Oryx Press.

McClure, C. R., Owen, A., Zweizig, D., Lynch, M. J., & Van House, N. A. (1987). *Planning and role setting for public libraries: A manual of options and procedures.* Chicago: American Library Association.

McCook, K. de la Peña. (1992, Winter). Where would we be without them: Libraries and adult education activities, 1966–91. *RQ, 32*(2), 245–253.

McCook, K. de la Peña. (2000, May 1). Ending the isolation of poor people. *American Libraries, 31*(5), 45.

McCook, K. de la Peña. (2011). *Introduction to public librarianship* (2nd ed.). New York: Neal-Schuman.

McDonough, K., & Cohen, M. (2006). Open for business: The NYPL Science, Industry and Business Library takes stock. *Library Quarterly, 25*(1/2), 75–90.

Milone, N. (2011, November/December). Public libraries and the homeless. *Public Libraries, 50*(6), 13–22.

Molz, R. K., & Dain, P. (1999). *Civic space/cyberspace: The American public library in the information age.* Cambridge, MA: MIT Press.

Monroe, M. E. (1979). Adult services in the third millennium. *RQ, 18*(3), 267–273.

National Center for Educational Statistics. (NCES, 2002). Programs for adults in public library outlets. http://nces.ed.gov/surveys/frss/publications/2003010/index.asp?sectionid=6

National Endowment for the Humanities (NEH). (n.d.). http://www.neh.gov/divisions/bridging-cultures

Nelson, S. (2001). *The new planning for results: A streamlined approach.* Chicago: American Library Association.

Nelson, S. S., & Public Library Association. (2008). *Strategic planning for results* (Fully rev. ed.). Chicago: American Library Association.

Norman, C. D., & Skinner, H. A. (2006). eHealth literacy: Essential skills for consumer health in a networked world. *Journal of Medical Internet Research, 8* (2): e9URL: http://www.jmir.org/2006/2/e9/

Nyack Public Library. (n.d.). http://nyacklibrary.org/adultservices

Panz, R. (1989). Library services to special population groups in the 21st century. *Journal of Library Administration, 11*(1/2), 151–171.

Poe, J. (2006, Spring). Information and referral services: A brief history. *Southeastern Librarian, 54*(1), Article 8. Available at: http://digitalcommons.kennesaw.edu/seln/vol54/iss1/8

Prasad, P. (2009). Reference services to senior groups in the San Antonio Public Library. *Reference Librarian, 50*(1), 99–108.

Scott, R. (2011). The role of public libraries in community building. *Public Library Quarterly, 30*(30), 191–227.

Smith, C., Logsden, K., & Clark, M. (2005). Consumer health information services at Iowa City Public Library. *Library Trends, 53*(3), 496–511.

Technology Assistance for Individuals with Disabilities Act. (1988). http://www.naset.org/techassist2.0.html

Urbaniak, T. (2012). The public library and intangible cultural heritage: The Storyteller-in-Residence program of the Cape Breton Regional Library. *Journal of Library Innovation, 3*(2), 33–42. http://www.libraryinnovation.org/article/view/194/382

U.S. Department of Education. (2000, November). Learning without limits: An agenda for the Office of Postsecondary Education. http://www2.ed.gov/offices/OPE/AgenProj/report/AgendaProjectReport.pdf

Van Fleet, C. J. (1990). Lifelong learning theory and the provision of adult services. In K. M. Heim & D. P. Wallace (Eds.), *Adult services: An enduring focus for public libraries* (pp. 166–211). Chicago: American Library Association.

Van Fleet, C. J. (1995). A matter of focus: Reference services for older adults. *Reference Librarian, 49/50,* 147–164.

Vavrek, B. (1995). Rural information needs and the role of the public library. *Library Trends, 44*(1), 21.

Wente, J. (1979). What are "adult services"? *RQ, 18*(3), 231–234.

Westport Public Library. (n.d.). http://www.westportlibrary.org/services/maker-space

Wilson, L. R. (1938). *The geography of reading: A study of the distribution and status of libraries in the United States.* Chicago: American Library Association and the University of Chicago Press.

Yarrow, A., Clubb, B., & Draper, J.-L. (2008). *Public libraries, archives and museums: Trends in collaboration and cooperation* (IFLA Professional Reports, No. 108). The Hague: International Federation of Library Associations and Institutions. http://www.ifla.org/files/assets/hq/publications/professional-report/108.pdf

Young, H. (Ed.), with Belanger, T. (1983). *The ALA glossary of library and information science.* Chicago: American Library Association.

Zionts, N. D., Apter, J., Kuchta, J., & Greenhouse, P. K. (2010). Promoting consumer health literacy: Creation of a health information librarian fellowship. *Reference & User Services Quarterly, 49*(4), 350–359.

PART II

Tools and Techniques

"By three methods we may learn wisdom: First, by reflection, which is noblest; Second, by imitation, which is easiest; and third by experience, which is the bitterest."

—Confucius

"The only source of knowledge is experience."

—Albert Einstein

CHAPTER 4

Planning for Adult Services

In this chapter, we will examine the way libraries plan for adult services by learning about the community that the library serves, the individuals in that community, and their information needs. To learn about the community, the library conducts an analysis of the community's makeup. Based on the results of the community analysis, a community information needs assessment is conducted. Community analysis can be defined as "nothing more than the division of the community into its component parts, the peculiar characteristics of the community elements—including characteristics, needs and behavior are identified and their significance established" (Evans, 1976, p. 441). Community needs assessment is described as gathering "accurate information representative of the needs of a community. Assessments are performed prior to taking action and are used to determine current situations and identify issues for action. Needs assessments establish the essential foundation for vital planning" (Taylor, n.d.). Assessment focuses on information needs, services provided, and the adequacy of the services as they relate to the identified need for information.

In this chapter, we will also review the history of community analysis in libraries and the tools for conducting community analysis and community needs assessment. Resources and methods for planning library services based on community analysis and assessment will be examined.

Whether one is planning a one-time short program or a major programmatic change in adult services, a successful enterprise is not something that just happens—it takes planning that is informed by knowledge of the community. The importance of establishing knowledge of the community cannot be overestimated. Greer and Hale (1981) emphasized that a thorough knowledge of the community is critical when establishing goals and objectives on which planning is based. Indeed, "it is the foundation of a responsible library policy" (p. 30). Library services can be anticipated and projected from the results of a community analysis. Resources can be allocated, staff trained and organized, and budgets prepared.

HISTORY OF COMMUNITY ASSESSMENT AND ANALYSIS IN LIBRARIES

Community assessment and analysis, which can be described as an essential part of the reference librarian's toolkit, seem to be synonymous terms; yet some make the distinction that analysis is the collection and detailed examination of data about a community to understand it, while assessment is the careful consideration of the information or data known about a community to determine the importance or priority of various elements within or components of the community. For example, analysis might involve understanding the generational groups within the community that the library services, while assessment would determine priorities related to maintaining or expanding library services for each group by considering each group's needs and the corresponding existing community resources. Analysis and assessment go hand in hand. The early literature used the term "analysis," and for the sake of simplicity, this term will be used for the remainder of this section to include both analysis and assessment.

Community analysis is not new to librarianship. At the close of the nineteenth century, Mary Cutler believed librarians' responsibilities included conducting community studies to understand underlying constructs of the community and apply these to library services. To do this, a librarian should "be a careful student of his own town ... know its history and topography, its social, political, business, literary and ecclesiastical life ... city officers, party bosses, the labor leaders, members of the board of trade, manufacturers, and leading women in the society ... those who shape the charitable organizations" (Cutler, 1896).

The first published study of a library community was undertaken in 1908 by the Brownsville Branch of the Brooklyn Public Library. The study consisted of a description of the Jewish immigrant population in the community (Solis-Cohen, 1908). A similar study conducted in 1919 by the Rivington Street Branch (now Lamb's Church of the Nazarene) of the New York Public Library was more detailed and in-depth. In this study, the authors are said to have demonstrated the importance of knowledge of the community for library management. The Rivington study was criticized as subjective and based on almost random observations. After the Rivington study, the use of more formal methods was recommended (Williamson, 1919).

Community surveys were conducted using Neighborhood Survey Cards, which were printed and distributed by hand to homes in the community. The cards were later collected with library application cards. The Graduate

Library School of the University of Chicago provided the major move toward the utilization of community analysis in library management during the 1930s. Faculty members Louis Round Wilson, Carleton Joeckel, and Douglas Waples engaged in community analysis, developing techniques and providing examples that others could follow. They articulated the types of data to be collected and methods of collecting them. Some of their work was summarized by Carnovsky and Martin (1944) in *The Library in the Community: Papers Presented before the Library Institute at the University of Chicago, August 23–28, 1943*. By 1976, Kunz had incorporated the use of census data in community research, community analysis was well established, and *Library Trends* devoted an issue to the topic. Evans (1976) stated that "Community analysis is as basic to library management as the physician's diagnosis is to the practice of medicine" (p. 454). He pointed out, however, that primary methods such as descriptive surveys and historical research did not provide answers to some of the questions that managers needed answered. In 1960, the American Library Association (ALA) published *Studying the Community: A Basis for Planning Library Adult Education*, a work on community analysis, as part of the ALA Library Community Project (1955–1959). The work was intended to serve as a handbook for the study of adult education needs and is useful for all types of community studies. It contains sample questionnaires and survey reports.

In 1982 Greer and Hale developed a structured form of community analysis that integrates techniques used by social science researchers into "a systematic process of collecting, organizing and analyzing data about the library and its environment" (p. 358). The process focused on four perspectives: individuals, groups, agencies, and lifestyles (Sarling & Van Tassel, 1999, p. 8). This approach, called the Community Analysis Research Institute (CARI) model, became the tool for conducting library community analysis.

The ALA and the Public Library Association (PLA) also developed tools to help librarians begin planning by developing goals and objectives for library services. *Planning and Role Setting for Public Libraries*, released in 1987, outlined public library roles which are profiles of library service emphases (McClure et al., 1987). The roles provided a "menu" for identifying the most appropriate roles for the library to fill. Ten years later, this approach was changed.

The PLA released a new tool in 1998, *Planning for Results: A Library Transformation Process* (Himmel et al., 1998), and the planning process moved from selecting library roles to looking at service responses planned to meet identified community needs. This publication emphasized the link between community needs and library services. To implement the "service response model" for planning for library services, librarians had to identify the makeup of the community and their needs for library services.

To adequately address the needs of adults in their community, librarians learn about and understand the implications of these needs so that they can plan appropriate services to offer in their libraries. The methods and tools for studying the community and using the results of the study will be explored in this chapter. Collection and analysis of data for planning will also be discussed.

STUDYING THE COMMUNITY

Community analysis is integral to understanding the information needs and cultures of the community that a library serves. Evans (1976) stated that knowledge of the community served by the library is an essential foundation for library management but was concerned that librarians had not always practiced community analysis. Hiller, Schillie, and Self (2004), making the same observation nearly 40 years later, said that despite the importance of community analysis, few librarians possessed the skills or experience to perform an effective community assessment and analysis. They went on to say that community assessment and analysis is an ongoing process that identifies the population served by the library, their socioeconomic profiles, library and information needs, and patterns of library use.

As the twentieth century advanced, people wrote about the need for librarians to know their communities. Warnecke (1975) felt that public librarians need to gather and organize current, documented information concerning the community's background, needs, and interests. This information should then be used to build the library's collection, programs, and community relationships. Without this continued diligence, the library could lack real meaning to the community.

"Customizing information services to address information needs requires knowledge of the clientele, in this case its communities" (Grover, Greer, & Agada, 2010, p. 43). To acquire this knowledge, data must be systematically collected by conducting a community analysis, which is "a systematic process of collecting, and analyzing data about the library and its environment. It is designed to assist the administrator in choosing from alternative patterns of satisfying residents' information needs and interests" (Greer & Hale, 1982, p. 358). Community analysis involves breaking down the community into its components. The aim is to identify the characteristics and information needs of the identified groups within the community (Eisner, 1981).

As Larry Bone (1976) points out, "a library cannot be a living, growing and changing force in any community unless it remains sensitive to the character and the needs of the community it serves" (p. 430). He goes on to clarify that community analysis must be an ongoing management activity; that is, for a librarian to remain sensitive to community needs, the community must be studied on a regular basis, with additional community analysis when significant changes are detected or implied by events in the community such as the employment, housing, or population changes or forecasts.

Evans (1976) divides library community analysis into community character-istics and the significance of these characteristics. He argues that knowledge of the community to be served is essential for library management and that com-munity analysis provides the foundation upon which appropriate services can be developed to meet the community's real needs.

To develop adult services, public librarians first begin by determining the background, needs, and interests of adults in the entire community. This involves gathering the following types of information:

- Community socio-demographic information such as age, gender, race, ethnic groups, and educational levels
- Information about the local community
- Organizational data about schools, businesses, health-related groups, nonprofit groups, and other local institutions
- Data related to the community's business and commerce
- Data related to the geographic area the library serves
- Data related to transport patterns within the service area
- Data related to information services provided by other organiza-tions (Hiller, Schillie, & Self, 2004).

Let's look closer at the kinds of information to be gathered.

Socio-demographic information is the starting point of any community analysis and involves collecting data about the population's characteristics. While this analysis focuses on the adults in the community and their needs, socio-demographic data are collected for the whole community to help determine the necessary balance between services (and supporting budget) for the children in the community versus the adults in general and then for various segments of the adults in the community (e.g., older adults).

The analysis can be accomplished by looking at existing data sources and retrieving relevant data. Needed information can be found from data readily available through existing data sources such as U.S. census data from the decennial census figures. U.S. census data offers a great deal of demographic information, including race, age, and employment or those who are unem-ployed. The Census Bureau provides demographic estimates of selected age groups (U.S. Census Bureau, 2010). It also provides information on projected population growth via the American Community Survey (ACS) pro-gram. To locate more detailed demographic information for your library's ser-vice area, libraries may look in census tracks. American Factfinder can also be used to find statistical information about a particular community.

State and municipal agencies can provide more focused community data. Data can also be obtained from internal library reports such as gate counts and number of registered borrowers. Factors such as the number of single parents and their needs or the number of college graduates in the community can influence which services will be offered.

Once a librarian locates demographic information, additional help can be found in the Public Library Geographic Database (PLGDB). This resource, developed by Florida State University's School of Information Studies, includes the locations of 16,000 public libraries mapped at 1999 geographic location with data sets from the 2000 U.S. Census figures (Koontz, Jue, McClure, & Bertot, 2004). Community information retrieved from census sources can be visually presented using geographic information systems (GIS). Adkins and Sturges (2004) state that GIS allow the librarian to visually represent and manipulate information about his or her community by connecting geographically bound data such as census demographics to other geographically bound data. Using GIS to map an area increases the librarian's awareness of the communities surrounding his or her library and can be helpful in planning services to complement other available resources.

COMMUNITY ANALYSIS DATA

Greer and Hale (1982) suggest that community analysis should be conducted from four perspectives: (1) demographic data, (2) community groups, (3) agencies, and (4) lifestyles.

Demographic data should provide information on the numbers and characteristics of people living in the area. Census figures and updates are the primary source of demographic data, though other sources can also provide additional information. For example, planning agencies and political groups help verify the census data. Greer and Hale (1982) point out that finding the total population of an area may be difficult because the number is a political issue. Demographic data provide information about age groups, household size, income, education and employment levels, income levels, and other useful items about the community. Every state has a state data center that uses Census data to compile a variety of state and local data. The data can be found in town profiles.

Community groups can be studied through observation; researchers recommend that librarians gather impressions of the community groups and not just gather demographic data about them. This approach can provide insights into the existing sense of community. The librarians can create categories of characteristics and observe local groups keeping these categories in mind to learn more about the type of community the library serves. Monitoring the newspapers can provide a treasure trove of the nature of groups in the community, which, combined with demographic data, can influence the type of services needed.

Agencies are a source of information for community analysis. An agency is "a corporate body located in the library service area for the purpose of providing service or product to local residents" (Greer & Hale, 1982, p. 363). A systematic review of agencies' services and activities will provide helpful information to help a library better understand the community's information needs.

Lifestyles found in the community can be assessed via a questionnaire based on a number of data gathering tools. The resulting survey can be made available at the library, on the library's website, and through various organizations and businesses in the community. Questions of interest might concern individuals' preferred activity level (e.g., very active and healthy, leisurely but healthy, sedentary without worrying about health); socialization (e.g., active in clubs and community groups, active with friends and taking in new experiences, more spur of the moment); and health (e.g., remain as active and involved as possible; let limitations dictate the level of activity to be provided).

After a thorough review of the information gathered from these various sources, the librarian can begin to examine the existing library services for adults so that he or she can determine gaps in services as well as improvements that are needed for existing services.

After analyzing the community's demographic characteristics, business information, the library service area, transportation patterns, and the services of other organizations in the area, existing library services need to be examined so that gaps can be closed and needed improvements can be made. This is the time when library staff needs to "look around." While looking around, the staff begins collecting information about what is inside the library and analyzing the information so that they can make decisions. *Community Analysis Methods and Evaluative Options Handbook: The CAMEO Handbook* (Group et al., 1993) was based on work done in the 1980s on planning, role setting, and output measures. It is a step-by-step guide for public library planners. It provides instructions on how to look around and provides worksheets and checklists for each activity observed. While this resource is 20 years old, it is still valid. It suggests that the examination of current library services include the following information, which gives you a sense of what you presently have available. This resource contains worksheets to aid in the collection of the different types of data discussed earlier. The worksheets were developed from the work of Greer and Hale (1981) and address the following aspects:

- The facilities—physical plant and its adequacy for various services—parking, access, space, and other needed resources
- Analysis of the resources:
  - Book collections—size, composition, and age of collection
  - Non-book resources—number of databases, eBook readers

- Analysis of services available—the various services provided by the library and when they are provided:
  - Hours of operation
  - Circulation patterns
  - Reference and readers' advisory services
  - Programs and special services
  - Services currently not offered
- Analysis of the user and nonuser—people who use the library and potential users who do not currently use the library either because they are unaware of the services or have no way to get there
- Relationship between the library and the community:
  - Business community
  - Groups using the facility

METHODS OF COLLECTING DATA

The library needs to collect data about the environment in which the library exists as well as the services currently offered. Two kinds of data are collected: primary data and secondary data. Secondary data has already been collected for some other purpose within the library or as a byproduct of some library function, for example, circulation or reference transactions. Secondary data is easier to locate because it exists in different forms and in organizations whose function it is to collect data, such as the Census Bureau and the state library. It is available to those who know what they need and those who know the most likely source in which to find it. Access to this type of information from outside agencies through online searching grows daily. Primary data is collected from the original source for the study at hand. Collection of primary data is time consuming and expensive.

The library can collect primary data by conducting an environmental scanning; preparing a strengths, weaknesses, opportunities, and threats (SWOTS) analysis; organizing focus groups; collect observations; conducting interviews; and using surveys.

Adults encounter a variety of situations in their life such as engaging in academic studies, work life, and entertainment, all of which result in different information and library service requirements. The librarian needs to consult the literature for recommendations on service responses, select services that are relevant to the information needs of the community, and implement the identified services based on the resources the library has to address the needed improvements. The literature suggests that library services include support for the following items:

- Lifelong learning
- Leisure time interests

- Information needs
- Community activities
- Cultural activities
- Recreational reading

TOOLS FOR COMMUNITY ANALYSIS

A number of management techniques were applied in community analysis in the twentieth century and continue to be used in the twenty-first century. The tools are discussed in this section.

Environmental Scanning

The ability to anticipate and adapt to changing environmental factors is necessary for successful management of any organization, including libraries. Morrison (1991) discussed that librarians need to have (1) an understanding of their communities, (2) an understanding of how the external environment relates to the library's internal environment, and (3) methods that will enable them to understand both environments and their relationship.

Environmental scanning is a tool that will help achieve the needs Morrison points out. It is "the acquisition and use of information about events, trends and relationships in an organization's external environment, the knowledge of which would assist management in planning the organization's future course of action" (Choo, 2002, p. 4).

In the process of gathering information about the library's environment, librarians should know that their library, similar to all organizations, is said to have two environments, an internal environment and an external environment. "Marketers often define the internal environment as the 'micro-environment' and the external is defined as the 'macro-environment.' This internal environment is interlocked in an invisible partnership with the external environment" (Koontz, 2006). Koontz stated that the environment in which the library exists and the materials and services the library offers ultimately affect library patrons. "The components of the library's internal environment are more immediate to the agency and are therefore better known. . . . The primary forces in the library's internal environment are customers, employees and professional staff, vendors/distributors and library stakeholders" (Koontz, 2006, p. 2). Each entity is affected by ever-changing external forces.

The external environment, or macro-environment, is the larger of the two, and it is affected by forces external to the library, including the state of the economy, infrastructure, legal and political restrictions, technological developments, media, competition, natural resources, and societal and cultural conditions (Koontz, 2006 p. 2). External conditions are subject to change in the same way as the macro-environment affects the internal environment. Because librarians manage and work in their internal environments, they are more familiar with the components of the internal environment (as they are closely tied to the operations of the library). Therefore, it is important for librarians to devote a greater effort to keeping track of changes in the external environment.

During environmental scanning activities, library managers try to know about and interpret changes taking place in the external environment. They identify strengths and weaknesses in the internal environment and are cognizant of the opportunities and threats to the organization and its environment. Some of this can be determined with a SWOT analysis.

Environmental scanning can also be achieved through user surveys, focus groups, statistical research, interviews, and observations. Librarians collect, select, and organize data as part of their day-to-day tasks. Koontz (2006) suggests that the same expertise be applied toward solving library problems. Guidelines suggested by experts for successful environmental scanning are:

- Seek signs of change. Review primary sectors (economic, social, etc.) for signs of change. For example, what changes in local, national, or global economies, technologies, and legal and regulatory factors will affect the library?
- Look for signals of potential events on the horizon. For example, when the federal government imposed Internet filtering, the impact on public libraries was immediate. At the local level, changes in elected officials affect priorities for agencies under their control.
- Beware that there are few guidelines on how to do scanning. You are your own expert.
- Write abstracts and scenarios that summarize your organization's internal and external environments (Morrison, 1991).

SWOT Analysis

SWOT analysis is a framework for defining the library's environments (Nelson & Public Library Association, 2001). SWOT analysis allows library staff to identify the positives and negatives within the library's organization (Strengths and Weaknesses) as well as outside the library's organization (Opportunities and Threats). By reviewing the results of the SWOT analysis, library staff can enrich their awareness and understanding of the situation in which the library operates. This it facilitates strategic planning and decision making, and it provides choices that can yield optimal resources and services to meet the needs of the community given the constraints and prospects. *The New Planning for Results* provides sample forms for completing a SWOT analysis of community needs. An example worksheet for a SWOT analysis is shown in the chart below.

SWOT ANALYSIS WORKSHEET

Strengths (internal)
- Public service–oriented
- Well-qualified and dedicated staff
- Ongoing professional development for staff
- Ongoing goal of developing quality collection and services
- Ongoing provision of patron access to information

Weaknesses (internal)
- Impact of budget on staff
- Impact of budget on facilities
- Lack of consistent communication among library units
- Lack of staff diversity

Opportunities (external)
- New staff hiring
- Outreach and marketing of library services
- Collaboration with outside government and other agencies
- Library as a place

Threats (external)
- Budget cuts
- Economic uncertainties
- Potential loss of staff
- Potential reduction in hours of operation
- Challenges having limited resources to stay current with changing technology

Completed by _____

Date completed _____ Library _____

Source of Data_____

TYPES OF DATA

Tools used to collect primary data are discussed in the following text. They include focus groups, interviews, observations, and surveys.

Focus Groups

Focus group interviewing is a data gathering technique used in qualitative research. A focus group involves an open, in-depth discussion with a small group of selected individuals led by a moderator to explore a predetermined topic of shared interest. Focus groups are group interviews with the goal of examining in detail people's perceptions about products and services (Walden, 2006). Focus groups involve presenting questions to the group and letting each participant respond spontaneously but managing participation so that each member has an opportunity to respond and no one member monopolizes responses.

Using focus groups to collect data differs from other interview methods because of the interaction between the group members as they answer the questions. Bryman (2004) identifies the interaction as the distinguishing element between interviewing and using focus groups. The technique usually addresses a specific subject that is explored in depth by the group. Focus groups are said to give insight into people's feelings, values, and opinions that would not otherwise be known. One of the disadvantages of the technique is that results from focus group research cannot be generalized to the general population, as the group members are usually not selected using sampling techniques.

With focus groups, data can be provided quickly at low cost compared to other techniques. They are also said to provide opportunities for stimulating ideas through the interaction of group members. Walden (2006) listed some disadvantages of the technique, including nonproduction of quantitative data, small number of interviews, lack of privacy, and difficulties in recording and analyzing open-ended responses.

The steps involved in the focus group process are planning the project, recruiting the participants, implementing the discussion sessions with the help of the moderator, and analyzing and reporting the answers (Walden, 2006). Connaway (1996) documents a number of library applications of the technique in decision making for evaluation of services in determining community needs and services. Higa-Moore and colleagues (2002) document the use of focus groups in the planning process in medical libraries. Focus groups are popular for assessing what people feel and why they feel the way they do.

Interviews

An interview is the act of asking oral quantitative or qualitative questions of participants. Quantitative questions are closed ended, have specific answers to select from, and can be categorized and analyzed. Qualitative questions are open ended, and respondents provide a response in their own words. Interviews are used to get more in-depth information about perceptions, attitudes, insights, experiences, or beliefs or as a follow-up to other techniques.

The three approaches to qualitative interviews may be combined when conducting an interview:

- Informal conversational interviews, the least structured approach, use questions or topics that are not predetermined or discussed. They tend to be spontaneous.
- Semi-structured interviews include an outline of topics to be discussed. The interviewer may vary the order of the questions.
- Standardized open-ended interviews are the most structured and include a set protocol of questions. The interviewer must use the exact wording and ordering of the questions.

Interviews, like all techniques, require careful planning. The following steps are involved in planning for interviews:

- Determine the focus of the interview. Include questions that will provide answers to the topic under investigation.
- Develop an interview guide or questionnaire. For informal interviews, no interview guidance is needed. For semi-structured interviews, an interview guide may include specific topics to be covered in the interview. For a structured open-ended interview, all the questions for the interview should be developed ahead of time.
- Select the number and type of people to be interviewed. The number will be determined by the total number of participants, or population represented, resources, and interviewers available to conduct the interviews.
- Train the interviewers so that they know how to conduct an interview and how to use the interview guide.
- Ensure the respondents' confidentiality and provide them with information about how their confidentiality will be protected.
- Pilot test the interview guide or questionnaire. Pilot testing allows one to determine questions that may be confusing or misinterpreted and to learn if changes need to be made to the interview guide.

Interviews are useful for gaining insight into and context about a topic. They allow respondents to describe what is important to them and are useful for gathering quotations and stories. Disadvantages are that they are susceptible to bias, time consuming, and expensive compared to other methods and may seem intrusive to the respondent (CDC, 2009).

Observations

Observation is a way of gathering data by watching events or behaviors, or noting physical characteristics in physical environments. Observations can be covert (no one knows they are being observed) or overt (the subjects know they are being observed). The advantage of covert observation is that people are more likely to behave naturally if they are not aware that they are being watched. Observation may be direct or indirect. Direct observation occurs when processes or interactions are observed as they occur, for example, observing a reference interaction between a librarian and a patron. Indirect observation occurs when the results of interactions or behaviors are observed after the fact. Observations can be used in community assessment to gather data on individual behaviors or interactions between people. They can also be used to learn about a physical setting where an activity is going on to help understand the event. Like all data collection techniques, observation needs to be planned. The following are the steps for conducting observations:

- Determine the focus of the observation, the questions you want to answer through the observation, and which areas to focus on for data collection.
- Design a system for data collection, decide the specific items you want to collect data on, and determine how to collect the information. The three primary methods of collecting observation data are:
  - o Recording sheets and checklists are the most standardized way of collecting observation data and may include both preset questions and responses.
  - o Observation guides list interactions, processes, or behaviors to be observed. There is space to record open-ended narrative data.
  - o Field notes are the least standardized way of collecting data, and they do not usually have preset questions or responses. Field notes can be open-ended narrative that may be written or dictated onto a tape recorder. Note: Any of the three methods may be used, or a combination may be used to collect observation data.
- Select the site of the observation, making sure it is representative of what you want to observe.
- Select the observers, librarians, and professional staff or volunteers.
- Train the observers in the use of data collection techniques to ensure the collection of high-quality and consistent data.
- Time the observations appropriately. Programs and processes follow a sequence of events. Observation must be scheduled to follow the components of the activity that will answer the questions for which answers are needed (CDC, 2008).

Observation as a data collection technique has some advantages. Data are collected where and when an event is happening, the technique does not rely on people's willingness or ability to provide information, and data collection allows the observer to directly see what people do rather than relying on what people say they do. Disadvantages of observation as a data collection technique are that observation is susceptible to observer bias and the "Hawthorne effect" (people perform better when they know they are being watched). The process can be expensive and time consuming compared to other data collection methods and does not explain why people behave as they do.

Surveys

Surveys are used to collect information from a wide range of persons who work in or use the library, including all staff and volunteers. Library users (including community residents) are surveyed. The data are gathered through a carefully developed instrument that is pretested to clarify questions that might be confusing. Within the community, it should be administered to individuals identified—if at all possible—through a sampling procedure. This is not easy, and a librarian might wish to consult a statistician to conduct this procedure. Administering to a sample population chosen this way is more likely to provide accurate findings; however, the reality is that such research usually requires special funding to conduct.

Surveys may include personal interviews, telephone interviews, and questionnaires (mailed or web-based). The use of web-based survey techniques has grown exponentially with the development of web-based survey and evaluation systems such as SurveyMonkey and SurveyWriter. These programs collect and analyze the data and the results are reported to the organization that ordered the survey. Surveys tend to be difficult and time consuming. Four groups are typically surveyed by librarians: staff, citizens, students, and library users. Here is more information about each group:

- Staff: Covers staff attitudes, priorities for service, what services should be added or eliminated, evaluation of library services, and job satisfaction. This type of survey is easy to administer, and the staff are most informed about library operations. It also helps them feel like they are part of the planning process. Some disadvantages are that staff may focus on internal management problems rather than on service, and they may also be protective of their own service area. Further, the time it takes to complete an intensive survey may disrupt library services.
- Citizen: Includes participation in community groups, library use patterns, knowledge of library services, use of the library, priorities for service, access to library service, and convenience of library services. This type of survey can help determine information needs such as importance or depth of need, satisfaction with services being provided by the library, and preference for priority service roles. Some of the advantages of this kind of survey are that the librarian is able to obtain opinions and perceptions of all citizens rather than just library users, it can verify demographics from secondary data, and it can create ownership of the library (whether the respondents use it or not. Some disadvantages are that citizens may not know enough about the library to provide the needed input, it can be difficult to obtain accurate data on information needs, and people may not be able to articulate their information needs.
- Student: Asks the same types of questions as library user surveys in the next bullet point. The major difference is that student surveys are usually conducted in academic library settings.
- Library user: Covers topics such as access and ease of use of the library. It may also ask about the resources available and their

usefulness, opening hours and days library is open, and interest in and attendance at special programs.

Once the data has been collected it may be compared with the list provided by PLA on basic library services.

COMMUNITY NEEDS ASSESSMENT

The terms "community analysis" and "community needs assessment" have been used interchangeably in the literature. However, there is a difference. Community needs assessment is the ongoing process by which the current situation in the community is assessed, and an accurate appraisal of the current situation is its objective. Community needs assessment builds on the results and data collected during community analysis. It should be an integral part of a reference librarian's "toolkit" for the twenty-first century. Yet relatively few reference librarians possess the skills or experience necessary to perform effective community needs assessment (Hiller et al., 2004). The objectives of a community needs assessment are to identify the communities served (this is accomplished by conducting a community analysis), know their characteristics, understand the communities' library and information needs, and relate to the mission and goals of the library and the communities in which it exists. The process identifies the population served by the library and its socioeconomic characteristics, its information and library needs, and patterns of library use. The information gathered through community needs assessment is used to improve library services. It allows the library to target specific information needs to specific groups in the community. Methods of assessment use existing information, such as community data that were collected during the community analysis and they use data from reference staff observations, library use statistics, acquisition data, interlibrary loan requests, and computer log data. The information is analyzed to provide insight into current services. The existing data do not provide information on needs, satisfaction, or priorities, or about who nonusers are. The library needs to know this type of information, and assessment requires that libraries collect this type of information from direct user input. The most common methods of collecting data are the same as those used when collecting data during community analysis, surveys, focus groups, interviews, and observations. Additional methods include community meetings and usability studies. Usability studies involve giving people some tasks to complete. They are then asked to answer questions about the design model or process of completing the tasks. The responses are recorded and are used to evaluate the efficiency of the protocol used to complete the task.

Community needs assessment involves assessing who users and potential users are as well as identifying underserved demographic groups and underserved geographical areas. It also involves assessing services to determine heavily used services, underutilized services and the reasons for underutilization, poorly performing services, and new services that are needed. The information gathered from these assessments is used to plan for improving library services. The results may also be used to design a marketing plan for the library. Community needs assessment is an ongoing process because the library exists in a constantly changing environment, and the needs assessment must be carried out constantly for the library to be able to offer effective services and remain viable and relevant to its community as it seeks to address its information needs.

SERVICES TO BE ADDED OR IMPROVED

Based on the results of the community analysis and needs assessment, the librarian should identify new services that can be added to existing services that will improve the overall service response. Based on analysis of the collected data, services that will be added or improved upon are selected using the service responses described in Chapter 3. With your results, you can now begin to plan and implement the services needed in your library and also to fix any problems with present services. In this way, you will be providing the best resources to the adults in your service area, and you will begin to reach your goal of serving all the adults in the community. You will use information on service responses and best practices as guidelines to plan and implement services.

The purpose of a community analysis is to help librarians choose how to allocate resources for adult services. This understanding of community is essential for library planners if they are to develop appropriate and effective services for their library users. Each library must provide services tailored to the identified needs of the community. Urban libraries that serve diverse populations such as low-income, blue-collar, and ethnic populations need to develop different services from those developed by librarians in the suburbs who serve a more homogenous, affluent community. It is essential that all librarians—not just adult services librarians—be familiar with methods of conducting community analysis and community needs assessment. Community needs assessment has the potential to provide valuable insights into the information needs of the population it serves and help the decision-making process related to improving library services.

REFERENCES

Bone, Larry. Introduction. *Library Trends*, 24(3), 429–432.
Bryman, A. (2004). Focus groups *Social Research Methods* (2 ed.). New York: Oxford University Press.

Centers for Disease Control and Prevention (CDC). (2008, December). *Data collection methods for program evaluation: Observation.* Evaluation Briefs, No. 16. Retrieved from http://www.cdc.gov/HEALTHYYOUTH/evaluation/pdf/brief16.pdf

Carnovsky, L., & Martin, L. (Eds.). (1944). The library in the community: Papers presented before the Library Institute at the University of Chicago, August 23–28, 1943. Chicago: University of Chicago Press.

Choo, C. W. (2002). Environmental scanning as information seeking and organizational knowing. *Sprouts: Working Papers on Information Systems,* 2(1).

Connaway, L. S. (1996). Focus group interviews: A data collection methodology. *Library Administration & Management,* 10(4), 231–239.

Cutler, M. S. (1896). Two fundamentals. *Library Journal, 21*(October), 2.

Eisner, J. (1981). *Beyond PR: Marketing for libraries* (LJ Special Report #18) (p. 25).

Evans, C. (1976). A history of community analysis in American librarianship. *Library Trends,* 24(3): 441–457.

Greer, R. C., & Hale, M. L. (1981). Data collection. In J. Eisner (Ed.), *Beyond PR: Marketing for libraries* (LJ Special Report #18, pp. 30–32). New York: Library Journal.

Greer, R. C., & Hale, M. L. (1982). The community analysis process. In J. Robbins-Carter (Ed.), *Public librarianship: A reader* (pp. 358–367). Littleton, CO: Libraries Unlimited.

Group, T. C. L., Cooper, S., Bolt, N., Lance, K. C., & Webster, L. (1993). *Community analysis methods and evaluative options: The CAMEO handbook.*

Higa-Moore, M. L., Bunnett, B., Mayo, H. G., & Olney, C. A. (2002). Use of focus groups in a library's strategic planning process. *Journal of the Medical Library Association,* 90(1), 86–92.

Hiller, S., Schillie, J., & Self, J. (2004). *Community assessment: An essential part of the reference librarian's toolkit.* Paper presented at the World Library and Information Congress: 70th. IFLA General Conference and Council, Buenos Aires, Argentina.

Koontz, C. (2006). *Environmental scanning: Discover what is happening outside of the library doors.* Paper presented at the World Library and Information Congress—72nd IFLA General Conference and Council, Seoul, Korea. http://www.ifla.org/V/ifla72/index.htm

Koontz, C. M., Jue, D. K., McClure, C. R., & Bertot, J. C. (2004). The public library geographic database: What can it do for your library? *Public Libraries,* 43(2), 6.

McClure, C. R., et al. (1987). *Planning and role setting for public libraries: A manual of options and procedures.* Chicago: American Library Association.

Morrison, J. L. (1991). "Environmental Scanning." In M. A. Whitely, J. D. Poeter, & R. H. Fenske (Eds.), *A primer for new institutional researchers.* Tallahassee, FL: The Association for Institutional Research.

Nelson, S. S., & Public Library Association. (2001). *The new planning for results: A streamlined approach.* Chicago: American Library Association.

Sarling, J. H., & Van Tassel, D. S. (1999). Community analysis: Research that matters to a north-central Denver community. *Library & Information Science Research,* 21(1), 7–29.

Solis-Cohen, L. M. (1908). Library work in the Brooklyn ghetto. *Library Journal, 33,* 485–488.

Taylor, T. (n.d.). Community needs assessments. Learning to Give. Retrieved from http://learningtogive.org/papers/paper16.html.

Walden, G. R. (2006). Focus group interviewing in the library literature: A selective annotated bibliography 1996–2005. *Reference Services Review, 34*(2), 21.

Williamson, C. C. (1919). Efficiency in library management. *Library Journal, 44*, 67–77.

RESOURCES FOR COMMUNITY ANALYSIS

American Fact Finder, http://factfinder.census.gov/

American Community Survey, http://www.census.gov/acs/www/index.html

GIS, http://erg.usgs.gov/isb/pubs/gis_poster/

U.S. Census, http://researchguides.library.wisc.edu/content.php?pid=109927

SUMMARY FILES

Public Library Geographical Database, http://www.geolib.org/PLGDB.cfm

Summary File 1, http://www.census.gov/2010census/news/press-kits/summary-file-1.html

Summary File 2, http://www.census.gov/2010census/news/press-kits/sf2/summary-file-2.html

Summary File 3, http://www.census.gov/mp/www/cat/decennial_census_2000/summary_file_3.html

Summary File 4, http://www.census.gov/census2000/SF4.html

SWOT Analysis, http://en.wikipedia.org/wiki/SWOT_analysis

WEB RESOURCES

Cooper, S. M., Bolt, N., Lance, K. C., & Webster, L. (1993). *Community analysis methods and evaluative options: The CAMEO handbook.* The Consulting Librarians Group in cooperation with MGT of America, Inc., for the Library of Virginia.

The New Planning for Results is an all-in-one guide that outlines a tested, results-driven planning process that has been revamped and streamlined to enable libraries to respond quickly to rapidly changing environments and transform services to effectively meet changing community needs. Chapter 2 provides an overview of identifying community needs in the context of a community vision. Workform B provides a template for gathering data about your community. The resource also includes a number of additional workforms for collecting data for planning.

CHAPTER 5

Assessment of Adult Services

Mary E. Brown, Ph.D.

Professor, Southern Connecticut State University

Assessment is a process in which we collect and consider information for the purpose of measuring or evaluating change. Assessment is something we do naturally as we go about our daily activities.

We might set the goal of traveling to work without encountering routinely heavy traffic; then we try perhaps different departure times or different routes until we are satisfied with the resulting outcome. We find a recipe that does not produce a food dish as we would like it, so we change proportions of ingredients until we are satisfied with the resulting outcome. What we choose to focus on, what we choose to alter, and what we choose to evaluate depends upon what criteria or goals we set.

Our goal may be to have the least stressful drive to work, with least stressful defined as less traffic and a more scenic route. We may not find the magical formula that satisfies all requirements at the same time, and we may need to make tradeoffs such as a more crowded drive along a pleasant, scenic route or a less crowded drive along a more monotonous, uninteresting route. One alternative may not fit all days or situations. One day the crowd-free but uninteresting drive may be preferred, while another day the scenic but more crowded drive may be preferred. Library programs and services are no different.

While we may have high attendance as the optimal goal for all programs, which will result in high awareness or learning or entertainment impact, we may find that all goals are not obtainable simultaneously. Each program or service should have individual goals, while the array of programs and services represents a more balanced set of goals. For example, we may set as an overall goal for all adult services programming some programs with wide appeal and large attendance and other programs with substantial learning reported by attendees.

In setting objectives for these goals, we may feel it is important to have two high attendance events each year. While awareness and learning are desired outcomes, the primary goal is to have a large audience coming away with the feeling they greatly enjoyed the program, whether leisure entertainment or stimulated learning. They would come again to other programs.

The librarian may also feel it is important to have the objective of one event each month in which those who participate come away feeling they have learned something new and significant such as awareness and/or learning a new skill or new knowledge. The librarian, while desiring a large attendance, is willing to run these events for a small number of participants. Together, these events make for a balanced program that achieves the broader set of programming goals.

Certainly library staff can see the numbers of attendees at each event and how those numbers change from event to event, and they can observe reactions of the attendees through their facial expressions and their comments both to other attendees and to library staff. While this may be sufficient for library staff to know their plans have been successful or to identify elements of the program planning that are problematic or need a bit of fine-tuning, this *personal knowledge* is likely to fail to meet what those outside the library need in order to justify the value received or resulting from current budgets, to justify future budgets, or possibly to justify the need for the library or its services.

WHY CONDUCT ASSESSMENT?

We currently live in an era of answerability and accountability, and reliable measurement and clear documentation are the tools that help us responsibly satisfy both for our constituents and funding agencies. To document the path toward meeting the program's goals and justify its cost and relevance, assessment is needed. Each program event calls for specific types of assessment, depending upon the objectives. These may be measures of attendance or measures of impact on awareness, learning, or entertainment. The overall adult services programming also needs to be assessed as to how well the slate of programs and services meets the overarching goals of adult services as a whole.

WHO SHOULD CONDUCT ASSESSMENT?

Anyone who wants to measure and/or document the outcomes of an initiative or event conducts assessment. At a very personal level, we need to look no further than penciled lines with dates running up doorjambs for evidence of assessment instruments. In this case, we are measuring a growing child's height at periodic intervals. The penciled lines give us a visual that allows us to compare change from year to year. We can compare the growth lines for two children. We can measure the distances between marks and determine the growth trend or average growth rate. We can say the information both as marks transferred to a paper rule and as a table of dates and measured heights. We have a record of collected data that we can pull out at family reunions to verify a claim of which niece or nephew was tallest at age six.

Anyone who is accountable for their work—whether to colleagues, supervision, stakeholders, or funding agencies—should conduct assessment. Just as recorded heights from each birthday can become critical information to have available at a family reunion, collected data about programs and services and from different perspectives can become critical information to have available when funding, budget, or promotion times roll around.

Similar to most things, if you have a large enough budget, you can find someone who is an expert in the moneymaking business of planning, conducting, and summarizing assessment for you. However, few library budgets, especially in an economic downturn, can afford to hire any outside agency to manage their assessment needs.

Many librarians may call up memories of college courses in research methods that may have been successfully avoided or, if taken, became numbers tucked into journal articles that they recognized as statistics but weren't quite certain what they meant. Many students do try to shy away from *research*, *assessment*, and *statistics* because they have the perception that these are complex and difficult topics that require an expert. While this may be true for some research, we have already suggested with the opening example that assessment is something you already do naturally. You will find that tallying up numbers and then calculating percentages provide descriptive statistics that are the mainstay of many assessments. In any situation, a pinch of intuition and common sense is a good foundation for those who have not formally studies research methods.

HOW DO WE CONDUCT ASSESSMENT?

The Online Dictionary of Library and Information Science (ODLIS; http://www.abc-clio.com/ODLIS/odlis_A.aspx) tells us that "assessment is accomplished by various methods, including direct observation, analysis of feedback obtained through interviews, user surveys, testing, etc." In our library world, it really begins before that. To have effective assessment, we need to begin with an assessment plan, which should have several characteristics:

- It should be based on the mission and goals of the library.
- It should be ongoing with periodic reflections on a group of individual assessments, such as all adult services assessments every three months or all assessments of a certain event services over several seasons or years.
- It should be designed to improve programming and services (not just collect data about them).
- It should collect information from various points of view (such as attendees, patrons in general, community in general, library staff) using a variety of methods (questionnaires, focus groups, observations from events).
- It should be developed by those (staff, volunteers, patrons) working with the program(s)/service(s).
- It should be well organized and fit seamlessly into library/program operations.

Let's take a look at each of these characteristics. With the first, assessment should be based on the mission and goals of the library. From the library's mission and goals, a vision and goals for adult services as a whole is developed as is a vision and goals for each program and service within adult services. This is not as daunting as it might seem. Consider a few library mission statements you might find in the literature to help when establishing the mission, vision, and goals for adult services. Some examples are shown in the following text as the definitions of these terms are clarified.

To begin, it is best to clarify the terms "vision," "mission," "goals," and "objectives." A succinct publication on vision, mission, goals, and objectives comes from the University of Maine's Cooperative Extension Publications: *Bulletin #6107, Vision, Mission, Goals & Objectives ... Oh My!* (Singer, 2011). Some of their wording helps clarify these terms.

While the terms "vision statement," "mission statement," and "goals and objectives" easily retrieve explanations when searched on the Internet, there is not always a clear consensus of definition or exemplars for these terms. It is not uncommon to get the feeling goals and objectives are used interchangeably; then to find other sources that link each term to a timeline of use, such as long-term, short-term, or a given number of years such as three to five years or up to a year. You may find "mission" described in terms of purpose, then later find other sources that seem to treat "mission" and "purpose" as two different concepts. I have sat in a room observing a committee arguing over whether stated program goals and objectives are in fact goals and objectives, and then they have argued about what constitutes a goal and an objective. Yet, mission, goals, and objectives (MGO) are common terms tossed out as needed for planning as well as assessment and often expected to be on display for the public. The University of Maine's "Vision, Mission, Goals & Objectives ... Oh My!" offers a succinct and workable explanation and worksheet for group planning. Notwithstanding this fine resource, following are brief explanations of each of these four terms using concepts if not terminology often found in their discussion; the explanation are couched in adult services. Following each brief explanation is an example of how a vision statement, mission statement, goal, or objective might be worded.

- *Vision* is the framework for the future: the mental picture or dream of the purpose of adult services and what values are important to maintain and why.
  An example after the UK Department of Health's vision for adult social care might be:

  Vision for adult services in the public library: Facilitating capable communities and active citizens built on the values of personalization (to meet the individual's needs), partnership (among the library staff, volunteers, and the community), plurality (recognizing individuals learn or take in information in different ways), protection (recognizing that the library is a resource for all citizens in the community), productivity (greater accountability for publishing information on the outcomes of programs and services and the segments of the community served), and people (ensuring all staff are well-trained and well-suited to develop, maintain, and deliver services that preserve the values set forth for adult services).

  Another example similar to the Ruth H. Young Center for Families and Children at the University of Maryland (http://www.family .umaryland.edu/) might be:

  The vision for adult services in the public library is an educated and productive citizenry that enhances the self-assurance, permanency, and well-being outcomes for the community.

- *Mission* is the clear, concise, and realistic statement that publishes the purpose established in the vision statement while describing the scope or boundaries of what adults services does, for whom, and how. An example might be

  To help the adult residents of Ourtown develop and maintain information literacy skills that match the current state of information access and to afford access to information and cultural heritage in multiple media and formats as best serves the adult residents of Ourtown.

- *Goals* are broad statements of what is expected to be achieved in support of the mission. Goals can be short-term covering the coming year, or long-term covering a few years. Goals need to be attainable. This does not mean they are dreams; they are things that are doable in terms of the resources available and needs and interests of the community. An example would be, "Improve access to information and cultural heritage for older citizens."
- *Objectives* are the translation of goals into specific, doable, measurable tasks. An objective states what will be done, to what extent, for whom, and by when. An example would be "Within the next calendar year, appropriate outreach initiatives will be established with 50% of the assisted living facilities in the community."

It is at the objectives level that assessment takes place. Successful objectives work toward achieving a goal. If it can be said a goal has been accomplished, it is likely that either an objective has been labeled as a goal or the expectation was that any minimal initiative would fulfill it.

Missions are generally a long-term description of purpose. The mission of adult services needs to reflect and be incorporated within the library's mission. Visions tend to be idealistic and to shift with leadership and local dispositions, though they need to be held in check by the mission. Goals and objectives change, in part due to assessment and reflection on what that assessment means in terms of the current goals and objectives. When a mission statement needs to be developed, it is nice to begin by first creating a shared vision among constituents; but it is the mission statement that is the commonsense and practical foundation. The vision is more idealistic and dreamy. Visions can create motive, but missions create direction.

Here is one library's mission statement: "The [Public Library] serves as a resource to provide information, education and recreation to [the citizens]. It lends books, offers timely, accurate reference services, and provides learning resources to support diverse educational goals for the out-of-school citizen." Another states: "We believe that libraries can change people's lives and are a cornerstone of our democracy. The [Public Library] provides opportunities for our residents and taxpayers to pursue lifelong learning, cultural and economic enrichment and enjoyment. To accomplish this mission, we offer free and open access to creative works, knowledge and information from diverse perspectives."

The first mission statement clearly gives three terms that cover adult services: to provide "information," "education," and "recreation." The second uses the terms "lifelong learning," "cultural and economic enrichment," and "enjoyment." Aligning these, one comes away with three common goals: resources (information, cultural and economic enrichment), learning (education, lifelong learning), and entertainment (recreation, enjoyment).

Some mission statements are a bit more allusive, for example, "The [Public Library] mission is to provide free resources that inspire reading, guide learning, and encourage individual exploration" or "The mission of the [Public Library] is to inspire lifelong learning, advance knowledge, and strengthen our communities." Another choice might be, "Our mission is 'to provide equal access to information and services that empower, enrich, and enhance the quality of life for all.' " Yet from these we can understand that resources and learning are goals, and within resources and learning there can be a good bit of range from academic scholarship to entertaining awareness.

Critical goals, explicit or implied, can be distilled from mission statements and a mission statement for adult services so that goals can be derived. While this may result in effective programming and services for adults, it is taking a bit of an if-you-build-it-they-will-come approach. An MLS student said in class, "If you don't ask people what they think, how do you really know?" It is best to start the process by asking adults what they think the vision, mission, and goals of adult services should be for the community.

If you recall, vision, mission, and goals are all fairly broad statements. While the essence of these drafted by the library staff may end up matching the essence of these drafted through a collaborative experience involving constituents, what the experience of developing the vision and mission statements and goals offers is ownership by those involved. For the library to be a collective part of the community, the community does need to feel it has an interest or ownership in what the library offers.

If adult services already has a vision, mission, and goals developed by staff, a day of activities with constituents can be undertaken to reaffirm that these are indeed a shared vision, mission, and goals, and such a day may provide an opportunity to restate them in language more natural to constituents.

To create or reaffirm a shared vision, include representatives of each of the major constituent groups. This means library patrons and nonpatrons, working adults, stay-at-home adults, adults with children, adults without children, active older adults, and older adults who require outreach. Be sure to stay current with local news to help you identify groups in the community you want to include. For example, one news article (Singer, 2011) featured the Depaul House in Germantown, Pennsylvania and its volunteer residential program for homeless men. These men were able to express themselves through art after taking classes in photography and creative writing taught by Temple University professors. While the resulting art was on display at the Painted Bride Art Center in Philadelphia, it could also have been on exhibit at the public library as a way to raise awareness of and make connections with citizens working to obtain employment, a bank account, and their own residence as well as with the social services and local university faculty helping them. Try to include representatives who reflect the whole of the adult service community. For example, if the community has several long-term care and assisted living facilities, the director of one of the facilities should be included. Think broadly and inclusively. Let the broad, inclusive group of constituents help establish priorities and explore ways to maximize limited budgets or ways to obtain additional funding.

To gather input from the groups or representatives of groups you have identified, you can use a focus group, interviews, questionnaires, or a combination of techniques. The ease of access to and size of groups to be reached as well as finding out what library resources are needed will help determine which gathering mechanisms to use. For groups with regular meetings—such as school parent organizations, church groups, or business groups—you may want to arrange for a few minutes to present the request for participation in creating a shared vision and asking members to complete a short questionnaire such as:

- What purpose should the public library serve for adult residents of the community?
- What is important for the public library's adult services to accomplish and why?
- What values should be embedded in the library's adult services?

A final space might be given to use for drawings, descriptions, or words the adults feel best represent their vision for adult services at the public library.

A fairly wide group of suggestions can be gathered this way, although analyzing them is a bit problematic (but doable; see later in this chapter). The results of such questionnaires can assist a group representative as well as library staff at a collaborative community vision-building meeting.

The same questions could be used to interview individuals or with small focus groups in which five to eight people (see later in this chapter for how to manage a focus group). When conducting interviews or focus groups, it is important for the facilitator to stick to the list of predetermined questions and limit additional questions to probes such as "Why?" "How do you mean that?" "Can you tell me more about that?" "Is there anything else?" "When did you do that?" "What happened exactly?" or "It didn't work?" to the comment "It didn't work." In response to a comment about something not working, an additional probe could be, "How did that make you feel?"

Never ask a leading question such as, "Did that make you feel like an outsider?" Such leading questions could lead participants to think you wanted them, for example, to feel like an outsider. This might make the person think he or she should give an answer to please you. Remember, participants are volunteering their time to answer questions to help, so it is not unheard of for them to give answers they think are desired. It is important to give them an empty canvas to paint what they feel.

Another error that some staff members or other researchers make in asking for input is asking participants to "answer honestly." While it may seem sincere and inviting to state and even restate that participants should answer honestly and give their "real opinions," this can be taken by participants to mean that the library staff expects them not to be truthful or that answers the library staff expect to get are not what they want to get. This is not good. A better way to approach this is to say you believe their thoughts and opinions will be valuable in designing or developing adult services and programs and setting priorities.

The outcome from this information from constituents may be used to reaffirm the vision, mission, and goals for adult services that also support the mission of the library. Later in this chapter, how to analyze narrative input that is collected will be discussed in more detail. At this point, assume this has been completed and a set of goals for adult services has been created. It is now time to develop objectives and a plan for assessing the outcomes of those objectives.

As stated earlier, assessment begins with a set of goals for adult services as a whole that support the mission of the library. Each program or service with adult services should also have its own goals, and these goals should support the goals of the adult services program as a whole.

Assessment should be ongoing, with periodic reflections on a group of individual assessments. An assessment cycle for adult services is set up as a whole process that includes data gathering, reflection on data gathered about individual events or services, and group reflection on all gathered data. For example, if overall planning for adult services is concluded each April for programming and services for the following September through August, a cycle of assessment might be:

- April: Annual Assessment and Planning Meetings; FIRST YEAR: Establish goals and objectives for Adult Services in general and for each program or service; Plan assessments to measure each objective for coming year. FOLLOWING YEARS: Review summaries of quarterly reflections over the past year; review and update goals and objectives for Adult Services in general and for each program or service based on review of reflections; Plan assessments to measure each objective for coming year; prepare a report on achievement status over the past year.
- September–November: Gather data.
- December 1: Group meeting for reflection on programs and services; review goals, objectives, outcomes, and usefulness of assessments and assessment instruments for each program or service; adjust assessment plans and measures as needed.

- December–February: Gather data; review goals, objectives, outcomes, and usefulness of assessments/assessment instruments for each program or service; adjust assessment plans and measures as needed.
- March–May: Gather data.
- June 1: Group meeting for reflection on programs and services.
- September: Semiannual Assessment Meetings; Review goals, objectives, outcomes, and usefulness of assessments/assessment instruments for Adult Services in general and for each program or service; Adjust assessment plans and measures as needed.
- September–November: Gather data.

A graphic chart of this cycle is shown in Figure 5.1.

Figure 5.1   Sample Cycle of Assessment

Year 1

Mar	Apr	May	Jun	Jul	Aug	Sep	Oct	Nov	Dec	Jan	Feb
	●										
						▨	▨	▲			
									▨	▨	▲

Following Years

Mar	Apr	May	Jun	Jul	Aug	Sep	Oct	Nov	Dec	Jan	Feb
▨	▨	▲									
	●										
			▨	▨	▲						
						●					
						▨	▨	▲			
									▨	▨	▲

○ Annual Strategic Planning Meeting for Adult Services

● Semi-Annual Assessment Meeting for Adult Services

▲ Quarterly Program Reflection Meetings by Initiative

Assessment should be designed to improve programming and services, not just collect data about them. Libraries are not vendors of contained information who measure input and output of quantities of materials and headcounts through the physical and electronic door. Rather, librarians today need to partner with their communities and support, if not be leaders in, helping residents become information literate and maintain lifelong learning. Therefore, assessment of library services and programs needs to be focused toward the learning they support rather than the number that attend programs or the volumes that circulate.

For assessment to be meaningful, it needs to feed back into planning as well as demonstrate how the stated objectives are being met. Objectives, by definition, are specific, measurable, and attainable. Where goals are more conceptual, objectives are more concrete. In operationalizing goals, questions to be asked include "What needs to be done?" "To what extent does it need to be accomplished?" "For whom is it to be done?" "By when is it to be accomplished?" For example, consider the goal of increasing programming for older adults.

To operationalize "Increasing programming for older adults" into an objective, four questions are answered:

- What needs to be done? Answer: increase the number of programs directed to older adults.
- To what extent does it need to be accomplished? Answer: 40% increase over last year's programs.
- For whom is it to be done? Answer: citizens aged 55 and older.
- By when is it to be accomplished? End of the year.

The objective then becomes, "By the end of the planning year, the number of offered programs geared toward residents 55 and older will be increased 40% over the number offered in the previous planning year."

To determine if this objective is met, the lists of programs geared toward residents 55 and older from the previous and current planning years will need to be compared using a simple rate of change formula,

[(number offered in current year) – (number offered in previous year) / (number offered in previous year)] * 100

The rate of change is calculated in three steps:

1. Subtract the number of programs offered in the previous year from the number of programs offered in the current year (to find the change, in raw numbers).

2. Divide this difference by the number of programs offered in the previous year (to find the rate of change as a proportion).

3. Multiply this quotient by 100 (to convert to rate of change in percent).

For example, if 15 programs were offered in the previous year and 20 in the current [(20 – 15) / 15 * 100], the percent of increase would be 33, just short of the set objective of 40 percent increase.

For a bit more complex initiative, let's consider this goal: "To promote the value of library services to the community." To operationalize this to an objective, we answer the four questions stated previously. Beginning with, "What needs to be done?" we decide that dollars and cents value may have more persuasive powers with constituents than values expressed in figurative language. We decide we want constituents to be able to put a dollar value on services they use. In searching, we come across tools developed by three agencies:

- The Massachusetts Library Association's (MLA) downloadable spreadsheet for calculating value of library services (http://www. ala.org/advocacy/advleg/advocacyuniversity/toolkit/makingthecase/ library_calculator)
- The Chelmsford (Massachusetts) Public Library's interactive web-based version of the MLA spreadsheet (http:// www.chelmsfordlibrary.org/ library_info/calculator.html)
- The Boone County (Kentucky) Public Library's library tax calculator that allows patrons to compare how much they paid in library tax (based on the value of their home) compared to the value of library services they used (http://www.bcpl.org/library/)

These three models allow you to develop a library use value calculator for adult services. Now you want to test the calculator to know how useful or informative patrons find it.

The second question asks, "To what extent does it need to be accomplished?" That is, what percentage of the participants need to find the library tax calculator "informative" before you can declare it worthy to use as a way to promote the value of adult services? We decide success will be achieved if "80% of participants in the pilot test rate the calculator as informative, easy to use, and increases their awareness of the value of library services."

"For whom is it to be done?" is the third question. Here we want to know how many participants we want to test the calculator. We decide "At least 50 patrons from each of the following life stages: young adult singles, parents of school-aged children, middle adulthood (40–60), older (over 60) adults."

"By when is it to be accomplished?" is the next question. We decide "The calculator will be developed by the end of [month], and the pilot will be completed by the end of [month]." Then the objective becomes: "By the end of [month] 80% of participating adult patrons will find a developed Library Use Value Calculator is informative, is easy to use, and increases their awareness of the value of library services."

Objectives need a plan of action. In the first example, the action plan was fairly simple: apply the formula. This meant that for previous and ending current years, the number of programs geared toward citizens 55 and older needed to be counted, and the math needed to be computed. In the latter example, there are more actions that need to be taken, some actions must be completed before others can be started, and there may be a repeat cycle (e.g., if success is not achieved, the calculator may be redesigned and then retested). Before patrons can use the library use value calculator and rate its usefulness, the calculator needs to be created. While there are models that can be used, they need to be adapted to the specific programs and services at the library, and it may take a bit of research and calculation to determine the value for the use of each of these.

Once the calculator is developed, it must be made available on a limited basis during the trial pilot, for example, only through a given computer in the library. A questionnaire is be developed that includes the three rating scales stated in the objective as well as demographic questions about age, marital status, age of any children, and so on. The calculator and the questionnaire should be tested by a few (between three and nine) adults to ensure it works as expected, the survey questions are clearly understood, and the procedure for overseeing the pilot and collecting the data is workable. Then the pilot test is advertised, and staff members are designated to oversee the pilot. As data is collected and analyzed, it is possible that one will discover that the calculator, the questionnaire, or the procedure for collecting data needs to be revised.

Assessment should collect information from various points of view using a variety of methods, and it begins with planning. In planning adult services and programs, a needs assessment is conducted to determine what services and programs residents want and which of those can be provided by the public library without negating other community services and programs and vice versa. Each service and program the library offers must have a purpose with associated goals and objectives. To determine these, the librarian may want to begin by creating with area residents a shared vision of adult services.

Begin with current library patrons, having representatives from various generational groups: traditionalists, born before the end of World War II; baby boomers, born between the end of World War II and the mid-1960s; Generation X, born between the mid-1960s and the beginning of the 1980s; and millennials, born after the beginning of the 1980s. Ask each to try to bring a friend or relative of the same generation with them who does not typically visit or attend programs at the library.

Using focus groups (participants who respond to questions through group discussion) or working groups (participants working together to accomplish a task), ask participants to first visualize the public library—the physical structure and its digital presence—as a place they can retreat to for information, entertainment, or socialization. Then ask that they write descriptive words or draw images that represent how they visualize their interaction with the library building or website. Ask participants to briefly explain their visions. Then ask the group to identify common themes. From this, craft a shared vision statement of the library's services and programs to the community.

This process can be repeated with two to three groups of eight to 16 participants. In the end, these statements are crafted into a single vision statement for adult services and programs. From the descriptive words and images, it may be possible to garner a list of services and programs envisioned by participants, grouping them into those most frequently mentioned and those less frequently mentioned.

This might be a good time to reach out to the broader group of library patrons with a survey. Surveys could be distributed within the library during a designated period, perhaps a week, or mailed to cardholders. Distribute questionnaires in sets of two, asking patrons to give the second to an acquaintance who is not a frequent user of or participant in adult services. Be sure to include an addressed envelope with return postage for a paper-based questionnaire or a URL for access to a web-based questionnaire (for a web-based questionnaire, it would be good to have a link to it from the library's homepage). Be sure to include questions that ask for demographic information such as gender, generational group, level of interaction with the library (web-only, building-only, combination), and frequency of that interaction (weekly, monthly, several times a year). It is also important to ask about the patron's availability to come to the physical library. In the questionnaire, it would be good to ask how well the vision statement matches their idea of adult services or for descriptive words if their vision is different. Include a list of services and programs, and ask if these items would contribute toward fulfilling the vision statement, what the patron would expect to gain from each service or program, and how likely the patron is to use such a service or attend such a program.

To keep patrons updated, you will want to have two locations—in the building and online. You will want to keep a running log on the library's website accounting for the created shared vision and purposes or outcomes of types of services or specific programs. Patrons should be able to see the progress, the current drafts of statements, and instructions on how they can add their input. It is likely best to give an end date for collecting input. You can then post the outcome and, if desired, give a second period for comments or reactions. This will permit wider input as well as help patrons feel a part of the process and outcome. The purposes and outcomes will comprise a major portion of this programs and services assessment. This will allow constituents to be aware that the library is seeking their input as well as keep them up to date.

Assessment should be developed by those working with the specific program or service. Those who work with a program or service most likely already have a wealth of observations as well as insights from those observations. This can be valuable in guiding the kinds of questions that should be asked and evidence or data that should be collected to document how well objectives and goals are being met. When the librarian is working with a researcher who has experience or expertise in designing assessment instruments, it is important to ensure that those who work with the program or service being assessed are included as co-researchers who have the experience or expertise in that program or service. Excluding or minimizing the involvement of staff who work with the program or service could result in a narrowly focused assessment that misses the opportunity to gain a broader understanding and fails to maximize the opportunity to enhance and enrich programs and services.

Assessment should be well organized and fit seamlessly into library and program operations. Assessment has three purposes, the first of which is demonstrating that the community was involved and had input when goals were developed. This is done through feeding back the results of the assessment into the planning process. This will demonstrate that the service or program has purposes, goals, and objectives that are based on community needs and input, and it will be used to evaluate how well the objectives have been met. To have a well-organized assessment plan that is not burdensome, it needs to be designed into the program operations rather than existing as a separate entity that must be worked on periodically.

Planning for assessment is always a part of planning for programming. Just as budget and promotion must be considered in planning for programming, so should assessment be part of planning for programming.

Assessment begins with community analysis and needs assessment, as covered in Chapter 4. This means creating a shared vision, which was covered earlier in this chapter. From this, a purpose and goals for adult services in general is developed and then objectives are set for each program or service. Assessment then shows if the needs and expectation of patrons are met and if objectives are being fulfilled.

SOME WAYS TO LOOK AT ADULT SERVICES

Other ways to look at adult services include shadow studies, checklists, and rating scales. Examples of each are given in this section.

In a technique called shadow studies, a careful record is kept of a patron's continuous behavior. This can be used to take a closer look at events in the library and analyze and interpret them for insights that could help improve services. Imagine a small public library that is concerned about the impact of the local senior center changing its morning library transportation service to the afternoon. This means the older adults are arriving at the same time as middle-school students who come to the library for the afterschool program. The concern is promoted by an observation which begins as Scene 1.

Scene 1: Reference desk   Time 3:21 p.m. to 3:22 p.m.

The reference desk area is in turmoil. A few young adults are seated at tables near the reference desk, but most of them are in the process of getting settled. As an older adult walks toward the reference desk, he glances around the area. As his glances meet those of the young adults standing around the area, his face has a puzzled look and his walk seems to slow. Just short of the reference desk he pauses, as if undecided whether to step in front of the lingering young adults to the desk. Suddenly, he turns, shoving the paper in his hand into his shirt pocket, and walks away from the reference desk.

Time 3:22 p.m. to 3:24 p.m.

The older adult walks briskly to the circulation desk then hesitates a distance away from another group of young adults gathering near the circulation area. His glaze wanders around the room. He looks for a while back at the reference desk. Then he quickly walks to the front doors and exits the library.

Scene 2: Reference desk   Time 10:13 a.m. to 10:14 a.m.

The reference desk area is in turmoil. A few adults are seated at one of the tables near the reference desk. As an older adult walks toward the reference desk, he glances around the area. As his glances meet those of the reference librarian, his face has a puzzled look and his walk seems to slow. Just short of the reference desk he pauses, as if undecided whether to step up to the desk. Suddenly, he turns, shoving the paper in his hand into his shirt pocket, and walks away from the reference desk.

Time 10:14 a.m. to 10:17 a.m.

The older adult walks briskly to the circulation desk, then hesitates a distance away. His glaze wanders around the room. He looks for a while back at the reference desk. Then he quickly walks to the front doors and exits the library.

Scene 3: Reference desk   Time 3:33 p.m. to 3:35 p.m.

The reference desk area is in turmoil. A few young adults are seated at tables near the reference desk, but most of them are in the process of getting settled. As an older adult walks toward the reference desk, he glances around the area. As his glances meet those of young adults standing around the area, his face has a puzzled look and his walk seems to slow. Just short of the reference desk he pauses, as if undecided whether to step in front of the lingering young adults to the desk. Suddenly, he turns, shoving the paper in his hand into his shirt pocket, and walks away from the reference desk.

3:35 p.m. to 3:38 p.m.

The older adult walks briskly to the circulation desk, then hesitates a distance away from another group of young adults gathering near the circulation area. His glaze wanders around the room. One of the young adults looks up, waves at the older adult, and walks toward him. The older adult greets the younger adult then takes the paper from his pocket and shows it to the younger adult. The older adult and young adult walk toward the reference area engaged in a conversation, and the young adult is gesturing as if pointing out areas of the library. The young adult takes a book off the shelf and hands it to the older adult. Then they proceed to the copy machine. After photocopying a few pages and setting the book on a nearby table designated for reshelving, the two walk back toward the circulation desk. The older adult waves and leaves the library, and the young adult rejoins his friends.

Workshop Participant 001

Organizational skills
_____ 1. Works in an organized manner
_____ 2. Employs time management
_____ 3. Maintains a clear focus on information problem

Problem-solving skills
_____ 1. Uses or modifies strategies that solve a similar problem
_____ 2. Develops new strategies

Communication skills
_____ 1. Communicates and defends strategies used
_____ 2. Communicates and defends conclusions reached

Comments:

If an assumption was ventured on the basis of the first observation alone, a far different conclusion might result than after considering the second and third observations. Planning to make observations over a variety of situations, times, and observers can aid in trying to identify what is really going on. Sufficient observations should be conducted to give confidence that enough information was captured to understand the core behavior and recognize the situational elements and their impact on the core behavior. When conclusions are based on a single observation or on only one point of view, the observer could be jumping to impulsive and flawed conclusions.

Checklists

Checklists aid observation in that they help focus the observer's attention on the presence, absence, or frequency of a behavior. Imagine a public library is offering workshops in using library resources to strengthen job skills and look for employment. To document whether each participant demonstrated the skills taught in the workshop, a checklist is developed by first listing the behaviors to be observed and actual sequence of behaviors. The behaviors are then categorized and grouped together by similar traits or attributes. All relevant and specific points of behavior are included on the checklist. Space is also provided for relevant notes or comments.

A single checklist could also capture the behaviors of a group of participants. Imagine a public library is offering a workshop for caregivers in storytelling and reading aloud, and it wants to record read-aloud behavior at the beginning of the workshop and again at its conclusion.

Read Aloud activity at [beginning/conclusion] of workshop
Participant:

			(Check if observed)		
Activity:	1	2	3	4	5
Voice is relaxed					
Voice is not too soft or too loud					
Rate (tempo) is not too rushed					
Book held so listener can see pictures					
Book held so reader can maintain eye contact with listener					
NOTES:					

Rating Scales

Rating scales are useful for gathering information from patrons on their attitudes or opinions. Rating scales can take a variety of forms: numeric, categorical, graphic, or pictorial.

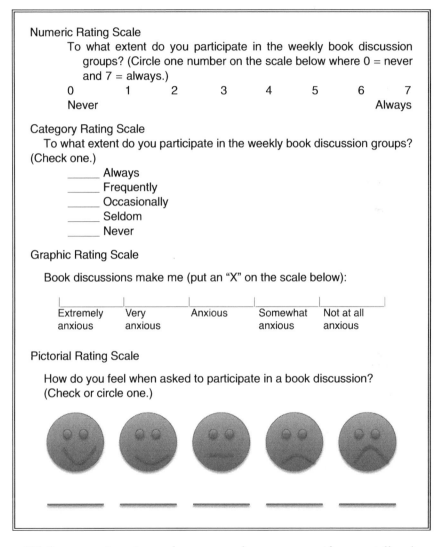

While a numeric rating scale may seem better to quantify, especially when you are going to report the mean average rating, it is not always the better scale for capturing participants' feelings. Nor is the mean average necessarily the better statistic to report. Do not underestimate the emoticon's ability to capture a good representation of the participants' feelings.

SOME WAYS TO ANALYZE OPEN-ENDED RESPONSES

Sometimes it seems best to give participants the opportunity to write narrative responses rather than check items on a list. For example, if a goal is to create a welcoming and comfortable area for reading, asking the participant

---

Dear Adult Patron,

   We are asking for your help in designing a dedicated Adult Services area within the library. After completing this questionnaire, please return it to either the marked Survey Collection Box located at the circulation desk or the Survey Collection Box located at the reference desk.

1. Please describe your ideal area for how you use or would like to use the library and what should be done to create an ideal Adult Services area in the library.
2. How do you or how would you like to use the library? (Please check all that apply.)

___ through a computer to access electronic resources

___ to borrow books

___ to identify books that might interest me

___ to socialize with others

___ to escape my usual routine

___ to have a quiet place to read

___ to wait while my children attend programs/use the library

___ to learn more about technology and newer resources

___ other (please specify)

3. I am:

___ under 18   ___ 18–21   ___ 22–30   ___ 31–45

___ 46–55   ___ 56–65   ___ 66–75   ___ over 75

4. I have (please check all that apply):

___ children under age 5

___ school-aged children

___ children in college

___ adult children

___ grandchildren

___ children for whom I provide care

___ parent or other adult for whom I provide care

___ other (please specify)

5. I am (please check all that apply):

___ employed at home

___ employed part-time

___ employed full-time

___ not currently employed

___ considering or looking for employment

___ retired

___ other (please specify)

6. I am:

___ female___ male

Thank you for your participation! Please return your completed questionnaire to a Survey Collection Box located at the circulation desk or at the reference desk.

to select from a list of choices will certainly give limited input, and you may miss becoming aware of wonderful ideas that could be implemented. There are, however, times when you are limited in what can be implemented, and therefore you would want to use a list of choices. If there are no limitations, open-ended questions are likely the better way to gain input. For example, a one-page data collection instrument might include the information given in the chart on page 92.

While questions 2–6 can be tallied to report the percentage of participants who marked each response option, question 1 allows a wide range of narrative input. You may already have some general features about which you want input such as location in the building, type of seating or furniture, and type of lighting. For these you can read each response and list the words written by the patron that address each of these features. If you did not already have specific features in mind, when reading through responses you will find common ones emerging. Either way, you will arrive at a point where you are grouping together terms that are describing the same thing but likely in different words or arrangements of words. If very few questionnaires are being analyzed, you could make a photocopy of each and then cut the copy into phrases that express a concept and sort these into piles that represent distinct concepts. This may bring back memories of reading Sina Spiker on how to create a back-of-the-book index (http://uwpress.wisc.edu/books/1781.htm).

The key to analyzing narrative or open-ended responses is categorization. You want to read through the responses first to get an idea of the common themes or categories being expressed in the narratives. Make a list of these, for example:

Furniture – chair – comfortable
Furniture – chair – back support

Furniture – table – group
Furniture – table – individual study
Furniture – newspaper racks
Lighting – reading
Lighting – natural
Location – isolated
Location – central
Features – quiet room
Features – game room
Resources – readers' advisory
Resources – new publications display
Resources – newsletter

On a second reading, you can then tally the themes or categories that are expressed in each questionnaire.

An ample supply of well-written texts is available that are excellent to help with research design, questionnaire design, and methods of analysis. This chapter has neither the purpose nor the space to summarize these. It is hoped that the few examples given within this chapter can serve to help in drafting a basic assessment plan and reasonable instruments.

SUMMARY

Assessment begins with planning. In planning adult services and programs, we need to conduct an environmental scan and needs assessment (see Chapter 4) to determine what services and programs residents want and which of those can be provided by the public library without negating other community services and programs and vice versa. A shared vision of adult services is created with a representative group of the community. Each service and program that is to be offered in the library should have a purpose with associated goals and objectives. An assessment plan is built into adult programming so that it is seamless and ongoing. Outcome assessment is given regular reflection to compare the results to the set objectives.

What is learned from this reflection is then used to plan future programming. All assessment is documented to demonstrate to various stakeholders that the community had input into planning, service and program objectives were based on community needs and expectations, and set objectives were measured from a variety of perspectives.

BIBLIOGRAPHY AND READINGS ON RESEARCH

Books on How to Conduct Research and Assessment in the Library

Beck, S. E., & Manuel, K. (2008). *Practical research methods for librarians and information professionals*. New York: Neal-Schuman.

Durrance, J. C., Fisher, K. E., & Hinton, M. B. (2004). *How libraries and librarians help: A guide to identifying user-centered outcomes*. Chicago: American Library Association.

Johannsen, C. G., & Kajberg, L. (Eds.). (2005). *New frontiers in public library research*. Lanham, MD: Scarecrow.

Powell, R. R., & Connaway, L. S. (2004). *Basic research methods for librarians* (4th ed.). Westport, CT: Libraries Unlimited.

Wallace, D. P., & Van Fleet, C. (Eds.). (2001). *Library evaluation: A casebook and can-do guide*. Englewood, CO: Libraries Unlimited.

Wallace, D. P., & Van Fleet, C. J. (2012). *Knowledge into action: Research and evaluation in library and information science*. Santa Barbara, CA: Libraries Unlimited.

Wildemuth, B. M. (2009). *Applications of social research methods to questions in information and library science*. Westport, CT: Libraries Unlimited.

Articles Reporting on Research Dealing with Adult Services in Public Libraries

Baker, N. (1995). Adult services. *RQ, 35*(2), 169–172.

Butcher, W., & Street, P.-A. (2009). Lifelong learning with older adults. *APLIS, 22*(2), 64–70.

Prasad, P. (2009). Reference services to senior groups in the San Antonio Public Library. *Reference Librarian, 50*(1), 99–108.

Scott, R. (2011). The role of public libraries in community building. *Public Library Quarterly, 30*(3), 191–227.

Senkevitch, J. J., & Sweetland, J. H. (1994). Evaluating adult fiction in the smaller public library. *RQ, 34*(1), 78–89.

Zionts, N. D., Apter, J., Kuchta, J., & Greenhouse, P. K. (2010). Promoting consumer health literacy: Creation of a health information librarian fellowship. *Reference & User Services Quarterly, 49*(4), 350–359.

Other Articles that Can Be Applied to Research Dealing with Adult Services in Public Libraries

Carter, T. M., & Seaman, P. (2011). The management and support of outreach in academic libraries. *Reference & User Services Quarterly, 51*(2), 162–171.

Frumkin, J., & Reese, T. (2011). Provision recognition: Increasing awareness of the library's value in providing electronic information resources. *Journal of Library Administration, 51*(7/8), 810–819.

Lankes, R. D. (2012). Joining the conversation. *Teacher Librarian, 39*(3), 8–12.

Robinson, L. (2011). Library and cultural service convergence: A case study of the City of Wanneroo, Western Australia. *APLIS, 24*(4), 160–166.

Singer, D. (2011, August 14). Arts program helps homeless men express their reality. Philly.com. http://articles.philly.com/2011-08-14/news/29886620_1_homeless -men-homeless-people-art-exhibits.

Terrile, V. C., & Echols, S. M. (2012). They don't leave their lives at the door, but neither do we: Changing our minds about changing teens' behaviors. *Young Adult Library Services, 10*(2), 19–23.

Williams, P., & Edwards, J. (2011). Nowhere to go and nothing to do: How public libraries mitigate the impacts of parental work and urban planning on young people. *APLIS, 24*(4), 142–152.

Suggested Journals for General Reading on Research

Canadian Journal of Information and Library Science
Information Processing and Management
Journal of Education for Library and Information Science
Library and Information Science Research
Library Collections, Acquisitions & Technical Services
Library Quarterly
Library Trends
Reference & User Services Quarterly
Technical Services Quarterly

PART III

Types of Services for Adults

"How wonderful it is that nobody need wait a single moment before starting to improve the world."

—Anne Frank

CHAPTER 6

Readers' Services

In this chapter, the historical background of readers' services in public libraries, and the evolution of readers' advisory (RA) services from readers' services, will be examined. The different types of readers' services and concepts in public libraries, including reference and the readers' advisory interview, will be discussed. Activities that provide access to all categories of reading materials, fiction and nonfiction, will also be addressed. Techniques and strategies for offering readers' advisory services, their forms and their levels of services, as well as tools for implementing RA will be presented. The integration of web-based technology in the implementation of RA services and training for RA services in the twenty-first century will be reviewed.

HISTORICAL BACKGROUND FOR RA

Services for readers in public libraries in the early 1900s were known by various terms such as "reading guidance," "readers' advisory service," "readers' consultants," "reading counselors," and "readers' assistants" at different times (Rubin, 1982, p. 95). The early 1920s saw the establishment of "readers' bureaus" in many public libraries, which were set up to provide reading guidance separate from information (reference) departments (Rubin, 1982). The advantage of the separate departments is that ready resources and procedures, and perhaps environments, could be designed for the different functions. This meant, however, that a patron seeking help finding factual information as well as selecting personal reading materials needed to visit two separate departments in the library.

Public libraries from their beginnings have been involved in *providing* information (reference) and reading materials (RA) to their patrons, but the concept of *helping readers choose* what to read came into focus in the late nineteenth century.

Rubin (1982) reminds us that "aid to readers" is a cornerstone of library philosophy that dates back to 1885 when Melvil Dewey referred to it as the "modern library idea" (Dewey, 1885). The activity of assisting patrons in identifying books of interest was initially tied to the educational objective of libraries described by John Cotton Dana in his draft of *A Library Primer* as a place where patrons could obtain a self-administered education with reading guidance from librarians. Dana believed that "the public library is chiefly concerned not in the products of education, as shown in the finished book, but in the process of education as shown in the developing and training of the library users, of the general public" (Dana, 1899, p. 132).

The functions of reference service were first articulated by Samuel Green in his paper "Personal Relations between Librarians and Readers" (Green, 1876). These are reflected in present-day reference service, but they are not the same as meeting educational objectives.

Lee (1966) classified into four hierarchical levels the services provided by librarians to meet patrons' educational objectives. The most basic level is the provision of materials; the next level adds to this provision of personal assistance; the third level adds to this the provision of stimulation (to motivate or promote reading); and the final level adds the provision of services to special groups.

In discussing her service paradigm for public libraries, Dresang (1982) felt that public service was an "urgent duty" and should not be avoided. Her fundamental functions were information, instruction, guidance, and stimulation.

In the 1880s and 1890s, librarians trained to assist library users as they sought information became necessary with the implementation of separate reading rooms. Initially, separate reading rooms were set up for the reference collection and services, and separate readers' bureaus were set up to provide reading guidance. The first designated readers' bureau was established in 1923 at the Chicago Public Library.

The new activity was initially referred to as "assistance to readers," which became known as "reference work." Public libraries in large cities started offering classes for "reference assistants" (Bopp & Smith, 2011).

Readers' services in libraries have been referred to by different names, including "readers' consultants," "readers' counselors," "readers' assistants," and "readers' advisers." In 1885, the St. Louis Public Library added library "hostesses" to welcome patrons and assist them in the library. Other libraries followed suit: the Washington, D.C., Public Library in 1905, the Chicago Public Library in 1923, and the New York Public Library in 1929. The New York

Public Library became the first public library to set up a readers' advisers office in 1934 (Rubin, 1982, p. 95).

Readers' guidance continued to be provided in public libraries. The service went through a number of cycles. The 1930s were said to be the "golden age" of RA. The service grew rapidly during this time. One study stated that in 1935, there were 63 readers' advisers in 44 libraries (Monroe, 1963, p. 2). The pioneers of readers' services in public libraries include Jennie Flexner, New York Public Library; Mable Booton, Cleveland Public Library; Margery Doud, St. Louis Public Library; and Marion Hawes, Enoch Pratt Free Public Library in Baltimore (Rubin, 1982).

The 1940s saw a decline in the growth of RA, and it had nearly disappeared by the 1950s. Rockwood and Shores (1957) explain one reason for this decline is that while effective RA reached too few people, another reason was that the organizational structure of public libraries changed from centralized to decentralized, and readers' services started to be provided in different parts of the library and by all library staff.

Bopp and Smith (2011) pointed out the difference between the "classic" readers' advisers who interviewed patrons to understand their needs and selected library resources to meet those needs, and today's readers' advisers who provide reading materials, current awareness services, and library use instruction to help users understand the library and learn how to be aware of new books relevant to their reading interests.

CONTEMPORARY RA SERVICE

The 1980s saw a renewed interest in RA services in public libraries. In 1984, librarians in the Chicago area established Adult Reading Round Table to focus on adult reading interests. Librarians in other metropolitan areas began forming RA associations. During this decade, Betty Rosenberg published *Genreflecting: A Guide to Reading Interests in Genre Fiction*, a book that is credited as being one of the key events in spurring the revival of RA (Maatta, 2010). This revival created interest in what has been described as "contemporary readers' advisory" consisting of an organized program promoting both fiction and nonfiction discretionary reading for the purpose of both satisfying reader needs and advancing a culture's goal of a literate population (Crowley, 2005).

RA today links readers not only to books, but also to author resources, multimedia resources, and all formats of published information. Tools include resources such as commercially created bibliographies, databases, and all types of lists. Readers' advisers consult websites, listservs, blogs, and discussion groups to help readers find the right books and resources for their reading interests. Social networks have become an integral part of implementing contemporary readers' advisory services in public libraries. They help create online communities through which readers can communicate with each other. In these communities, members share personal information as well as interests and participate in discussions. A number of public libraries have developed social networking spaces to reach both users and nonusers of library services. The sites allow for two-way communication between readers and library staff. They also provide a way to announce events and post other information about library events and RA programs. Libraries also post information about new acquisitions of books, videos, and DVDs.

Many authors have used sites such as MySpace and Facebook to reach their readers, and sometimes they create spaces for their favorite characters or series. Popular social network sites for RA are LibraryThing, Shelfari, and GoodReads.

The development of electronic formats such as eBooks has added a new dimension to the tasks of readers' advisers. As Dunneback (2011) points out, expanding the formats in which books are available expands the appeal of reading books. Readers' advisers need to be technology advisers in addition to assisting with content, and the format used to access the story expands the appeal to the story. Readers' advisers have to be familiar with the technology they use so that they can educate readers about how to use the technology.

RA SERVICES FOR SPECIAL POPULATIONS

Contemporary RA is also involved with helping develop a literate population. RA is therefore also concerned with literacy issues and the development of new readers. Not all adults are able to engage in leisure reading. Approximately 30 million adults in the United States have less than basic literacy skills, and approximately 11 million are nonliterate in English. These individuals need to be able to engage in leisure reading. Public libraries collaborate with outside agencies such as Literacy Volunteers of America, providing space and resources for tutoring. Literacy Volunteers of America provides basic adult literacy programs such as GED preparation and English as a Second Language programs for immigrants and adult new readers. Readers' advisers can help these readers by providing resources through the library collection that are appropriate for their reading levels and ability. Librarians have to look for clues to help identify this category of users, many of whom are unlikely to reveal their limited reading ability. Maatta (2010) recommends that advisers identify books with high interest for readers with low vocabulary, and she recommends that advisers talk with new readers as well as literacy tutors to find out what elements interest new readers. In addition, librarians must become part of the larger learning community if they are to be effective in meeting the needs of the new adult readers.

Access to collections that suit the needs of adult learners will help create a welcoming environment for these users.

Patrons with disabilities must also be considered in the provision of RA services. Patrons with disabilities make up a large proportion of library patrons and benefit from services that accommodate their disabilities by providing reading materials in other formats. The National Library Service for the Blind and Physically Handicapped (NLS) can help provide materials in Braille or talking books. Large print books should also be part of the resources provided for patrons with visual impairments. Patrons with disabilities need books and resources that match their interests in formats they can use. "Providing services to adult learners and people with disabilities is a winning situation for the entire community. Increased access to reading materials and information encourages lifelong learning which ultimately improves the overall health of the community" (Maatta, 2010, p. 235).

The 1990s saw a resurgence of RA services to individuals as well as groups. A number of authors emphasized the importance of the service, explaining that the advisory service helps the library reach more patrons and provide services to the community at large (Ross, 2011; McCook & Rolstad, 1993). Public libraries have been establishing readers' advisory services as separate services within the public services function. Librarians have established additional components such as book discussions. They have enlisted the help of professional organizations in their efforts. Some public libraries focused readers' advisory activities on helping readers with fiction and other recreational reading materials (Saricks & Brown, 1997). With the emergence of lifelong learning as well as the need to address life situations and health issues, helping readers find nonfiction materials has become an integral part of readers' advisory services in public libraries of all sizes.

Public libraries in the twenty-first century need to provide additional readers' services to address the changing demographics of their communities and the growth of virtual services to remote patrons, and they need to apply technologies designed to take the services to patrons who cannot come to the library. Models of service that include specialized services such as services to new adult readers will be examined in the following section.

RA SERVICE CONCEPTS

The purpose of RA is articulated by Opening the Book Ltd. as " The best book in the world is quite simply the one you like best and that is something you can discover for yourself, but we are here to help you find it." This purpose is in contrast to reference service, which brings in the knowledge of the librarian to evaluate the material. Reference service is assistance provided by the library staff to patrons to help satisfy their information needs.

RA services guide readers to reading materials relevant to their reading interests. The differences in definition predict the difference in services provided.

RA is a special extension of reference service, which is defined by Joan Reitz as including "answering substantive questions; instructing users in the selection of appropriate tools and techniques; conducting searches for patrons; directing users to library resources, evaluating information, and referring patrons to resources outside the library; keeping reference statistics; and developing the reference collection" (Reitz, 2004, p. 602). In contrast, RA has been described as the core business of the public library (Shearer & Burgin, 2001). The function of the readers' adviser is to understand the needs of readers and help them choose materials to meet their needs. A number of definitions of the concept can be found in the literature, including:

> ... a patron centered library service for adult leisure readers. A successful readers advisory service is one in which knowledgeable, non-judgmental staff help fiction and non fiction readers with their leisure reading needs. (Saricks, 2005, p. 1)

Shearer (1996) defines it in terms of the activity involved:

> An exchange of information between two people with the purpose of one person's suggesting text for the other's reading interest. ... The text suggested in the transaction is expected to meet a recreational, emotional, psychological or educational need. (p. 3)

The various definitions offer the framework within which the service is provided in public libraries, clarify methods used to link patrons to books that they are interested in, and create an awareness of the resources that the library has to help patrons find books that satisfy their reading interests. The service is reader centered, and all staff activities need to focus on readers along with their needs and reading interests. To be able to provide this service, the readers' adviser has to have the following skills:

- Understand the reader's needs
- Know something about books, both fiction and nonfiction
- Be familiar with the library's collection
- Know the resources needed to support RA services
- Know of the role of reading in the life of the reader (Shearer & Burgin, 2001)

Understanding the reader requires interaction and communication with the reader. This is accomplished by conducting an RA interview.

THE RA INTERVIEW

The RA interview is considered one of the basics of readers' advisory service. Just like in a reference interview, the success of the service depends on how effective the reference interview transaction is. Readers' advisers are expected to be proficient in conducting interviews. A number of techniques for conducting an RA interview are found in the literature (Saricks & Brown, 1997). The RA interview has been defined as "a conversation between the adviser and the reader about books" (Saricks, 2005, p. 75). It is a transaction that differs from a reference interview in that its objective is identifying possibilities rather than a specific answer. The role of the readers' adviser is that of an adviser and not an expert; he or she acts as a consultant to his or her readers. The same techniques applied in the reference interview are applied in an RA interview—providing a welcoming atmosphere, setting the tone, getting the facts from the reader via open-ended questions during the conversation, and listening carefully to readers in order to understand their needs. The adviser then provides the necessary information and follows up to make sure that readers received what they needed. Saricks (2001) recommended that advisers suggest a range of books instead of recommending specific titles. Suggestions should be based on information received from the reader during the transaction.

RA RESOURCES, FICTION AND NONFICTION

To advise patrons, readers' advisers need to know their own collection and something about types of books in general. The collection consists of literary fiction, genre fiction, and nonfiction.

Fiction

Fiction material makes up 60 percent of the total circulation in most public libraries. Familiarity with fiction (both genre fiction and literary fiction) is necessary for readers' advisory work. Literary fiction tends to be character driven with focus on prose. Genre fiction, or popular fiction, tends to be plot driven and written for the masses; these readers may or may not be familiar with the particular genre. The texts are usually grouped into categories that share similar characteristics such as theme, appeal, and setting.

Maatta (2010) identified eight distinct mainstream genres: adventure, fantasy, historical fiction, science fiction, romance, horror, suspense or thrillers, and westerns. Within these genres are subgenres and a category of emerging genres such as chick lit and street lit. A number of publications are devoted to the study of fiction genres, including *Genreflecting: A Guide to Popular Reading Interests* and *The Readers' Advisory Guide to Fiction Genre.*

Trott (2009) suggests that maintaining and building knowledge of genres is the most challenging aspect of RA services. Knowledge of elements of appeals within genres is therefore critical to successful RA. "Keeping up with the reading community's interests," Trott tells us, "has never been more complex or more challenging," a situation that is not likely to change. Readers' advisers need resources that will help them, for example, good reviews, publishers' lists, and selection and evaluation tools (Trott, 2009).

Nonfiction

Nonfiction is a literary genre or collection that does not have an accepted definition. Instead, it is defined by what it is not. Literary fiction is not a genre. While there is a cultural appeal difference between literary fiction and popular fiction, the same techniques used to guide RA in finding popular or genre titles can be used to identify literary fiction titles of interest to a patron. Nonfiction literature therefore runs the gamut of human experience, such as adventure, travel, business, historical, and biographical. Readers' advisers need to be familiar with the characteristics of nonfiction just as they are expected to be familiar with fiction.

Wyatt (2007) divides nonfiction into two categories of purpose: task books and nontask books. Task books are needed to complete a task, such as how-to books. Nontask books are texts that readers want for various reasons, such as learning, exploration, and self-improvement. The readers' adviser has to determine which type of nonfiction the reader needs and provide books to satisfy the need. For task books, needs can be satisfied by using locational resources such as the library catalog to locate the item by conducting a subject search on the task for which the book is needed. For the nontask book, the readers' adviser has to provide advice and guidance based on some knowledge and understanding of the nature of nonfiction literature. Just as there are elements of appeal in the fiction genre; such as pacing, characterization, storyline, and setting, these elements are used to study the different fiction genres. Similar elements of nonfiction literature are articulated in the literature (Wyatt, 2007).

According to Wyatt (2007), four elements are used to study nonfiction: (1) narrative context, (2) subject, (3) type, and (4) appeal. Each of the elements is intertwined with the others and with sub-elements within each category.

The *narrative context,* or story, provides the context within which the reader can relate to the story or event. The dialog, setting, and plot are said to provide the framework within which the reader can experience the story, adventure, or events that the book tries to present.

The *subject* allows the contents to be classified using existing classification schemes of knowledge that make it easy to identify the topics addressed in the book. The subject is of vital importance, as it is the hook that gets the reader's attention.

The *type* classification provides information about kinds of nonfiction, such as biography, memoirs, adventure, short stories, and anthologies.

Appeal is similar to the concept of articulating a book's appeal outlined by Saricks and Brown (1997, chapter 3). Wyatt (2007) points out that the various elements of appeal in nonfiction are linked to the title's narrative, subject, and type and that they all work together to make up the total reading experience. Readers' advisers have to understand these elements, recognize them, and be able to articulate them. "Learning how to articulate them is fundamental to non-fiction readers advisory service" (Wyatt, 2007, p. 10). Wyatt provides more information about the elements and how to recognize and articulate them in his book on the subject.

The readers' adviser needs to prepare for reader interactions by thinking about books and knowing how to talk about books. The key to a successful RA is learning how to think about books, which the literature suggests is a three-step process: (1) begin with the book's appeal, that is, what makes the book a good read; (2) group the book with other titles and authors that have similar appeal; and (3) consider how authors and titles fit within a genre (Saricks & Brown, 1997).

The readers' adviser needs to be able to articulate the book's "appeal" (the elements in the book that make the book enjoyable to read) and have knowledge of similar authors whose works share similar elements of appeal. Ross and Chelton (2001) indicated that matching the mood of the reader with material suggested is an important aspect of the interview. The assumption is that the readers' adviser has the knowledge and skills to do the job.

TECHNIQUES AND STRATEGIES OF RA SERVICE

A variety of techniques and strategies of RA service are available. Strategies can take one of two forms:

- Active RA
- Passive RA

Forms of RA Services

Active RA involves direct contact with the reader, either face to face or through remote electronic interaction. This direct contact includes the RA

Forms of RA Services

Passive	Active
Annotations	Reference transactions
Booklists	Book discussions
Book displays	Author visits
Signage	Book talking
Book marks	Book clubs
Bibliographies	Online book discussions
Newsletters	Social networking tools
Bestsellers	Form-based readers' advisory

interview or transaction, programming that involves book discussions, author visits, book talks, online book discussions, and book clubs. Passive (or indirect) RA involves the creation of annotations, displays, arrangements, spine labels, marketing, bookmarks, bibliographies, booklists, and other materials that the reader can use as an aid or advisory in the absence of direct communication with the readers' adviser. These are both shown in the chart above.

A good RA service should be made up of both active and passive strategies. The nature of the mix of services depends on the needs of the patrons in the community, the library facility and the spaces available to conduct RA, and the resources available to support the services. Smith suggests that a good way to look at RA services is in terms of the level of service the library can provide.

LEVELS OF SERVICE

Smith categorizes RA into three levels of service: basic, enhanced, and exemplary. The factors used to demarcate the levels of service are:

- Frequency—how often a service is delivered
- Scope—the coverage and population impacted by the service and staff
- Involvement—the extent of staff involvement, which may be combined with the regular library tasks or the assignment of a staff to RA services exclusively

Basic Level of Service

Part of the service response of the library to the needs of the community includes, as defined by McCook (2004):

- Selection of resources for the library's collection
- Providing access to the collection, including instruction and RA and guidance
- Reference and information services
- Activation of use of the library's resources for individuals as well as community groups (McCook, 2004, p. 184)

This level of service involves the commitment of space, collection, staff, and resources to the needs of the community for fiction, nonfiction, and other forms of books and periodicals and formats (print, digital) of resources. In most libraries, the RA service is treated as a core service that is integrated with other services with no separate readers' advisory department. All staff members are expected to participate in the delivery of the service.

Enhanced Level of Service

This level of service provides a focused service to fiction readers as one of the service responses. RA service is a coordinated function of the library, with staff assigned to managing the implementation of the readers' advisory function. At this level of service, the library provides a budget, designates a separate space with signage and service desks, and provides RA training so that all public service staff can participate in providing the service. The library staff is involved in active as well as passive RA services, such as book talks, hosting author visits, creating reading lists, and participating in programming. Librarians promote and market the service. The service is provided as outreach in both physical and virtual environments. The library website has a separate section dedicated to RA services.

Exemplary Level of Service

This level of service has all the elements of the enhanced service. In addition, the library offers a major service in support of readers and reading that is formalized and integrated into other public services in the library. The services are proactive and are provided outside the library (e.g., outreach) as well as inside. Services include an RA service desk, reading roundtables, and web-accessible services. Staff members provide book talks in the library as well as to community groups. The library commonly sponsors author visits and uses mass media such as radio and television to promote and market its services. The library organizes online discussion groups and book clubs, uses social networking tools to promote the services, and offers collaborative activities with patrons. Staff create guides and resources to meet users' interests (Minnesota Development, 2000).

Public libraries have become the main resource for leisure reading for adults. They have expanded their collections beyond print to other formats such as audio books, eBooks, and graphic novels. Moyer (2010) articulates that RA services have expanded beyond leisure reading and advocates an "integrated readers' advisory" approach to RA. She explains the concept: "It is a whole way of looking at and thinking about library materials that incorporates the techniques of readers' advisory and multiple media that make up the modern library collections. It is a way for you and your library users to maximize your library resources by finding connections between them" (Moyer, 2010, p. xii).

In considering RA services, librarians have to consider reading technologies other than the book. These technologies include audio books, electronic books, and multimedia such as DVDs and other resources, including movies and music that readers and viewers may request. Technologies changed, for example, when Playaways arrived on the market. They are small battery-operated audio devices about the size of a deck of cards with digital content such as an audio book preloaded. This device requires the user to insert headphones or earbuds, press play, and listen. Many librarians have started providing both Kindle and Nook readers and buying books to place on them. The iPad and the application (app) for downloading books to a cell phone are also new technologies on the market. The continuing development of such new devices must be taken into consideration when implementing RA services for the contemporary reader of the twenty-first century.

ONLINE RA AND WEB 2.0

Online RA is a logical step in the age of the Internet. Wilson pointed out that it is imperative for libraries to offer online services to woo back patrons lost to Yahoo and online bookstores such as Amazon. Since Wilson's directive in 2001, public libraries have responded by creating entire websites dedicated to books.

Three examples are the Charlotte Mecklenberg County Public Library in North Carolina, the Hennepin Public Library in Minnesota, and the Morton Grove Public Library in Illinois. Publishers and vendors have helped the process by developing electronic databases and resources devoted to RA, such as Novelist by EBSCO and RA Online by Libraries Unlimited. OCLC has created the fiction tool Syndetic Solution, which offers catalog elements such as tables of contents, summaries, annotations, and reviews for librarians to use in developing readers' advisory resources.

Some libraries offer online book clubs such as Readers' Club (see http://www.readersclub.com). Virtual reference strategies have made it possible for librarians to use chat, Instant Messaging (IM), and Short Message Service (SMS) to promote RA. Some public librarians are proactive and solicit information from readers using a reading interest form much like email reference forms. Information collected using these forms allows librarians to match patrons' reading interests with items in the collection. This has resulted in the implementation of form-based RA. The first RA form was offered in 2003 by the Williamsburg Regional Library in Williamsburg, Virginia. Librarians there suggest that the RA form is a noninvasive way to obtain the profile of their readers and that it provides documentation that can be used for follow-up support for RA activities. More information on developing and delivering the form is provided in the literature (Hollands & Trott, 2006).

With the development of Web 2.0 technologies, librarians have taken up the challenge and have integrated technology into the delivery of library services, including RA services. Barry Trott and Jane Jorgenson recommend that librarians provide "proactive and reactive" readers' services using Web 2.0 tools, taking readers services to readers and dealing with individual requests for resources (rickilibrarian, 2010). The tools include blogs and wikis along with other social networking tools that can be used to communicate with readers as well as build reading communities. *Blogging for a Good Book* by WRL is a good example of integrating blogging into RA services. Examples of Web 2.0 RA services include wikis as well as a collaborative community of readers such as Goodreads, LibraryThing, and Shelfari. Social networking sites such as Facebook, MySpace, and YouTube are also used by libraries to provide RA services. Maatta (2010) reminds us that social networks offer a wide range of functions, from adding user profiles to joining groups and offering opportunities to contribute content to the site. Librarians have to determine which tool to use depending on the level of service and the resources they have to support the service.

Examples of methods of providing online RA include:

- Library websites with links to RA-related information
- Access to lists, for example, bestseller, *New York Times*, publishers' lists, online databases, Novelist, Overbooked
- Annotations that provide, more information on posted items
- Form-based email-based services
- Chat RA, an RA-related chat by readers' advisers
- Online newsletters and alert services
- Online discussion groups, book discussions

TRAINING FOR READERS' ADVISERS

The need for training readers' advisers has been addressed in the literature. Quinn (2008) suggests that training for readers' advisers should be competency based. The competencies were first articulated by the State of Minnesota Career Renewal Training for Library Employees and were developed using RUSA reference guidelines (Quinn, 2008). Competencies include knowledge of fiction and nonfiction, particularly popular authors and titles, and understanding readers.

Watson (2000) expressed the need for a specific preparatory course for readers' advisers. The need to integrate Web 2.0 in teaching reference and RA was addressed by Moyer and Weech (2005). The difficulty of training RA staff was discussed by Saricks and Brown (1997).

Implementing Training for Readers' Advisers

To implement successful RA service, training for the library staff has to be part of the strategy. Smith (2000) introduced the concept of a "competency-based approach to readers' advisory training." Smith and others developed four broad areas of competencies and, within those areas, 130 individual competencies for RA services. The four broad areas are:

- Background in fiction and nonfiction literature
- Understanding people as readers and readers' as people
- The appeal of books
- Readers' Advisory Transaction (Duncan, 2000)

These four broad areas of competencies and the 130 individual competencies they suggest should be the framework for implementing competency-based training for RA services.

A background in fiction and nonfiction is an essential competence for readers' advisers. Readers' advisers need to be familiar with fiction and the genres, know the characteristics of specific genres, and be able to talk about them, not only as books, but also the cultural context in which the books are written. Books are written with the context of life experience and conclusions, which are always changing and evolving. This is reflected in the emergence of nonfiction genres. Readers' advisers must be involved in continuing education to build on the knowledge they have, integrating new concepts and genres both in fiction and nonfiction. They have to be familiar with the reasons for selecting and evaluating fiction and nonfiction materials. They also have to be familiar with other forms of materials, electronic and multimedia resources, that are now included in what their readers and viewers want.

A new approach to readers' advisers that has an impact on the competences is the "Whole Collection" readers' advisory services, which goes beyond the current connection between reader and book based on the concept of appeal, taking into consideration the entire library collection. Whole Collection RA moves beyond the title-to-title paradigm to include consideration of all elements of the collection—fiction and nonfiction, audio books, music, art, movies, and electronic resources (Wyatt, 2006).

Wyatt, in recommending Whole Collection RA, believes that the approach will enrich the experience of the book, giving the reader more to choose from and making the most use of the collection. The Whole Collection approach exposes the reader to a world of nonfiction literature that would not be as accessible in the title-to-title approach.

Understanding people as readers and readers as people requires that readers' advisers understand the value of the reading experience and how readers interact with the reading experience. Readers' advisers need to be aware of the diversity among readers, consider the differences in the diversity of RA services, and be accepting of each individual reader's tastes and interest.

Understanding of a book's appeal and articulating that appeal is at the heart of RA services. Readers' advisers need to be trained in how to understand a book's appeal and the appeal of alternate formats and ways of connecting with the reader in a readers' advisory transaction, for example, in-person interview, phone discussions, email exchange, and interactive advising from the library website. This is an essential part of training for RA services and is just as important to the process as the reference interview. The RA interview has been said to be more complicated than question negotiation in a reference interview (Baker, 1992).

Training for RA in addition to the competencies outlined earlier in this chapter requires a solid background in reference materials and tools on which the special knowledge base for readers' advisers will be built. Since these librarians are expected to deliver passive and active RA services, they have to be trained in programming and outreach services. All aspects of public services need to be included in the training. Also, readers' advisers need to have a high level of technology skills to be able to integrate emerging tools and application into readers' advisory services.

Readers' advisers must be able to promote and market their services to both their readers and the community at large. RA is the "core business of the public library" (Shearer, 1998, p. 114) and as has been said previously, library educators should do more to help provide the knowledge and skills necessary for this important service. This will be discussed in the final chapter of the book.

REFERENCES

Baker, S. L. (1992). Readers' advisory services. A call for more research. *RQ, 32,* 166–169.

Bopp, R., & Smith, L. C. (2011). *Reference and information services: An introduction* (4th ed.). Santa Barbara, CA: ABC-CLIO, Libraries Unlimited.

Crowley, B. (2005). Rediscovering the history of readers advisory service. *Public Libraries, 44*(1), 38.

Dewey, M. (1885). Twenty-seventh annual report, address given at the Brooklyn Public Library. New York: Brooklyn Public Library, 9–10.

Dresang, E. T. (1982). Service paradigm: An introduction. In G. Schlacter (Ed.), *The service imperative for libraries: Essays in honor of Margaret E. Monroe* (pp. 13–20). Littleton, CO: Libraries Unlimited.

Green, S. S. (1876). Personal relations between librarians and readers. *Library Journal, 1,* 74–81.

Hollands, N., & Trott, B. (2006). Improving the model for interactive readers' advisory service. *Reference & User Services Quarterly, 45*(3), 205–212.

Lee, R. E. (1966). *Continuing education for adults through the American Public Library 1833–1964.* Chicago: American Library Association.

Maatta, S. L. (2010). *A few good books: Using contemporary readers' advisory strategies to connect readers with books.* New York: Neal-Schuman.

McCook, K. de la Peña. (2004). *Introduction to public librarianship.* New York: Neal-Schuman.

McCook, K. de la Peña, & Rolstad, G. O. (Eds.). (1993). *Developing readers' advisory services: Concepts and commitments.* New York: Neal-Schuman.

Minnesota Development. (2000). Talking with Readers: A workbook for readers' advisory. https://books.google.com/books/about/Talking_with_Readers.html?id.

Monroe, M. E. (1963). *Library adult education: Biography of an idea.* New York: Scarecrow.

Moyer, J. (Ed.). (2010). *Integrated advisory service: Breaking through the book boundary to better serve library users.* Denver, CO: Libraries Unlimited.

Moyer, J. E., & Weech, T. L. (2005). The education of public librarians to serve leisure readers in the United States, Canada and Europe. *New Library World, 106*(1/2), 67–79. doi: 10.1108/03074800510575366

Quinn, S. (2008). Reading rewards: The evolution of a train the trainer course for public library reader advisers. *Australasian Public Libraries and Information Services, 21*(2), 44–55.

Reitz, J. M. (2004). *Dictionary for library and information science.* Westport, CT: Libraries Unlimited.

Rickilibrarian. (2010, March 24). Readers' advisory 2.0: The next dimension. Retrieved from http://ricklibrarian.blogspot.com/2010/03/readers-advisory-20-next-dimension.html

Ross, C. S., & Chelton, M. K. (2001). Readers' advisory: Matching mood and material. *Library Journal, 126*(2), 52–55.

Rubin, R. J. (1982). Guidance. In G. Schlachter (Ed.), *The service imperative for libraries: Essay in honor of Margaret E. Monroe* (pp. 94–119). Littleton, CO: Libraries Unlimited.

Rockwood, R. H., & Shores, L. (1957). Research in readers' services. *Library Trends, 6*, 160–170.

Saricks, J. (2005). *Readers' advisory service in public libraries* (3rd ed.). Chicago: American Library Association.

Saricks, J., & Brown, N. (1997). *Readers' advisory service in public libraries* (2nd ed.). Chicago: American Library Association.

Shearer, K. (1998, Fall). Readers' advisory services: New attention to a core business of the public library. *North Carolina Libraries* (Online), *56*(3), 114–116.

Shearer, K. D. (1996). *Getting the reader to the next book*. New York: Neal-Schuman.

Shearer, K. D., and Burgin R. B. (Eds.). (2001). *The readers' advisor's companion*. Englewood, CO: Libraries Unlimited.

Smith, D. F. (2000, Winter). Talking with readers: A competency based approach to readers' advisory service. *Reference & User Services Quarterly, 40*(2), 135–142.

Trott, D. (2009, March 29). Building on a firm foundation: Readers' advisory over the next twenty-five years. RUSQ Blog. Retrieved from http://blog.rusq.org /2009/03/29/building-on-a-firm-foundation-readers-advisory-over-the-next-twenty-five-years/

Watson, D., & RUSA CODES Readers' Advisory Committee. (2000). Time to turn the page: Library education for readers' advisory services. *Reference & User Services Quarterly, 40*(2), 143–146.

Wyatt, N. (2006). Reading maps remake RA: Re-create a book's entire universe on-line, and transform readers' advisory. *Library Journal*, 38–42.

Wyatt, N. (2007). *The readers' advisory guide to nonfiction*. Chicago: American Library Association.

RESOURCES FOR READERS' ADVISORY SERVICE

Annotated bibliography of books, journal articles, blogs, and websites, http://rusa.metapress.com/content/m0237t7367240534/fulltext.pdf

A list of print resources for readers' advisory, http://tinyurl.com/78amujs

A readers' advisory wiki, http://liswiki.org/wiki/Readers%27_advisory

Free resources for readers' advisory, http://libguides.fau.edu/content.php?pid=127350&sid=1092990

LibGuide for readers' advisory, http://bestof.libguides.com/readersadvisory

Morton Grove Public Library, http://www.webrary.org/rs/rslinks.html

Nonfiction readers' advisory, http://www.rburgin.com/sites/ranf.html

Nonfiction by subject, http://www.cmrls.lib.ms.us/ra_list_nf.htm

Readers' advisory booklists, http://mvcc.libguides.com/content.php?pid=78508&sid=582474

Training for readers' advisory, http://www.slideshare.net/brendajhostettler/readers-advisory-training

Workshop, http://infopeople.org/training/redefining-readers-advisory-2011

CHAPTER 7

Library Services to the Business Community

This chapter reviews the history of library services to the business community by public libraries and examines the service response models used by public libraries to support the business community. It identifies the types of responses that are needed in the twenty-first century.

Library service to business has been a part of public library services since the beginning of the public library movement in the middle of the nineteenth century. A number of public libraries established special services to the business community. New York Public Library established the Economics Division of its reference department in 1911, and later, a combined business and technology department became part of public library services in Fort Wayne, Indiana; Portland, Oregon; and, in 1913, in Minneapolis, Minnesota, where a separate business branch was opened in 1916.

In the late 1940s through the 1960s, there was great interest in offering services to business. In 1946, the American Library Association (ALA) Council adopted a four-point program that articulated the potential role of libraries in the economic life of the community. ALA asked libraries to "ascertain areas of community economic opportunity, define the extent of library service, discover sources through which library service may be supplemented, and by a positive program through all media and channels, inform the community of the library's role and resources" (Valstein, 1959).

Public libraries have a history of providing information services to local businesses, including individualized assistance and printed guides to business resources. These services have evolved into websites and other electronic sources, small business seminars, participation in economic development networks, and freestanding small business information centers. In 1904, John Cotton

Dana, one of the pioneers in the field of special librarianship, established the Business Branch of the Newark (New Jersey) Public Library. By 1929, public libraries in 20 of the largest cities in the United States had separate business branches or business departments, and another 11 libraries combined business with another special department (Welch, 2005, p. 282).

Part of libraries' interest in providing such services was rooted in humanitarian considerations. But another aspect was that libraries understood that they had a role to play in the economic life of their communities. With this understanding, libraries began to answer questions related to why they should offer information services to business and industry. The history of public library services to the business community shows libraries trying to figure out the form, extent, and mechanism for the delivery of library services. Still today, the how and why questions related to public library services to business continue to be raised by the library community. In recent years, public libraries have become a valuable resource to business leaders, small business persons, budding entrepreneurs, and job seekers (Bleiweis, 1997).

Weiss and colleagues (2011) explain that to achieve continuous growth in today's knowledge-based economy, businesses require access to timely, accurate, and relevant information as well as the skills and competence to effectively use the information. They state that the business owner who is equipped with this information has an edge in the challenging marketplace and that small businesspeople who lack both an awareness and access to existing unique industry resources find themselves at a disadvantage in the current information-driven business arena (Weiss, Serlis-McPhillips, & Malafi, 2011, p. 6).

The literature highlights that it is in the library's best interest to cultivate the business community as library users because the success of the businesses in the community is crucial to the economic health of the community the library serves as well as that of the library it serves. It is also stated that the library gains supportive, appreciative patrons who can be counted on to sponsor library events and help promote the library as a whole (Weiss et al., 2011).

In this new digital era and amid economic transformation, the business of public libraries is being recast, and libraries have become valuable resources in building local economic bases. The World Wide Web has revolutionized the Internet by making a wealth of information easily available to anyone with a computer and Internet access. Public access to digital information and technology is now a draw for libraries, and public libraries are playing active roles in addressing such pressing urban issues as literacy, workforce training, small business vitality, and community quality of life. Library employment and career resources are preparing workers with new technologies. With an array of public computers, Internet access, and media products, public libraries are a first point of entry for many new technology users (Urban Libraries Council, 2007).

In addition to using technology to deliver library services to the community in general, libraries can use technology in ways not possible before, such as to repackage information into a more focused and usable format for business users. New ways public libraries are able to assist by repackaging existing information include:

- Pinpointing existing customers and targeting new ones
- Identifying and evaluating competition
- Locating industry benchmarks and forecasts
- Examining retail sales and consumer data for any U.S. zip code
- Evaluate local, regional, and national business climate
- Study market trends and market research reports (Weiss et al., 2011)

USERS OF BUSINESS SERVICES

The array of individuals that patronize public libraries ranged in the early days from industrial workers, mechanics, and apprentices, to owners of small and medium-sized businesses. Other patrons included professionals, local businesses, self-employed entrepreneurs, consultants, nonprofit groups, marketing specialists, managers, job seekers, employees of corporations, people who were laid off and exploring new ventures, and anyone who needed accurate and fast business information. These many different types of users called for focused service responses to satisfy the various information needs of a wide variety of people that make up the business community. John Cotton Dana (1899) noted that while "the vast extent" of material in the library was related to business, few members of the business community are familiar with or know about the resources the library has to offer. The situation is much the same today; in particular, small and medium-sized business entities could benefit from understanding the resources freely available to them through the public library. Pankl (2010) advocates that public libraries market their business resources in particular to small businesses.

MODELS OF SERVICES

Manley (1940) identified two paths to business library development: "business library development in the last thirty years has followed two roads—relatively few selective business collections maintained by public libraries and the many specialized collections in business corporations directed by special librarians" (p. 14).

The literature currently identifies three models of library service related to the business community:

1. Freestanding business reference collections that are found mainly in large metropolitan libraries and that are modeled after John Cotton Dana's Newark, New Jersey, business reference library. This model is devoted to business resources and is often located in business

districts, downtown areas, or close to the chamber of commerce. The New York Public Library is a good example of this model. The New York Public Library's Economics Division was established in 1911. Similar libraries were started in city centers such as Binghamton, New York; Brooklyn, New York; Charlotte, North Carolina; Chicago; Simsbury, Connecticut; St. Paul, Minnesota; and Washington, D.C. Major foreign library systems such as those in Vancouver, British Columbia, and Adelaide, Australia, have also established business information centers. One of the largest business centers in the United States is the Science, Industry, and Business Library (SIBL) of the New York Public Library (Welch, 2005, p. 283).

2. The creation of a separate business reference collection within the branch of the main library.
3. The integration of business resources within the general reference collection.

In a study of library services to business, Fenner (1953) discusses two major options for the delivery of services to the business community: (1) a branch located away from the main library, and (2) a specialized department within the main library. In the branch option, the service facility is usually located close to the business community. As businesses spread out to the suburbs and industrial parks, the proximity to business was no longer an advantage, and the option of establishing a department within the main branch provided the benefit of allowing a patron to have access to all the library's resources in one place. Fenner noted that it was not necessary to duplicate parts of the main collection in the branch business library because the patrons were primarily from the professional, managerial, or administrative staff of businesses. When business services are a department in the existing library, visitors to the department tend to be a diversified group that includes students, home makers and other patrons that use the main library (Fenner, 1953).

Services to businesses as well as other organizations in the economic community have, over time, followed each of these service models. In the late twentieth century, however, libraries tended to focus services on specific groups within the business community: entrepreneurs, chambers of commerce economic development entities, and state and local governments.

RESOURCES FOR SERVICES TO THE BUSINESS COMMUNITY

To adequately provide services to the business community, the library needs to develop a collection relevant to the information needs of all segments of the business community. Information about collection development (including general business sources, yearly selection of outstanding business reference sources, and the best of the business websites) can be found in guidelines articulated by the Business Reference and Services Section (BRASS) of the Reference and User Services Association (RUSA) of the ALA (http://www.ala.org/rusa/sections/brass). Recent books from ALA devoted to business information and services include the *ALA Guide to Economics and Business Reference* (2011) and *Making Sense of Business Reference: A Guide for Librarians and Research Professionals* (Ross, 2011).

Different types of resources have been highlighted as must-haves for all business reference collections and include:

- Business plans, including sample business plans such as Business Plan Pro, Business Plan Handbook, and Small Business Resource Center, which are all Gale Cengage Learning resources. Pankl (2010) pointed out that the public library is virtually the only place aspiring entrepreneurs can go for information to fill in the blanks for their business plans.
- Demographic and psychographic data, which is needed for writing business plans that require estimates for demographic, consumer expenditure, retail sales, and other information that is used to generate maps and reports. Examples of this type of research are Demographics Now, a Cengage Learning database that provides the types of data discussed here. *SRDS: Local Audience Market Analysis* is a report that provides some of the needed information for designated market areas (DMA). *U.S. Life Styles* provides access to information on household income, home value, and shopping profiles that can be searched by geography even to zip codes. Other reports include *Market Profile Analysis: Consumer and Business Demographics Reports*, which reviews demographic and market data for specific U.S. geographic regions.
- Industry surveys such as *First Research* by Dun & Bradstreet and *Standard & Poor's NetAdvantage*
- Directories of all types, such as Reference USA, Dun & Bradstreet Million Dollar Directory, and Thomas Net, that provide information on manufacturing and other industries.
- Trade associations' publications and periodicals.
- Special industry resources that provide information for specific industries at the local level, such as building, construction, and labor rates; concrete and masonry cost data; and data that would not ordinarily be available if it were not collected by the library from local sources.
- Legal and government sources that have to do with requirements and relevant legislation.
- International business resources that allow local businesses to maintain up-to-date awareness of global economic issues and ecommerce activity.
- Resources for nonprofits.

- Career and job search resources. Especially in hard economic times, all aspects of job search, resume writing, and job promoting activities should be provided. It is recommended that libraries create annotated lists of new career information and link them to service announcements and tools for exploring job opportunities. Test preparation resources should also be provided.

SERVICE RESPONSES

Service responses are based on Martin's (1983) philosophy that "libraries need to focus on providing a few services well rather than providing a lot of services poorly" (Garcia & Nelson, 2007, p. 1). Public libraries have developed service responses based on several documents published by the Public Library Association, including *Planning and Role Setting for Public Libraries: A Manual of Options and Procedures* (Charles R. McClure & Public Library Association, 1987), *Planning for Results: A Public Library Transformation Process* (Ethel E. Himmel, William J. Wilson, & Revision Committee of the Public Library Association, 1998), *The New Planning for Results: A Streamlined Approach* (Sandra S. Nelson & Public Library Association, 2001), *Public Library Service Responses 2007* (June Garcia & Sandra Nelson, 2007), and *PLA Service Response Workbook: Build Successful Enterprises: Business and Non-Profit Support* (Public Library Association, 2011). Each library needs to base its service responses on the needs of the community (in this instance the needs of the business community). Establishing a collection and services for the business community begins by taking stock of what the library currently offers and then deciding whether a separate area will be used to collect these resources or whether a guide (print and digital) will be used to create a guide to available resources. Then a decision needs to be made about which new or expanding services to focus on.

Some service responses that a library may choose to focus on include:

- Business and career information and job placement services. One of many examples is the Memphis Public Library's JobLINC Job and Career Center, a new library service model (Urban Libraries Council, 2007). Services include an extensive collection of materials on career selection, educational opportunities, resume and cover letter writing, interviewing, and test preparation. There are also listings of available jobs in the Memphis area, aid in locating training opportunities, one-on-one assistance in conducting job searches and preparing for interviews, and job readiness workshops (http://www.memphislibrary.org/joblinc).

- Reference assistance that is available in person or by phone, email, or chat, for help with business information needs, services, or resources.
- Ready reference services, which are walk-in or telephone services.
- In-depth or extensive research assistance by appointment or on a walk-in basis.
- Assistance with using online databases, including directory, patent, and trademark searching as well as how to search electronic or web-based business resource guides.
- Public-use computer equipment for preparing resumes.
- Links to business, investment, bid and procurement, and job placement Internet sites and government information, including access to government procurement and tax information.
- Hosting of business-related seminars and workshops, such as how to start a business, resume writing, and job interview training.
- Collection of resources that include print sources such as directories, how-to guides, stock and bond guides, business magazines, state and local codes, patent and trademark information, and construction codes along with electronic resources that include business directories, business databases, business planning software, and online stock and bond resources. Most of these resources may not be affordable for small and medium-sized business (Welch, 2005), supporting the need for the public library to be the business information center for the community.

As public libraries try to provide services to the business community, they have to deal with some barriers that prevent them from doing their job, which in the early days included lack of space, lack of staff, and lack of funds. The same barriers still exist today. By partnering with the business community, the public library may be able to develop strategies and resources to overcome the barriers.

SERVICES TO SMALL BUSINESS

Small businesses are an integral part of the economy of any region. Small businesses make up 99.7 percent of U.S. employers, and they accounted for 64 percent of net new jobs created between 1993 and 2011 (i.e., 11.8 million of the 18.5 million net new jobs). From mid-2009 to 2011, small firms (20–499 employees) led larger ones in the creation of new jobs and accounted for 67 percent of net new jobs (SBA, 2012).

Small businesses are a vital part of the economy of North America and other parts of the world. Approximately 85 percent of all new employment is created by small businesses; however, 75 percent of all new businesses fail within the first three years. One of the main reasons is lack of knowledge.

Access to accurate and current information is important to small businesses in their day-to-day operations as well as start-ups. Public libraries and librarians need to provide specialized services to support small businesses in the community at all stages of their existence. Some public libraries have developed services to serve the special needs of small business, including the use of technology to help with new approaches to service. The New York Public Library Science and Industry Business Library (SIBL) has been in the forefront of the application of technology, with mass adoption of the Internet and customization of information and instructional services for small businesses (McDonough & Cohen, 2006).

New York Public Library combined the collection of two of its branch divisions—Science and Technology, and Economic and Public Affairs—with the materials of the mid-Manhattan Central Library to form the Science and Industry Business Library (SIBL) with a focus on business, science, and technology literature that is relevant to industry. SIBL librarians have developed hands-on training for electronic resources and patent searching, and they provide seminars by business experts. They have a small business website that provides links to business support groups, forms, permits, business plans, and a metro calendar of training and networking events. They have moderated forums on how-to topics for business. They provide on-site business counseling with the help of volunteers from the Service Corps of Retired Executives (SCORE) and full-time employees that staff the business center in the library. Visit the library's site at http://www.nypl.org/locations/sibl.

Smaller public libraries have followed the lead of the NYPL by providing services to small businesses. The Hartford Public Library in Connecticut created the Small Business Center. Services include linking to the resources of the Small Business Administration (SBA), providing information on applying for SBA loans, navigating the government procurement process, and providing information and workshops on grants and the grant application process. See http://www.hplct.org/library-services/adults/small-business-services.

In Ohio, the Public Library of Cincinnati and Hamilton County has a Government and Business Department that handles reference requests. The department offers workshops, seminars, and materials for small business owners, job seekers, and investors. They have a job information center that provides resources to support all aspects of job searching such as resume writing, interviews techniques, and career information (Klinck, 2005). See http://www.cincinnatilibrary.org/main/go.asp.

Similar job information centers with links to job openings and government jobs sites can be found in many small and medium-sized public libraries. The Association of Small Business Development Centers (ASBDC) provides resources for the development of small business centers in public libraries. More information is available at http://www.asbdc-us.org/.

Public libraries have provided a variety of services, including 24/7 access to some resources, to better fit into the small business owner's schedule. Some libraries provide resources for the nonprofit sector, including resources on foundations through a foundation center and workshops on grant writing as well as a number of online grant resources. See, for example, the Hartford (Connecticut) Public Library's services to nonprofits at http://www.hplct.org/library-services/nonprofits.

LOCAL ECONOMIC DEVELOPMENT AND PUBLIC LIBRARIES

Economic development programs involve people, the use of technology, and information. Public libraries are uniquely situated to participate in local economic development activities because they are in the business of providing access to information as well as using technology to deliver services to patrons. A number of journal articles and studies make the case that public libraries can positively impact local economic development efforts and produce mutually beneficial results for libraries and the business community (Glass et al., 2000; Bleiweis, 1997; Walzer & Gruidi, 1996). Bleiweis (1997) points out that libraries depend on the tax base, which is supported largely by business, "and should therefore have vested interest in the support of the tax base" (xiv). According to Gutsche (2011), public libraries are involved in contributing to the human dimension of economic development. They have stepped into the gap to help workers in need of twenty-first-century skills, to provide job search help, and to offer a broad spectrum of other services and connections to community agencies. Libraries have programs to help the unemployed, offering workshops on resume writing and interviewing techniques. They also try to help people gain enhanced twenty-first-century skills in information literacy.

Gutsche (2011) outlined five library lifelines for the unemployed:

1. Advanced technology literacy. Libraries provide computer literacy classes and workshops, thereby providing the basic skills needed to navigate the increasingly online job application environment to people who otherwise have little access to such computer training.
2. Job seeker support. Many libraries use social media technology to support job seekers, and some libraries have taught job seekers to build personal websites to showcase their skills. For example, the Russell (Connecticut) Library (http://www.russell library.org/) has implemented a new job search paradigm with LinkedIn for job seekers.

3. Information to support local entrepreneurs and attract new business to the area by providing information about the town, school system, and other details about the area.
4. Advanced financial literacy via workshops with the help of financial experts related to managing finances and finding creative solutions to financial problems.
5. Connections and collaborative opportunities with outside relevant agencies. Libraries provide information on partnerships and mechanisms for fostering collaboration.

Libraries are said to be logical partners for local economic development initiatives. Their open structure and access to digital collections and technology training put them in a position to help communities transition from manufacturing and service economies to high-tech and information economies. In a study by the Urban Institute of the Urban Libraries Council about the impact of public libraries on economic conditions, it was found that the role of public libraries is shifting from passive recreational reading and research institutions to active economic development agents. The report documents four areas in which local government agencies are working together to achieve benefits for individuals, agencies, and the community:

1. Early literacy services that are contributing to long-term economic success. They provide services needed to build an educated workforce that is needed by the twenty-first-century workplace.
2. Library employment and career resources that are preparing workers to use new technologies. Internet access and training provided by public libraries help build the technology competence needed to navigate online job search and application tools.
3. Small business resources and programs that lower barriers to market entry. Libraries provide information on current business products and trends. They work with local and state agencies to provide business development data. Library resource and training facilities help reduce operating costs for local and small business agencies.
4. Library buildings, which are catalysts for physical development. The library as a place is welcoming to business owners and other patrons. Libraries have tremendous foot traffic and are perfect for interaction. (Urban Libraries Council, 2007)

By fulfilling the information needs of small business, libraries make a measurable contribution to the community's economy (Pankl, 2010). The Urban Institute study concludes that public libraries are positioned to fuel not only new, but next, knowledge economies because of their role in building technology skills, entrepreneurial activity, and vibrant livable places.

The combination of taking a stronger role in economic development and their prevalence—16,000 branches in more than 9,000 systems—makes public libraries a stable and powerful tool for cities seeking to attract and build new businesses (p. 23).

TWENTY-FIRST-CENTURY PUBLIC LIBRARY SERVICES

E-Government Services

Online services have increased since the passage of the E-Government Act of 2002, and public librarians now assist many patrons with federal, state, and local government services that have moved almost exclusively online. Persons with limited or no Internet access, as well as persons who need assistance using technology or understanding and reading forms, rely on public libraries to access e-government services. In results from the 2009–2010 Public Library Funding and Technology Access Survey (PLFTAS), two-thirds of public libraries reported being the only provider of free public access to computers and the Internet in their communities, and 78.7 percent of libraries reported that they provide assistance to patrons applying for or otherwise accessing e-government services. E-government services provided by libraries include:

- Access to and assistance navigating e-government websites
- Assistance filling in forms and sending emails related to obtaining forms
- Help writing employment letters and resumes, completing employment and unemployment applications, and searching employment databases
- Assistance with the creation of email accounts
- Help locating government information such as assistance and grants, Medicare benefits, immigration and naturalization regulations, tax forms, and hunting and fishing licenses
- Training classes regarding the use of government websites, programs, and electronic forms
- Collection and dissemination of informative pamphlets on e-government services
- Web 2.0 tools to disseminate information
- Creation of an emergency information hub

The ALA has created an e-government toolkit to help libraries develop service roles for e-government (http://publiclibrariesonline.org/2013/04/e-government-service-roles-for-public-libraries/). The e-government service roles are based on two studies conducted in Florida in 2009–2010. The study identifies four potential e-government service roles for public libraries:

- Basic services
- Library-driven services
- Agency-driven services
- Collaborative services

Basic services are those that most libraries currently provide, such as reference, assistance for patrons who are applying for e-government help, and provision of Internet access and general training in the use of computers. They may also assist in emergency response actions in times of natural disaster.

When providing library-driven services, the library takes a proactive role in the provision of e-government services, offering training in the use of government websites, collecting and distributing informative pamphlets on e-government services, using social media to disseminate information, and becoming a hub for emergency information.

Agency-driven services are those that libraries provide to meet agency demands, providing staff to assist library users or providing space for meetings and training by agency personnel. Collaborative services require active partnership between government agencies and public libraries. These services include ongoing active library participation that includes meeting with local, state, and federal government personnel on a regular basis (Bishop, McClure, & Mandel, 2011; Bishop et al., 2010).

As the use of e-government increases, public libraries will have to expand their e-government service roles from basic to more collaborative. They can plan and meet with government agencies to determine what other services they need to be promoting. Bishop and colleagues said it is essential that public libraries and state library agencies engage in ongoing dialog about the role of public libraries in providing e-government services and that the ongoing dialog will serve to better coordinate the services and activities of libraries to prevent service duplication.

PROGRAMMING FOR THE BUSINESS COMMUNITY

The business community is unique in its need for information. Businesses operate during the day, so libraries need to plan their services to suit the schedule of business owners. Programming is said to be the best way to reach the business community, and business programming is the key to the success of public library services to this group. Public libraries have to consider proper scheduling of programs—evenings and weekends seem to be best because most businesses operate during the day. Libraries have to find knowledgeable speakers and program leaders, which can be found among local business owners, nonprofit organizations, and chambers of commerce. Programming provides opportunities for networking among participants. Some examples of business programing include an introduction to the business center, trade shows, job fairs, and online database searching workshops.

NETWORKING AND COLLABORATION

Public libraries in the twenty-first century must be proactive in promoting their services. They need to encourage networking and collaboration between the business community and within the community. Public libraries can provide the opportunity and means for networking during programming, and they can create lists of entities that are relevant to the needs of particular segments of the community. Weiss and colleagues (2011) contend that libraries can add networking to any program by starting a program with a networking session before the program actually begins. In addition, libraries can establish special business-to-business networking groups for people with similar interests.

Public libraries need to promote partnerships between businesses and community organizations to allow partners to gain from each other's expertise. Entities can partner when creating economic development plans by applying for grants and engaging in other activities that require participation of more than one group. Partnerships allow libraries to do more with less—they can work with government agencies, health centers, and nonprofits to extend and expand their services beyond the physical library environment. Community development is one area in which the library can partner with the town or local chamber of commerce, providing data and other information to support proposals. Public libraries should be in the community attending town hall meetings and public hearings, and they should participate in a meaningful way so that they know the information needs of specific projects and can ensure these needs are provided for.

MARKETING OF PUBLIC LIBRARY SERVICES TO THE BUSINESS COMMUNITY

Marketing library services is an ongoing activity, especially in the face of competition that libraries face from bookstores and other information-providing entities. Library marketing tends to focus on buildings, entertaining, and educational programming. Pankl (2010) suggests that library information products get lost in a kind of homogenization and that libraries must be perceived as not only committed to general community social objectives, but also desirous of people succeeding economically. Public libraries must market their collections, services, and activities.

Valstein (1959) provided a list of public library services that are beneficial to offer businesses. She noted that the library collection should cover the five M's of management, men, materials, marketing, and money. She goes on to say that service should be objective and current, business trends and initiatives should be anticipated, and community contacts should be close as well as diverse to provide the essential supplements to public library resources of referral and consultation. Publicity should be continuous, and specific advantage should be taken of all media communication. Her recommendations are still valid for libraries in the twenty-first century.

Libraries can play the role of a silent business partner. They are there for everyone through the cycles of life for when people need them more. The benefit is that the library is a trusted resource whether one is using it or not. Even though it is relevant to small business owners, it can be a silent partner for people in all works of life to help them find whatever information they need when they need it, provided they are aware of all that the library can provide.

REFERENCES

Bishop, B. W., McClure, C. R., & Mandel, L. H. (2011). E -government service roles for public libraries. *Public Libraries, 50*(3), 6.

Bishop, B. W., McClure, C. R., & Mandel, L. H. (2013). E-government service roles for public libraries. *Public Libraries Online, 52*(2). Retrieved from http://publiclibrariesonline.org/2013/04/e-government-service-roles-for-public-libraries/

Bishop, B. W., McClure, C. R., Mandel, L. H., & Snead, J. T. (2010). *PASCO County Library Cooperative e-government services in public libraries 2010: Final report of project activities.* Information Institute, Florida State University, College of Communication & Information, School of Library & Information Studies. Retrieved from http://ii.fsu.edu/content/download/38777/244546/Pasco_E-Gov_Final_Report_July28_10.pdf

Bleiweis, M. (1997). *Helping business: The library's role in community economic development; A how-to-do-it manual.* New York: Neal-Schuman.

Dana, J. C. (1899). *A library primer.* Chicago: Library Bureau.

Fenner, E. (1953). Business services in public libraries. *Special Libraries, 44*(July/August), 2.

Garcia, J., & Nelson, S. (2007). *Public library service responses, 2007.* Chicago: American Library Association. Retrieved from http://ryepubliclibrary.org/wp-content/uploads/2012/05/ALAserviceresponses.pdf.

Glass, R. H., Clifford, N., Harris, B., & Rose, C. (2000). *The role of public libraries in local economic development.* Lawrence Institute for Public Policy and Business Research, Kansas City: University of Kansas.

Gutsche, B. (2011, September 1). A boon to the workforce. *Library Journal*, p. 4.

Heim, K. M., & Wallace, D. P. (1990). *Adult services: An enduring focus for public libraries.* Chicago: American Library Association.

Himmel, E. E., Wilson, W. J., & Revision Committee of the Public Library. (1998). *Planning for results: A public library transformation process.* Chicago: American Library Association.

Klinck, C. (2005). Libraries: Mean business. *Ohio Libraries, 18*(2), 24–27.

Manley, M. (Ed.). (1940). *Business and the public library: Steps in successful cooperation.* New York: Special Libraries Association.

Martin, L. A. (1983). The public library: Middle-age crisis or old age? *Library Journal, 108*(1), 17–22.

McClure, C. R., Owen, A., Zweizig, D., Lynch, M. J., & Van House, N. (1987). *Planning and role setting for public libraries: A manual of options and procedures.* Chicago: American Library Association.

McDonough, K., & Cohen, M. (2006). Open for business: The NYPL Science, Industry and Business Library takes stock. *Public Library Quarterly, 25*(1/2), 75–90.

Movahedi-Lankarani, S. J. (2002). E-commerce: Resources for doing business on the Internet. *Reference & User Services Quarterly, 41*(4), 316–325.

Nelson, S. S., & Public Library Association. (2001). *The new planning for results: A streamlined approach.* Chicago: American Library Association.

Oppenheim, M. R., & Forte, E. J. (2012). *The basic business library: Core resources and services.* Englewood, CO: Libraries Unlimited.

Pankl, R. R. (2010). Marketing the public library's business resources to small businesses. *Journal of Business & Finance Librarianship, 15*(2), 94–103.

Ross, C. (2011). *Making sense of business reference: A guide for librarians and research professionals.* Chicago: American Library Association.

Small Business Administration (SBA) Office of Advocacy (2012). Frequently asked questions. Retrieved from http://www.sbecouncil.org/about-us/facts-and -data/

Urban Libraries Council. (2007). Making cities stronger: Public library contributions to local government development (p. 27). Washington, D.C.: Urban Libraries Council.

Valstein, R. (1959). Public library service to business. *Library Journal, 84*(May), 3.

Walzer, N., & Gruidi, J. (1996). The role of small public libraries in community economic development. *Illinois Libraries, 78*(1), 7.

Weiss, L., Serlis-McPhillips, S., & Malafi, E. (2011). *Small business and the public library: Strategies for a successful partnership.* Chicago: American Library Association.

Welch, J. M. (2005). Silent partners: Public libraries and their services to small businesses and entrepreneurs. *Public Libraries, 44*(5), 282–286.

RESOURCES FOR SERVICES TO THE BUSINESS COMMUNITY

American Library Association, http://www.ala.org/ala/issuesadvocacy/advleg/ federallegislation/govinfo/egovernment/egovtoolkit/index.cfm

Association of Small Business Development Centers, http://asbdc-us.org/

BRASS professional tools, http://www.ala.org/rusa/sections/brass/brassprotools/ professional

Hartford Public Library, http://www.hplct.org/library-services/adults/small-business
      -services
http://www.ala.org/ala/research/initiatives/plftas/index.cfm
http://www.memphislibrary.org/linc/joblinc
http://www.archives.gov/about/laws/egov-act-section-207.html
Memphis Public Library, PLFTAS
New York Public Library, http://www.nypl.org/locations/sibl
Russell Public Library, http://www.russelllibrary.org/reference/business.html
U.S. Chamber of Commerce Small Business Nation, http://www.uschamber
      smallbusinessnation.com/

CHAPTER 8

Lifelong Learning

This chapter defines lifelong learning, provides the historical context for adult education and adult learning in the United States and in libraries, and then describes the services needed for libraries in the twenty-first century. The lifelong learning needs of adults in relation to demographic, social, and technical changes at this time are examined. Modes of delivery for public librarians to adopt to meet the needs of their patrons are discussed.

Lifelong learning begins with adult education. Adult education has been described as any deliberately designed activity or program for an individual over the required school attendance age (Broschart, 1977) that extends beyond basic literacy (Zafft, Kallenbach, & Spohn, 2006). Adult education spans vocational and nonvocational areas as well as formal and informal learning.

ADULT EDUCATION TO ADULT LEARNING

Public lectures given by the Lyceum and the Lowell Institute of Boston in 1826 were the earliest form of formal adult education in America. The Chautauqua movement, which by the early twentieth century had grown from a camp-like educational and cultural event to a circuit of speakers and entertainers who travelled from town to town, introduced the formal discussion group and modified lecture system in 1873 (Scott, 1999).

Other agencies and associations became involved. The Department of Education of New York City introduced free public lectures in 1924, and in 1926, the Carnegie Cooperation organized the American Association of Adult Education, which merged with the National Education Association's

Department of Adult Education to become the Adult Education Association in 1951. The American Library Association (ALA) became officially involved in adult education in 1924. The literature indicates that the term "adult education" was virtually unheard of before that date (Knowles, 1980).

The 1960s saw economic and social changes, and poverty and illiteracy were and remain a problem. During the Lyndon B. Johnson administration, legislation known as the War on Poverty was introduced, and adult literacy became a concern. The result was the passage of the Economic Opportunity Act in 1964. Title II B of Public Law 88–452 created the first Adult Basic Education (ABE) program. The ABE program established a state and federal partnership to focus on the most basic educational skills for adults who have not completed secondary education. The Adult Education Act, passed in 1966, focused on increasing adult literacy skills. Libraries were already involved in providing adult education programs to foreign-born individuals and others that needed it because adult education has been a focus for public libraries since the beginnings of public library service in this country.

In 1991, the National Literacy Act was passed, creating the National Institute for Literacy (NIFL), which serves as a focal point for activities that support the development of literacy services. The goal of NIFL, according to McCook and Barber (2002), is to "ensure that all Americans with literacy needs have access to services that help them gain the basic skills necessary for success in today's workplace, family and community" (p. 67).

In recognition of the fact that the skills adults need as workers, parents, and citizens go beyond the ones learned in traditional adult education programs, the NIFL conducted a project under the Equipped for the Future Framework (EFF). The EFF project was designed to create a better adult literacy system through developed standards (Stein, 2002).

A number of studies show that adult education and lifelong learning help the creation of social capital (Coleman, 1986; Putnan, 2000; Schuller, Baron, & Field, 2000). Participation in lifelong learning is said to strengthen "the fabric of communities" and encourage "citizenship, cultural awareness and understanding" (Jones & Symon, 2001, p. 276).

ADULT EDUCATION TO ADULT LEARNING IN PUBLIC LIBRARIES

Van Fleet (1990) found that the trend from adult education provider-based study to adult learning self-motivated study started in the early 1970s. She states that some theorists in the 1970s were concerned that the emphasis on structured classroom activities could lead to an "over credentialed society." A better approach, they thought, might be to pay more attention to learners who planned their own activities and instituted their own criteria for study and learning (Van Fleet, 1990).

According to Van Fleet (1990), "Adult education tends to emphasize the teacher-student relationship and carries with it connotations of organized, extremely directed activity, while the concept of adult learning focuses on the independence of the learner" (p. 168). Researchers suggest that many adults undertake learning projects on their own and tend to avoid classroom settings (Findsen, 2006; Bentley, 1998). When learning is seen as a characteristic of the learner and not a commodity supplied by a teacher, it is said to be learner-centered. The objective of learning is for the learner to become more independent and motivated. Cross (1981) noted that in using the term "learning," "there is a continuum of freedom and self-direction implied" (p. 4). Van Fleet (1990) pointed out that that observers in many disciplines, from economics to psychology, emphasize the conceptual paradigm of lifelong learning, explaining that the philosophy incorporates the ideas of both adult learning and adult education but gives a broader perspective recognizing "that attitudes and skills of adults are based on childhood developments and that the growth and attitudes of a society reflect the personal development of its individual members" (p. 168). However, in the beginning, the term was "adult education."

Founding fathers of the public library movement attested to the educational imperative of the public library. Charles Adams—a trustee of the Quincy, Massachusetts, branch of the Boston Public Library—believed the basic purpose of the public library was to serve as a means of continuing self-education (Bostwick, 1914). Looking back to the first publicly funded town library in America—in Peterborough, New Hampshire, in 1833—we find that citizens voted to use tax revenues for the purchase of library books for the purpose of education beyond the school. In 1895, Henry Munson Utley, the librarian of the Detroit Public Library (1885–1912) and then president of the ALA, saw the library as a societal force that could provide educational opportunities for those who stopped formal schooling, in particular those who stopped early to earn a living. He saw the public library as the people's university. It can be concluded from these statements that the educational responsibility of the public library was to provide the means for adults to continue their education, whether as a surrogate for a formal education cut short or to extend learning beyond formal education.

The growth of public libraries and the establishment of the ALA in 1876 fostered their educational work and involved the development of library collections that included popular novels. Adult education opportunities grew in the 1890s with outreach and expansion of library services (Van Fleet, 1990). The growth of personal assistance to readers also became important during this time, and these outreach services were the start of community services in libraries. Some educational services such as readers' advisory (RA), which involved personal interviews and individualized learning plans, came to be accepted as the "cornerstone of public library services to the community" and the greatest contribution to the adult education movement of the first half of the twentieth century (Birge, 1981).

A number of ALA officials spearheaded the organization's formal foray into adult education services. Judson T. Jennings, ALA president at the 1924 ALA Conference in Saratoga Springs, New York, stated that "the third enterprise that I think we should undertake is an active participation in the movement for adult education" (1924, p. 153). At the same conference, Alexander Meiklejohn presented a session titled "The Library and Adult Education." The ALA executive board appointed the Library and Adult Education Commission to study adult education issues.

The Carnegie Corporation also helped the course of adult education services by providing financial support for studies on the topic between 1924 and 1926. William Learned, an employee of the corporation, published a book called *The Public Library and the Diffusion of Knowledge* in which he said that the city library had the potential to be "an institution of astonishing power—a genuine community university bringing intelligence systematically and persuasively to bear on all adult affairs," and if organized properly on a national level, "it would immediately take its place as the chief instrument of our common intellectual and cultural progress" (Lee, 1966, p. 56).

After the assault on democracy during World War I, education became an ideological weapon and was said to be a good soldier in the defense of democracy (Jennings, 1925). As librarians provided adult education to foreign-born individuals whose focus was on Americanization and vocational training, new roles for librarians developed. Charles Belden (1926) attributes at least one new role to the adult education movement, that of the readers' adviser, "a new sort of public servant" (p. 275).

Public libraries provided services to foreign-born as a special group of library users. A number of public libraries provided services in the language of the immigrants in their communities, for example, Milwaukee in 1913 and the Woodstock branch of the New York Public Library beginning in 1920. The transition to literacy services is a natural progression to services for foreign-born individuals and included Americanization, provision of books in immigrants' native languages, vocational training, and the library as a cultural center (Monroe & Heim, 1991).

Not everyone supported adult education activities in public libraries. Some skeptics said that "adult education was simply a faddish and unsatisfactory label for what has been going on for years. In short library education was criticized for being too ambitious, too gimmicky, too commercial, too activist, too demeaning and too expensive" (Rachal, 1989, par. 16).

However, the ALA continued to support and advance adult education activities. In 1925, the Commission on Library and Adult Education issued a provisional report that was followed in 1926 by an official report titled *Libraries and Adult Education*, another Carnegie Corporation–supported activity. The report identified a number of roles for libraries with regard to adult education, including (1) providing consulting and advisory services to individual learners, (2) providing information about adult education opportunities outside the library, and (3) providing books and other printed materials for adult education services offered by other organizations. Other recommendations dealt with the need for: (1) librarians and educators to make concerted efforts to interest the general public in reading, (2) "more humanized books," (3) better coordination of library adult education services, (4) larger and better lending collections, and (5) adequate funding (American Library Association, 1926, p. 10).

The commission acknowledged the vagueness of the term "adult education" and stated that it was not merely Americanization and vocational training or literacy, but rather it was based on the "great truth that education is a lifelong process" and that "adult education is a spiritual ideal, taking form in a practical purpose" (p. 13). The commission also recommended the establishment of a permanent ALA Adult Education Board that would undertake "experimental study" of adult reading habits, the publication of new courses in the Reading with a Purpose series, and "most important, a program of education that will arouse librarians, library trustees, educational authorities, and appropriating bodies to the possibilities of the library as an agent in adult education" (p. 107).

In 1926, the ALA commission was disbanded, and the permanent Board on Adult Education was established to take over the work of the commission. The change brought about more collaboration between ALA and the American Association of Adult Education (AAAE), which was the start of community organizations participating with libraries in adult education activities. In the 1950s, Stevenson (1956) expanded the focus of adult education to include analysis of community needs as a basis for planning library services. The Library Community Project was one of the program's initiatives, and it was an example of interagency cooperation and public library participation in community educational planning.

Public libraries have continued to provide adult education, renamed adult learning services, to the present day.

PUBLIC LIBRARY SERVICES FOR LIFELONG LEARNING IN THE TWENTY-FIRST CENTURY

Public libraries play a fundamental role in society. They serve as collectors and organizers of knowledge and information, and strive to provide access to resources in all formats to all people. As stated earlier in this book, the services that they provide are or should be designed based on community needs and available resources. These services are further influenced by the trends of the time, technology, demographic changes, and so on.

To design services for the twenty-first century, the nature and type of patrons and communities need to be understood in terms of emerging trends and their implications for library services. Three major trends in society in the twenty-first century are (1) technology, (2) demographic change, and (3) political and policy issues.

Technology Issues

Technology issues came after the move from the postindustrial society, starting from the late twentieth century when the economy was based on manufacturing consumption goods and moving to the information society in which the creation, distribution, diffusion, use, integration, and manipulation of information is the main economic activity. Advances in information and communication technology (ICT) propelled us into the information society in the 1980s. "The information society became a synonym for societal development" (Drotner, 2005, par. 5). "In such a society the levers of development involve information processing as the efficient and reliable generation, transfer, and retrieval of information where appropriation is often closely tied to formal sites of labor and education" (Drotner, 2005, par. 10).

One of the competencies necessary to live in this society is information literacy (Kuhlthau, 1993; Bruce, 1997), which denotes an individual's ability to access, retrieve, and process data of relevance to concrete problem solving and discussion making. Information literacy is closely tied to the technologies of computing, Internet access, knowledge, and responsible and reflective use of information.

The result of this change is librarians' increasing use of Internet-based resources and communication, which shifts librarians' attention to the virtual user rather than the physical library. Services such as digital reference and free access to large-scale databases and resources have become an integral part of the library's service (Drotner, 2005). Librarians have become providers of electronic information and access ports to information, and they are keepers of the cultural heritage of the communities in which they exist.

Because of today's move from the information society and economy to the knowledge society that started in the mid-1990s, knowledge is the primary production resource. The knowledge society is a competitive society with knowledge accessible to all persons, who are expected to have the skills to improve themselves. The difference between the information society and the knowledge society is that information focuses on raw materials, while knowledge focuses on the various ways people handle raw materials (Drotner, 2005). That is, in a knowledge society, individuals need multimodal competencies that "encompass the ability to access, but also to use mediatized forms of communication; it denotes the ability to retrieve and receive but also to produce such forms of communication" (Drotner, 2005, par. 20).

The creative competencies required to survive in the knowledge society are related to appropriation of media, ICTs, online interaction, and virtual cooperation. E-learning is an important concept in the knowledge society. The need for the individual to continue to learn increased with advances in ICT and in globalization. Medel-Añonuevo and colleagues (2001) explain the impact of globalization on lifelong learning, insisting that "globalization has produced outcomes and processes which make learning new skills and competencies [important]" (p. i). They go on to suggest that "it is no longer enough to have the same learning and working skills one had five years ago. Learning to learn, problem-solving, critical understanding, and anticipatory learning are a few of the skills and the core competencies' needed for all" (Medel-Añonuevo et al., 2001, p. i) at a time when 60 percent of all trades and jobs to be performed in the next two decades or so are not yet known (Medel-Añonuevo et al., 2001).

Demographic Change

Two major demographic trends in the United States have major implications for the delivery of library services. The first is an aging population, and the second is a growing immigrant population. The Pew Research Center projects that the U.S. population will increase by 48 percent between 2005 and 2050 (which is an increase of 142 million people), and nearly all the increase will be due to new immigrants and their U.S.-born descendants. People 65 years of age and older represented 12.9 percent of the U.S. population (one in every eight Americans) in 2009, and by 2030, older adults are expected to make up 19 percent of the population (almost one in every five Americans) (Administration on Aging, n.d.). This population growth is attributed to the aging of the baby boomers (people born after World War II).

The implications for library services are obvious. Services need to be developed for target populations—the elderly and people with disabilities. Services have to target baby boomers, who are more educated, are more affluent, and require services tailored to their needs. Marshall and Marshall (2010) indicated the aging population will affect all segments of society; therefore, the library can be a resource for other community organizations that need information for planning. Librarians need to partner with outside organizations to provide necessary outreach services to caregivers for adults who need information about health, nutrition, and social support agencies.

As the number of foreign-born residents increases, librarians should plan services for this target group in addition to literacy and citizenship services. Librarians have to advocate for this group, and libraries should serve as cultural centers and democratic spaces where diverse people can meet and interact.

IMPLICATION FOR LIFELONG LEARNING SERVICES

The widespread acceptance of the concept of lifelong learning by all, including policymakers, is documented in the literature (Field, 2013). Jones and Symon (2001) discuss that lifelong learning emphasizes "the vocational economic and skilling aspect of learning at the expense of how learning can benefit the individual, the community, and society in general, enriching lives in the cultural sense" (p. 269). They go on to explain that learning for learning without the expectation of career advancement or enhancement or financial returns for their efforts (p. 270) was eclipsed in the last decade of the twentieth century by a campaign to retain workers for employment in the capitalist economy.

In the same vain, Medel-Añonuevo and colleagues (2001) concurred that "lifelong education in the early seventies was associated with the more comprehensive and integrated goal of developing more humane individuals and communities in the face of rapid social change" (p. 4). A UNESCO report, *Learning to Be the World Education of Tomorrow* focused on a humanistic view of lifelong learning as a process that benefits individuals, communities, and society and that has the potential to address inequities, suffering, and other dehumanizing forces (Faure et al., 1972). The idealistic notions of self-improvement and civic engagement was said to have been replaced in the 1990s by fiscal concerns linked "to retraining and learning new skills that would enable individuals to cope with the demands of rapidly changing workplace" (Medel-Añonuevo et al., 2001, p. 4).

Jones and Symon (2001) explain the difference between these two concepts of lifelong learning in terms of their focus on human capital versus social capital. Human capital focuses on a vocational approach to lifelong learning and the "perceived need to skill the work force so that industry can operate in an increasingly competitive global market" (p. 269). Social capital, on the other hand, "concentrates more on civic society and networks in the family" (p. 275). Recognizing the link between economic prosperity and social cohesion, the World Bank describes social capital in terms of the relationships and norms of institutions that shape the quality and quantity of a society's social interactions and the cohesion among those interactions (World Bank Group, 2002).

Basic literacy services and English as a Second Language classes are essential for the influx of immigrants who are not literate in English. The definition of literacy has been expanded to include information literacy, media literacy, and multimodal literacy. Multimodal literacy, developed from

Kress and Van Heawant (2001), includes competencies needed in the knowledge society, the ability to access and use mediated forms of communications. It also includes entertainment, personal interactions, and performance. Librarians should plan to provide instruction to patrons so that they can acquire the requisite competencies to be able to use library resources.

McCook and Barber (2002) point out that funding for many adult lifelong learning and adult literacy programs has been set up in the context of economically driven ideology such as the Personal Responsibilities and Work Opportunity Reconciliation Act (PRWORA) of 1996; and therefore the focus, it seems, is on work-related lifelong learning with minimal attention to informal learning for personal enrichment. PRWORA reformed welfare laws by adding provisions that move people into work-related activities.

In support of the social capital theory discussed earlier in the chapter and citing a number of studies showing that adult education and lifelong learning help the creation of social capital (Coleman, 1986; Putnam, 2000; Schuller et al., 2000), Nancy Kranich, then president of ALA, described libraries as institutions "rich in social capital" where "people of all ages can share interests, and concerns, find information essential to civic participation, and connect to fellow citizens" (Kranich, 2001, p. 40). Stevens (2006) states that "when viewed through the lens of social capital theory, libraries as cultural agencies establish the conditions for generation of social capital, lifelong learning and the productive relationship between the two" (p. 539).

Public librarians must design their lifelong learning service responses based on the needs of their communities. One can assume that some librarians in both rural and urban libraries may focus more on programs to enhance human capital, while suburban librarians may focus on services to support the growth of social capital.

LIFELONG LEARNING SERVICES FOR THE TWENTY-FIRST CENTURY

Public libraries have historically provided services that impact lifelong activities such as adult literacy. Library services in the twenty-first century continue to support lifelong learning. Van Fleet (1990) suggested that with the adoption of lifelong learning concepts as an underlying philosophy for library services, libraries foster services that support adults sustaining personal growth through self-motivated pursuit of knowledge.

Some existing services may need to be reexamined in the light of factors in today's societal and technological trends. Literacy services and technology training and programming need to be modified to suit the changing needs of the community.

Literacy Services

The public library provides support for education through service responses from the New Planning for Results (Basic Literacy Services). These services, related to information literacy and formal learning support, adult basic literacy, pre-GED, GED, English as a second language, and family literacy, continue to be needed in the twenty-first century, though the extent of the need depends on the size and location of the library.

Adult literacy is a severe problem. A 2003 national assessment of adult literacy found that 31 million people (14 percent of Americans) 16 or older had "below basic prose literacy," and 48 million (22 percent) had "below basic quantitative literacy." The report points out that in a global economy, these low-literate adults are at a high risk of never escaping subsistence or below-subsistence labor markets. Their limited job skills are a drag to natural economic growth (Bosworth, 2007).

The importance of literacy to lifelong learning is articulated by the International Federation of Library Associations and Institutions (IFLA) in its core values. The professional priority of promoting literacy, reading, and lifelong learning promotes increased literacy for all people. Three primary literacies are addressed:

- Basic literacy, which is the ability to use, understand, and apply print, writing, speech, and visual information to communicate and interact effectively
- Reading literacy, which is the ability to decipher print and other forms of notations
- Information literacy, which is the ability to formulate and analyze an information need, identify and appraise sources, and locate, retrieve, organize, and store information. It also includes the ability to interpret and to critically evaluate whether the information need has been satisfied. (Raseroka, 2003)

The focus of information literacy is on developing a person's ability to learn how to learn and therefore provide a foundation for lifelong learning (Boekhurst, 2003). According to Harding (2008), information literacy is widely considered to be a survival requirement for life in the information age and a vital underpinning to lifelong learning. Most of the literature on the subject comes from academic libraries, where the concept is linked to bibliographic instructor and user education. Public libraries have not documented their involvement in information literacy activities. Rader (2000) and Johnson and Jent (2007) found that only 2 percent of the relevant research addresses public library involvement in information literacy activities, compared to 62 percent for academic libraries. Information literacy is important to all society (Bundy 2002). Public libraries are highly suited to promoting the development of information literacy and to encouraging life-long learning in their communities (Leininger, 2007). Libraries today have the ability to provide assistance with teaching technology skills to adults in the community.

TECHNOLOGY AND LIFELONG LEARNING

The twenty-first century has seen an explosion of information—there is now much more information and in many different formats. Libraries strive to have in their collections information in all formats that can be easily located and accessed for use. Harding (2008) observed that a key element of information literacy is the ability to locate and access information. Librarians provide training and support in information communication technology (ICT), which enables their patrons to navigate, explore, and evaluate information sources (Harding, 2008).

Public libraries provide computer literacy classes and Internet access. In the twenty-first century, librarians must plan more formalized training for targeted groups within the community such as older adults, teens, the home-less, and job seekers. Librarians have taken advantage of new technological trends including using digital information, increasing internal reference sources, adapting social networking tools to delivery of services, and col-laborating with other librarians and social entities. As part of preparing patrons for lifelong learning, librarians need to train patrons in the use of these technologies as they are introduced.

SERIOUS LEISURE AND LIFELONG LEARNING

Most visits to the public library are associated with leisure activities such as fiction reading and attending library programs of different kinds. The nature of leisure and its implications for public library services have become an important aspect of research in library and information science. Hartel (2003) found that a better understanding of the nature of leisure and its information dimension can enhance information provision to a large num-ber of public library users. Fulton and Vondracek (2009) point out that lei-sure continues to grow in importance in today's society. They go on to discuss the impact of leisure on our everyday lives, including information behavior, negotiation of technology in the pursuit of leisure activities, and social outcomes of our interactions though leisure.

Categories of leisure were initially developed by Stebbins, a sociologist, in the 1970s, as he provided the categories of serious leisure and casual leisure. Robert Stebbins defined serious leisure as "the systematic pursuit of an ama-teur, hobbyist, or volunteer activity sufficiently substantial and interesting enough for the participant to find a career there in the acquisition and expression of a combination of his special skills, knowledge, and experience" (1992, p. 3). Stebbins's definition of casual leisure contrasts with that of serious leisure. He defines as casual leisure "as an immediately, intrinsically rewarding, a relatively short-lived, pleasurable activity requiring little or no special training to enjoy it." (2009, p. 623).

Later, Stebbins added project-based leisure to the other concepts of leisure, defining project-based leisure as "a short-term moderately complicated, either one-shot or occasional, though infrequent, creative undertaking carried out in free time" (2009, p. 622). Project-based leisure involves planning and effort and may also require skill or knowledge. Yet, project-based leisure is not considered serious leisure and is not intended to develop into serious leisure. Project-based leisure is also not casual leisure. As an occasional or one-shot undertaking, it includes "widely spaced undertakings for such regular occasions as arts festivals, sports events, religious holidays, individual birthdays, or national holidays while creative stresses that the undertaking results in something new or different, showing imagination, skill, or knowledge" (Stebbins, 2009, p. 629).

The concepts of leisure and leisure reading are new to librarians, and the provision of popular fiction for readers in public libraries is one way to provide leisure. Fulton and Vondracek (2009) identify a variety of factors that have increased the focus on serious leisure such as the rise of free time among baby boomers now retired (or retiring), increased opportunities for lower-cost travel, with cheap-fare airlines. The rediscovery of leisure through the lens of other disciplines has encouraged library and information science researchers to explore this aspect of everyday information and social behaviors.

Serious leisure is said to be the systematic pursuit of amateur, hobbyist, or volunteer core activity that is highly substantial, interesting, and fulfilling. These groups of participants have to be supported with resources to continue their brand of serious leisure activities. In explaining concepts related to the serious leisure perspective, Stebbins (2009) provides a detailed explanation of the activities that each of the three groups are involved in and the ramifications related to library use and access to information.

Leisure research is not new to library and information science researchers, and a number of completed and ongoing studies are reported in the literature. Duff and Johnson (2004) and Yakel (2004) wrote about the information-seeking behavior of genealogists and family historians, and Dolance and Gilmour (2006) studied amateur scientists. Other researchers have focused on a variety of leisure-related topics such as small worlds, information literacy, e-environments, and hobbies. Chang and Su (Chang, 2009; Chang & Su, 2007) studied the world of tourist information with their exploration of backpackers' information-seeking behavior. They suggest that understanding the information-seeking and sharing behaviors of backpackers and others engaged in similar activities could impact how librarians organize information for this group to access it.

Burnett (2000) examined communication and information exchange in online environments, including music and blogs. Leisure studies have found their way into one multiuser virtual environment (MUVE), or Virtual World. Second Life provides people interested in a particular topic a virtual place where they can pursue their serious leisure activities through meeting others, socializing, participating in individual and group games, and creating and trading virtual property and services. Second life is intended for mature users. Richard Urban (2007) articulates the benefits of introducing leisure concepts to the understanding of MUVEs, saying that it reinforces that of virtual worlds, and adult activities require passion and commitment that provides benefits not only to the participants, but also to the community. He goes on to say that the profiles of serious leisure participants look much like the lifelong learners identified by the Institute of Museums and Library Services (IMLS) and other funding agencies. Thus, he thinks a closer study of MUVE may help librarians better understand how to make information seeking and information systems more compelling if not more fun. He states that libraries are important, if not essential, to the pursuit of serious leisure.

The concept of serious leisure has become such a focus of library and information science research and literature that an entire issue of *Library Trends* (2009) was devoted to the topic. In "Leisure and Its Relationship to Library and Information Science: Bridging the Gap," Robert Stebbins (2009) provides a "conceptual framework for understanding leisure and leisure activities, which can help guide researchers and practitioners working on the retrieval and dissemination of information about such activities" (p. 618). That framework distinguishes among casual (immediate, short-lived) leisure, serious (systematic pursuit) leisure, and project-based (complicated, short-term, creative) leisure. Urban (2007) points out that Stebbins believed "serious leisure activities are not necessarily 'fun' or 'play' in the traditional sense. . . . serious leisure goes beyond an individual activity and suggests a longer-term commitment, participation in a community and social recognition for their engagement" (p. 38). Stebbins's framework suggests that different forms of leisure may necessitate different models of service responses.

The literature identifies themes in current library and information science research on leisure. The researchers, in associating information with leisure, have examined leisure involvement from the perspective of pleasure. Leisure is said to cross socioeconomic boundaries such as age and culture. Leisure is said to be fun for everyone, from holidaymaker to hobbyist. "Furthermore, involvement in a leisure world has the potential to open prospects for lifelong learning and increased social inclusion. The resulting possibilities for library and information professionals and educators are exciting" (Fulton & Vondracek, 2009, p. 613). Public librarians need to understand these perspectives and their implications for services for serious leisure patrons.

They need to be familiar with the different types of leisure and the library patrons engaged in them so that they can respond with relevant services and information resources. Public libraries in the twenty-first century must provide services to support all aspects of serious leisure activities if they are to satisfy the lifelong learning needs of patrons.

REFERENCES

Administration on Aging, Department of Health & Human Services. (n.d.). Aging statistics. http://www.aoa.acl.gov/Aging_Statistics/index.aspx

American Library Association. (1926). *Libraries and adult education: A study by the American Library Association.* Chicago: ALA.

Belden, C. F. D. (1926). President's address: Looking forward. *Bulletin of the American Library Association, 20*(10), 273–278.

Bentley, T. (1998). *Learning beyond the classroom: Education for a changing world.* New York: Routledge.

Birge, L. E. (1981). *Serving adult learners: A public library tradition.* Chicago: American Library Association.

Boekhurst, A. (2003). Becoming information literate. *Netherlands Library Review, 52*(7), 298–309.

Bostwick, A. E. (Ed.). (1914). *Classics of American librarianship: The relationship between the library and the public schools; reprints of papers and addresses.* New York: H. W. Wilson. Retrieved April 28, 2013, from http://www.archive .org/stream/relationshipbetw00bostrich/relationshipbetw00bostrich_djvu.txt

Bosworth, B. (2007, December). *Lifelong learning: New strategies for the education of working adults.* Center for American Progress. Retrieved from http:// www.americanprogress.org/issues/2007/12/pdf/nes_lifelong_learning.pdf

Broschart, J. R. (1977). *Lifelong learning in the nation's third century: A synthesis of selected manuscripts about education of adults in the United States.* Washington, D.C.: Superintendent of Documents, U.S. Government Printing Office.

Bruce, C. (1997). *The seven faces of information literacy.* Blackwood: Australia Library Association.

Bundy, A. (2002). Essential connections: School and public libraries for lifelong learning. In M. Nimon (Ed.), *Connecting challenges: Issues for teacher and children's librarians.* Adelaide: Australia Library Association.

Burge, E. J. (1983). Introduction: Changing perspectives. *Library Trends, 31*(Spring), 513–523.

Burnett, G. (2000). Information exchange in virtual communities: A typology. *Information Research, 5*(4). Retrieved from http://www.webcitation.org/5YovosQUO

Butcher, W., & Street, P.-A. (2009). Lifelong learning with older adults. *Aplis, 22*(2), 64–70.

Canadian Library Association. (2006). Creating lifelong learning opportunities through partnership: A 30-year success story. *Feliciter, 6,* 244–246. Retrieved from http://www.cla.ca

Chang, S.-J., & Su, H. C. (2007). *The concepts of task and sources of information in leisure activities: A case study of backpackers.* Milwaukee, WI: ASIS&T.

Chang, S.-J. L. (2009). Information research in leisure: Implications from an empirical study of backpackers. *Library Trends*, 57(4), 711–728.

Cohen, W. J. (1975, November). Lifelong learning: A definition and a challenge. *Educational Leadership*, pp. 83–84.

Coleman, J. E. (1986). ALA's role in adult and literacy education. *Library Trends*, 34 (Fall), 207–217.

Collins, J. (2004). Education techniques for lifelong learning: Principles of adult learning. *RadioGraphics*, 24(5), 1483–1489.

Cross, P. (1981). *Adults as learners*. San Francisco: Jossey Bass.

Dolance, T., & Gilmour, R. (2006). Libraries, information, and amateur scientists. *Technical Services Quarterly* 23(3), 1–18.

Drotner, K. (2005). Library innovation for the knowledge society. *Scandinavian Public Library Quarterly*, 38(2). Retrieved from http://www.splq.info/issues/vol38_2/07.htm

Duff, W. M., & Johnson, C. A. (2004). Where is the list with all the names? Information seeking behavior of genealogists. *American Archivist*, 66(Spring/Summer), 79–95.

Faure, E., Herrera, F., Kaddowa, A., Lopes, H., Petrovsky, A., Rahnema, M, & Ward, F. (1972). *Learning to be: The world of education today and tomorrow*. Paris: United Nations Educational Scientific & Cultural Organization (UNESCO).

Field, J. (2013). Learning through the ages? Generational inequalities and inter-generational dynamics of lifelong learning. *British Journal of Educational Studies*, 61(1), 109–119. Retrieved April 28, 2013, from http://www.academia.edu/2790270/Learning_through_the_ages_Generational_inequalities_and_inter-generational_dynamics_of_lifelong_learning

Findsen, B. (2006). Social institutions as sites of learning for older adults: Differential opportunities. *Journal of Transformative Education*, 4(1), 65–81.

Fulton, C., & Vondracek, R. (2009). Introduction: Pleasurable pursuits: Leisure and LIS research. *Library Trends*, 57(4), 611–617.

Håggström, B. M. (2004, March). *The role of libraries in lifelong learning: Final report of the IFLA project under the Section for Public Libraries*. Public Libraries Section: http://www.ifla.org/VII/s8/index.htm

Harding, J. (2008, December 1). *Information literacy and the public library*. Australasian Public Libraries and Information Services. Retrieved from http://www.thefreelibrary.com/Information+literacy+and+the+public+library.-a0190747227

Hartel, J. (2003). The serious leisure frontier in library and information science: Domains. *Knowledge Organization*, 30(3/4), 228–238.

Innocent, N. (2009). A revolution in lifelong learning. *Public Libraries*, 24(4), 30–32.

Jennings, J. T. (1924). Sticking to our last. *Bulletin of the American Library Association*, 18, 150–156.

Jennings, J. T. (1925). Third general session: Adult education. *Bulletin of the American Library Association*, 12, 121–123.

Johnson, A., & Jent, S. (2007). Library instruction and information literacy, 2005. *Reference Services Review*, 35(1), 137–186.

Jones, I., & Symon, G. (2001). Lifelong learning as serious leisure: Policy, practice and potential. *Leisure Studies*, 20(4), 269–283.

Kendall, M. (2000). Lifelong learning through computer-mediated communication: Potential roles for UK public libraries. *New Review of Libraries and Lifelong Learning 2000*, 81–101.

Kenneally, A. (2004). Public libraries in learning communities. *Aplis, 17*(3), 104–109.

Knowles, M. S. (1980). *The modern practice of adult education.* New York: Cambridge, The Adult Education Company.

Kranich, N. (2001). Libraries create social capital. *Library Journal, 126*(19), 40–41.

Kress, G. R., & Van Heawant, T. (2001). *Multimodal discourse: The modes and media of contemporary communication.* New York: Oxford University Press.

Kuhlthau, C. C. (1993). *Seeking meaning: A process approach to library and information services.* Westport, CT: Ablex.

Lee, R. E. (1966). *Continuing education for adults through the American public library* (pp. 3–11, 116–119). Chicago: American Library Association. Retrieved from http://www.questia.com/read/71925855

Leininger, M. (2012). Information literacy and public libraries. WebJunction. Retrieved August 15, 2013, from http://www.webjunction.org/documents/webjunction/Information_Literacy_and_Public_Libraries.html.

Marshall, J., & Marshall, V. (2010). New patterns of aging: Implications for libraries and cultural institutions. In P. Rothstein & D. D. Schull (Eds.), Boomers and beyond: Reconsidering the role of libraries. Chicago: American Library Association.

McCook, K. de la Peña, & Barber, P. (2002). Public policy as a factor influencing adult lifelong learning, adult literacy and public libraries. Reference & User Services Quarterly, 42(1), 66–75.

Medel-Añonuevo, C., Ohsako, T., & Mauch, W. (2001). *Revisiting lifelong learning for the 21st century.* Paris, United Nations Educational Scientific & Cultural Organization (UNESCO): Institute for Education.

Monroe, M. E., & Heim, K. M. (Eds.). (1991). *Partners for lifelong learning: Public libraries and adult education.* Washington, D.C.: Office of Library Programs, U.S. Department of Education, Office of Educational Research and Improvement.

Moyer, J. E. (2007). Learning from leisure reading: A study of adult public library patrons. *Reference & User Services Quarterly, 46*(4), 66–79.

Putnam, R. D. (2000). *Bowling alone: The collapse and revival of American community.* New York: Simon and Schuster.

Rachal, J. R. (1989, March). The American library adult education movement, 1924–1933. In R. Rohfeld (Ed.), *Breaking new ground: The development of adult and workers' education in North America.* Proceedings from the Syracuse University Kellogg Project's First Visiting Scholar Conference in the History of Adult Education, March 1989. Retrieved from http://www-distance.syr.edu/rachal.html

Rader, H. (2000). A silver anniversary: 25 years of reviewing the literature related to user instruction. *Reference Services Review, 28*(3), 290–296.

Raseroka, K. (2003). IFLA president acceptance speech. 60th IFLA General Conference Closing Ceremony, August 8, 2003. Retrieved from http://ifla.queenslibrary.org/IV/ifla69/papers/205e-Raseroka.pdf

Schuller, T., Baron, S., & Field, J. (2000), Social capital: A review and critique. In S. Baron, J. Field, & T. Schuller (Eds.), *Social capital: Critical perspectives* (pp. 1–38). Oxford: Oxford University Press.

Scott, J. C. (1999). The Chautauqua movement: Revolution in popular higher education. *Journal of Higher Education, 70*(4), 389–412.

Smith, M. K. (1996, 2001). Lifelong learning. *The Encyclopedia of Informal Education.* Retrieved from http://www.infed.org/lifelonglearning/b-life.htm

Stebbins, R. (1992). *Amateurs, professionals and serious leisure.* Montreal: McGill-Queen's University Press.

Stebbins, R. (1997). Serious leisure and well-being. In J. Haworth (Ed.), *Work, leisure and well-being* (pp. 117–130). London: Routledge.

Stebbins, R. A. (2006). *Serious leisure: A perspective for our time.* New Brunswick, NJ: Aldine Transaction.

Stebbins, R. A. (2009). Leisure and its relationship to library and information science: Bridging the gap. *Library Trends, 57*(4), 618–631.

Stein, S. (2000). *Equipped for the future content standards: What adults need to know and be able to do in the 21st century.* Washington, D.C.: National Institute for Literacy.

Stein, S. (2002, Winter). ABC's of EFF: Reading's role in Equipped for the Future. *EFF Voice, 3*(1), 1. Retrieved from http://eff.cls.utk.edu/PDF/vol_3_no_1.pdf

Stevenson, G. T. (1956). The role of the public library in adult reading. In N. B. Henry (Ed.), *Yearbook of the National Society for the Study of Education, 56*(2), 114–135.

Urbana, R. (2007). Second life, serious lesuire on LIS. Bulletin of American Society for Information Science and Technology . 33(6), p 38–40.

Utley, H. M. (1851). A public library. *Massachusetts Teacher, 4*(8), 2.

Van Fleet, C. (1990). Lifelong learning theory and the provision of adult services. In K. M. Heim & D. P. Wallace, *Adult services: An enduring focus for public libraries* (pp.166–211). Chicago: American Library Association.

Van Fleet, C. J. (1995). *Public libraries, lifelong learning, and older adults: Background and recommendations.* Washington, D.C.: Department of Education, Office of Educational Research and Improvement, Educational Resources Information Center.

Veal, R. E. (2009). Understanding the characteristics, concerns, and priorities of adult learners to enhance library services to them. *Reference Librarian, 33*(69), 113–118.

World Bank Group. (2002). *World Development Report 2002: Building institutions for markets.* New York: Oxford University Press.

Yakel, E. (2004). Seeking information, seeking connections, seeking meaning: Genealogists and family historians. *Information Research, 10*(1), 10–11.

Zafft, C., Kallenbach, S., & Spohn, J. (2006). *Transitioning adults to college: Adult basic education program models.* Boston: World Education.

CHAPTER 9

Services to Diverse Populations

In this chapter, library services for diverse populations will be discussed. The chapter will focus on populations that are distinguished by ethnicity, race, or cultural heritage. The demographics of each group will be identified, and the relevant services and how they are currently being delivered will be reviewed.

DIVERSE POPULATIONS

According to the Pew Research Center, the U.S. population will increase to 438 million by the year 2050 from 296 million in 2005, with 82 percent of the increase coming from immigrants arriving between 2005 and 2050 along with their U.S.-born descendants. If these changes continue, the demographic profile in the coming century will change dramatically, which will have implications for the delivery of all services, including library services. By the year 2050, nearly one in five Americans (19 percent) will have been born in foreign countries. The result of these trends will be a change in the racial and ethnic makeup of the population. It is estimated that the percentage of non-Hispanic whites will decrease from 67 percent to 47 percent by 2050, and the percentage of Hispanics will rise from 14 percent in 2005 to 29 percent in 2050. It is estimated that blacks, who made up 13 percent of the population in 2005, will maintain their share of the population through 2050. Asians, who made up 5 percent of the population in 2005, will likely make up 9 percent of the population in 2050. Immigrants are projected to be the drivers of national population growth in the twenty-first century. Libraries must prepare to provide services that are tailored to the needs of the new demographics. One size will not fit all, and the current model of library services for adults must be modified to fit population trends. This chapter will review services provided to the major ethnic populations, African Americans, Asian Americans, Hispanic Americans, Native Americans, and immigrants who for the most part are non–English speakers.

ETHNIC MINORITIES

In a 1981 statement, the Public Library Association (PLA) defined the role of the public library as serving individuals without regard to race, citizenship, age, educational level, economic status, or any other conclusion or qualification. That role has become more a shifting demographic (Kravits, Lines, & Sykes, 1991). The four major minority groups—African Americans, Native Americans, Hispanic Americans, and Asian Americans—in the year 2000 made up nearly one-third of the U.S. population. By 2010, it was estimated that the four groups made up about 35 percent of the population, an increase of 5 percent from the year 2000 (Santa Cruz, 2010).

African Americans

The history of public library services to African Americans parallels the social and societal problems of segregation and lack of access for African Americans in the early twentieth century. A New York state law required that a slave be taught to read the Bible by age 18 or be set free, so church-related schools became the earliest access to reading materials for blacks. Blacks were prohibited from using libraries, so they formed their own. The Philadelphia Library Company of Colored Persons was founded in 1833 by Robert Purvis (Wheeler & Johnson-Houston, 2004), which was the beginning of "Negro Libraries."

Following the landmark *Plessy v. Ferguson* Supreme Court decision in 1896 in which the court stated that absolute equality does not extend to social rights and upheld the growing practice of social segregation of the races (McBride, 2006), African Americans living in large cities such as Charlotte, North Carolina, and Houston, Texas, had public libraries with independent governance. The Carnegie Corporation provided money for the construction of branch libraries for Negros. The Auburn Avenue Branch of the Carnegie Library of Atlanta opened in 1921 as Atlanta's first public library branch for African Americans. Closed in 1959, the branch reopened in May 1994 as the Auburn Avenue Research Library on African American Culture and History (http://www.afpls.org/aboutaarl).

The Negro library service to African Americans followed the "separate but equal" policy of the local culture and politics. Differences in accommodations included separate branches, rooms, entrances, and days of service.

In some places, African Americans received only bookmobile services (Wheeler & Johnson-Houston, 2004). The development of academic libraries at historically black colleges led to improvements in library services for African Americans in general. Special collections and facilities became the natural step in the progression of library services for African Americans, which brought the building of special facilities and operations in all types of libraries—special, public, and research collections—for example, at the libraries of Johnson Publishing Company (the largest African American–owned publishing firm in the United States and publisher of *Ebony* magazine) and Amistad Research Center in New Orleans, "the nation's oldest, largest and most comprehensive independent archive specializing in the history of African Americans and other ethnic minorities" (http://www.amistadresearchcenter.org/).

Three U.S. public library systems established special facilities dedicated to preserving and disseminating the black experience. The Schomburg Center for Research in Black Culture at the New York Public Library opened in 1905. The Schomburg collects, preserves, and provides access to materials documenting black life and promotes the study and interpretation of the history and culture of peoples of African descent (http://www.nypl.org/locations/schomburg). More recently, the African American Research Library and Cultural Center was opened in Broward County, Florida, in 2002 (http://www.broward.org/Library/LocationsHours/Branches/Pages/AA.aspx); and the Blair-Caldwell African American Research Library of the Denver Public Library was opened in 2003 (http://www.denverlibrary.org/content/blair-caldwell-african-american-research-library).

The twentieth century saw the integration of services for all as the new model for public libraries, integrating African Americans into mainstream users. Most libraries provided special collections for African American users within the main holdings. Service and special collections for African Americans tended to address this group's perceived socioeconomic-based information needs. Jones (1973) estimated that during the twentieth century, as much as half of the African American community was considered middle class and received services with other middle-class patrons, leaving most specialized services for African Americans focused on the disadvantaged or those living within the inner city. Thirty years later, the focus remained the same.

With library services to African Americans focused on those living in urban areas, specialized services focused on provision of information and referral services to social service agencies as well as provision of information related to health care, consumer issues, housing, job-related issues, and other outreach services relating to literacy services. Public librarians have two models of service to the African American community: (1) They offer services that focus on the social, cultural, and economic needs of African American patrons as part of the service response to the entire community. With this response, they create access to library resources by establishing hours of services that are convenient to both adults and children. (2) They collect materials by and about African Americans, as well as materials by people of other ethnic backgrounds interested in materials about African Americans. Information about medical and health information, biographical information on black colleges and scholarships, career developments, training resources, and resources on African history and culture are also collected.

In this service model, a variety of services and programs of interest to the African American community and other individuals are provided. Much intergenerational programming is aimed toward bringing parents as well as children to the library. Librarians also try to ensure diverse personnel, with African Americans and individuals from other cultural groups. These services, even though focused on African American patrons, are an integral part of the services provided by the library to all patrons. In some libraries—such as Jacksonville Public Library in Florida, the West Las Vegas Public Library, and the St. Louis Public Library—the resources are in special collections to make them more accessible to patrons.

The second model of service involves placing branch libraries in predominantly African American communities and making the collections, resources, and services relevant to the needs of African Americans. The use of outreach services such as bookmobiles, literacy programs, intergenerational programing, and collaborating with community organizations for programming has helped tailor library services to the needs of this group of patrons.

Public libraries in the twenty-first century provide essentially these types of service responses. The methods of delivery are heavily dependent on technology, and libraries have to provide services to advance the technical skills of patrons by providing technology training and Internet access so that the patrons will be able to compete in the current knowledge society of the twenty-first century.

Asian Americans

According to the 2010 census, Asian Americans make up 5.6 percent of the population of the United States; 14.7 million identified themselves as Asians and another 2.6 million as Asian Pacific, for a total of 17.6 million people. The Asian community is a combination of ethnic groups who are linguistically, educationally, culturally, and economically diverse and who live mostly in urban areas. California has the largest number of Asian Americans (3.8 million). Many do not speak English and are "linguistically isolated" (Keller, 1998). Because of their linguistic isolation or limited English-speaking ability, Asian Americans have not enjoyed the same level of library access and services as other English-speaking residents.

Zhang (2001) stated that traditional library services are not adequately designed to meet the needs of the diverse Asian community. He went on to explain that the major challenges faced by Asian newcomers and other Asians are primarily in the area of communicating in English and finding gainful employment. He identified their information needs as acquiring English language instruction study materials, finding immigration forms and requirements, seeking information on locating housing, and finding jobs, health care, and social benefits.

The information-seeking behavior of Asian immigrants is directly related to both experience and culture. Free public library services are not offered in most Asian countries, and libraries are associated with academic institutions or government agencies. Libraries are reading places for storybooks, and most Asian immigrants are not aware of all the other services public libraries can provide. Meeting the information needs of Asian Americans continues to be a huge challenge for public librarians. A number of recommendations have been suggested to address the challenges of serving such a diverse group, including:

- The development of Asian-language collections with materials categorized so that they can be accessed via the catalogs. Some librarians, especially in California, apply special Chinese, Japanese and Korean cataloging (CJK) techniques in addition to the normal cataloging of items.
- Resource sharing with large libraries.
- The role of bilingual staff cannot be overemphasized. The hiring of Asian American librarians has been suggested by one national organization within the ALA, the Asian Pacific Americans Library Association (APALA). The Council on East Asian Libraries (CEAL) provides outreach services and helps to recruit Asian-speaking people into the profession.
- Outreach activities and partnership with Asian community organizations are strongly recommended. Community organizations are helpful in their support of the library.

Chinese organizations led fund-raising effort that resulted in building a permanent branch of the Los Angeles Public Library (LAPL) branch in Chinatown, and they still support the library by continuing to raise funds. These funds are used to provide scholarships for Chinese library school students and to provide volunteers to conduct classes. This partnership and collaboration, even though labor intensive, is an effective way to promote library services to Asians Americans. Other financial contributions are used to raise social consciousness and support volunteers (Zhang, 2001).

Public relations using materials in different Asian languages are needed for promotion of library services to Asian communities. The LAPL launched a successful multilingual and multicultural campaign to increase the use of the central and branch libraries in the city. The promotional materials included electronic formats. The model of service at the LAPL has become the standard for development of service to Asian American communities in other parts of the country. Additional ideas on serving Asian Americans can be found in *Harmony in Diversity: Recommendations for Effective Library Service to Asian Language Speakers* (Keller, 1998).

Hispanic Americans

Hispanic Americans from Spanish heritage and Latinos from Latin American heritage are part of a diverse, heterogeneous group with strong cultural values and use Spanish as their official language. They may be recent immigrants or fourth-generation citizens. Avila (2008) suggested that it is important to make a distinction between first-, second-, and third-generation individuals of Latin origin, as each group has unique characteristics along with different needs, expectations, values, and beliefs. Latinos may be from Mexico, Central America, Latin America, Puerto Rica, or Cuba.

According to the Census Bureau, there are 50.5 million Spanish-speaking people in the United States, up from 35.3 million in 2000 (an increase of 43 percent). They are the fastest growing minority group in the nation (Pew Research Center, 2013). New immigrants and their descendants account for 74 percent of the Latino population.

A review of the literature on library services to Latinos does not provide much information about the early history of such services. Guerena and Erazo (2000) felt that the scarcity of literature on the subject suggests that library services to Latinos is a relatively "new development." According to REFORMA, the National Association to Promote Library and Information Services to Latinos and the Spanish Speaking, Pura Belpré "was a talented author and storyteller who wrote and re-interpreted Puerto Rican folk tales. As the first Puerto Rican librarian in the New York Public Library system she pioneered the library's work with the Puerto Rican community" (REFORMA, n.d.). Belpré began work at the New York Public Library in 1921. Services to the Latino population grew with the 1964 passage of the Library Services and Construction Act (LSCA), which provided funding for libraries to improve services to Spanish-speaking people, including through bookmobiles and other forms of outreach.

In the early 1970s, a movement began to address the Latino community's need for library services, including:

- Development of Spanish-language and Latino-oriented library collections
- Recruitment of bilingual and multicultural library staff

- Promotion of public awareness of libraries and librarianship among Latinos
- Advocacy on behalf of the information needs
- Liaison with other professional organizations (REFORMA, n.d.)

REFORMA was established in 1971 as an affiliate of the ALA and continues to work with the ALA, including helping in the development in the 1988 *Guidelines for Library Services to Hispanic People.* These guidelines were revised in 2006 and approved in 2007. The *Guidelines for Library Services to Spanish-Speaking Library Users* are available at http://www.ala.org/rusa/resources/guidelines/guidespanish.

Hirst (2003) identified several policies and service areas that can impact Latino library usage: informational, collection, technology, programs, and outreach. She suggests some informational policy areas that may be modified to be more inclusive, such as including a commitment to multicultural library services, posting information in both English and Spanish, and explaining requirements for obtaining library cards so that the request for documentation is not viewed negatively. Amnesty periods for fines may be waived, and library flyers, notices, and other publications should be both in English and Spanish. Building a library collection in both English and Spanish would also be welcoming. Bennett (1998) noted that building collections in both languages can be a daunting task, and librarians should seek out Latin and South American publishers to help them locate Spanish materials published in the United States. Most libraries use technology to deliver services, and libraries serving Latinos must implement technology that will enhance access to resources such as bilingual search interfaces, Spanish-language databases, and language translation functions. Libraries help patrons learn how to use the technology and resources.

Programming should be provided in English as well as in Spanish when possible, and libraries can provide translators for services such as income tax clinics (Alire & Archbique, 1998; Alire & Ayala, 2007). Outreach services that include cultural events provide opportunities for collaboration and networking with Latino community organizations.

Libraries use the *Guidelines for Library Services to Spanish-Speaking Library Users* to plan services for this population. The guidelines were adopted in 1988 and modified in 2006, and they provide a starting point for libraries planning to set up services as well as information related to developing and selecting materials relevant to the needs of the group. They provide guidance on language of the resources, which should be bilingual in English and Spanish. It recommends that access to the collection should be facilitated with the use of Spanish-language subject headings. The guidelines also provide information on programming, community relations, and diversity of culture. Programming should reflect the culture and needs of the specific Spanish-speaking patrons in the community. They recommend collaboration and participation in the activities of Spanish organizations in the community. Other aspects of the guidelines deal with the provision of outreach services, including the need to continually analyze and access the nature of services and the information needs of patrons. The need to hire Spanish-speaking personnel at all levels in the library is discussed as part of recommendations for staffing services, and the recruitment of Spanish-speaking staff from graduates of library science programs is also recommended. Most library services for Spanish-speaking persons focus on services for first-generation Spanish-speaking adults. Services provided include English Language Services (ESL), provision of Spanish-language materials; resources to support general education (GED) classes; information on life skills, legal and consumer issues, and health information, as well as referral to social agencies. Programming for cultural enrichment should also be offered.

If public libraries are to serve the Hispanic community, librarians should understand the unique features about the population to be served such as the length of stay in the United States, language facility in Spanish and English, and the cultural subgroups to be served. Alire and Archbique (1998) point out that planning library services for patrons with different cultural backgrounds is a significant challenge, especially for public librarians in medium to large urban centers where the Latino population tends to be heterogeneous.

Native Americans

Native Americans represent the indigenous people of the United States, and they are unique in that, for the most part, they survive as intact political and geographical communities. Many Native Americans have migrated to larger, more densely populated areas. In the 2000 census, 4.3 million (1.5 percent) of the total U.S. population identified themselves as American Indian and Alaska native (U.S. Census Bureau, 2006). "We the People: American Indians & Alaska Natives in the United States" states that most Native Americans resided in four western states: New Mexico, Oklahoma, Arizona, and California (U.S. Census Bureau, 2006). Because they live mostly on reservations, which are significantly far away from public libraries, providing library services has proven difficult because reservations are mainly in rural areas The federal government tried to assist in the development of both tribal librarians through training grants and tribal libraries themselves. The Institute of Museum and Library Services (IMLS) continues to support tribal libraries; currently, IMLS offers Native American Library Service: Basic Grants, which are one-year, noncompetitive, and equally distributed awards to support existing library operations and to maintain core library.

Tribal libraries were set up to address the information needs of Native Americans. They were not much different from libraries in other rural communities. Tribal librarians began to be found on reservations in 1958, when the Colorado River Tribal Council established a library. Others followed in the 1960s when Vista volunteers started putting collections of books on the reservation. The St. Refer Akwesasne Mohawks in New York State as well as the Shoshones Bannock on the Fort Hale Idaho reservation established tribal libraries.

In the 1970s, federal funding made it possible for tribal libraries to be established. To facilitate funding awards, in 1977 the New York legislature passed a law that provided support for Indian libraries, making it possible for them to become full members of the state's public library system. Funding was provided for the establishment of a center to provide training and assistance to newly established tribal librarians (Hauptman, 1988). Training and Assistance for Indian Library Services (TRAILS) was set up by the University of Oklahoma in 1985 (Patterson, 1995).

In 1971 and 1972, the Indian Education Association in association with the National Commission on Libraries and Information Services (NCLIS) identified the need for information on employment, vocational training, legal and civil rights, health, service agencies that help Indians, local tribal history and culture, and native languages. To address these information needs, Patterson (1995) suggested that libraries located on or serving Indian reservations include records, treaties, business records, financial programs, land transactions, and all other aspects of tribal life. "In fact most tribal libraries are probably a combination Library/Archives/Record Centers and maybe even a Museum" (Patterson, 1995, p. 38).

This is never easily accomplished. Barriers to adequate services are articulated in the literature, including limited transportation to the library, limited hours of operation, lack of funding, and an inadequate and outdated collection. To address the situation, guidelines were established for service to diverse ethnic populations, of which tribal libraries are a part.

GUIDELINES AND POLICIES FOR SERVICE TO DIVERSE ETHNIC POPULATIONS

The ALA, under the auspices of its Reference and User Services Association (RUSA), has published several formal guidelines for services to different demographic populations. These guidelines were developed to help librarians establish and evaluate library services. These guidelines, which address services to people of different ethnic, cultural, and linguistic backgrounds, fall into two categories: (1) services to a specific linguistic group, such as Spanish-speaking people, and (2) services to multicultural groups. Two major guidelines provide a starting point for planning for services to multicultural populations: (1) *Guidelines for Library Services to Spanish-Speaking Library Users* and (2) IFLA Multicultural Communities: Guidelines for Library Services. *Guidelines for Library Services to Spanish-Speaking Library Users* were originally adopted by what was then known as the Reference and Adult Services Division Board of Directors in January 1988. It was revised in 2006 by RUSA and was approved by RUSA directors in January 2007. The guidelines are organized into four sections: (1) introduction; (2) collections and selection of materials, programs, and services; (3) community relations; and (4) staffing.

These guidelines formed a framework for the development and implementation of services to Spanish-speaking people. REFORMA, the national association that promotes library and information services to Latino and Spanish-speaking populations, would play a major role in the production of documentation needed to ensure that librarians would be able to adequately provide needed services and resources.

These guidelines provided the model for RUSA to create new guidelines for the development and promotion of multilingual collection and services (RUSA, 2007a; 2007b). They are designed to help librarians provide services and materials to non-native English speakers, all individuals regardless of the culture, ethnicity or language. These guides are also organized into the same four sections: introduction; collection and selection of materials; programs services and community relations; and staff. The content of the guidelines can be found at (http://www.ala.org/ala/mgrps/divs/rusa/resources/guidelines/guidespanish.cfm).

The International Federation of Library Associations and Institutes (IFLA) developed a more comprehensive set of guidelines in 1998 that was revised in 2011. The IFLA guidelines are based on the premise that library services to ethnic, linguistic, and cultural minority groups must be equitable. They recommend that library materials and access to networked information services be provided to individuals in their preferred language and that the collections and services reflect the cultures in the community that the library serves. The IFLA guidelines address eight major areas: funding and provision of library services, library materials, provision of cross-cultural materials and services, cataloging of materials, information services, library programs and community activities, staffing, and the needs of special groups. In 2006, the IFLA approved a similar document that emphasized the necessity of providing library and information services to underserved cultural and linguistic groups. In 2008, the IFLA manifesto was endorsed by the Inter-Governmental Council for the UNESCO Information for ALL Program.

The ALA continues to promote library services for minorities. In 1999 at the ALA mid-winter meeting, a formal Diversity Statement was adopted and a Diversity Office was formed. This office helps provide a forum for research, promotes awareness, and creates policies related to national diversity issues and trends.

To determine the impact of these guidelines and initiatives, a review of the literature on library services to ethnic and linguistic minorities reveals a number of articles on the topic. A number of authors—including Rios Balderrama (2006), Robbin (2000), and Josey and Abdullahi (2002)—present a historical perspective in the movement for diversity in U.S. libraries. They outline the changing demographics in the U.S. population and outline the difficulties of implementing diversity. Library and information science programs were told to include educational materials and experiences to sensitize future librarians to the importance of cultural diversity.

IMMIGRANTS AND NON-ENGLISH-SPEAKING POPULATIONS

The Census Bureau reports that 36.7 million (12 percent) of the U.S. population is foreign born and another 33 million (11 percent) are native born with at least one foreign-born parent. Thus, one in five people in the United States are either first- or second-generation U.S. residents. In 2011, there were 40.4 million immigrants living in the United States (Pew Research Center, 2013). These people are now considered the "emerging majority" rather than "minorities" (Quezada, 1992). They reside mostly in large cities in California, New York, Texas, Florida, New Jersey, and Illinois. Some states such as North Carolina, Georgia, and Nevada have seen an influx of immigrants in recent years.

Patrons or potential patrons who are immigrants are also referred to as foreign born. They speak other languages and little or no English. They are new immigrants who came to the United States seeking a better life, and some were running from political and other world conflicts. Most of these immigrants are adults and are heavily concentrated between the ages of 18 and 64. Immigration rates grew faster after the passage of the Hart-Cellar Act in 1965. Most of these immigrants joined their families in the United States to work and improve their standard of living.

Suarez-Orozco and Suarez-Orozco (2001) explained that upon arrival, immigrants are disproportionately poor and have lower levels of education and as well as fewer opportunities. They have limited English proficiency (LEP), which translates to lower wages. These people need to be assimilated into the native-born population and to learn English (the dominant language) so that they can function in society. This need to educate new immigrants creates a demand on libraries and other institutions to provide the services needed by this population. Cuban and Suarez-Orozco (2007) stated why immigrants come to the library. They come to read, improve their English, use computers, form community affiliations, and the reading enjoyments of their children. According to Nelson and the PLA (2008, p. 210), the library also serves as a "place" that provides a safe and enjoyable space for people to have open meetings, interact, and read. It also provides open and free access to networking.

Current library services do not adequately meet the great needs of new immigrant populations, who often use libraries for services such as English for Speakers of Other Languages (ESL), citizenship, and GED preparation courses. Public libraries are said to be "a place for immigrant self-education enlightenment and the study of democracy and English" (U.S. Citizens and Immigration Services, 2004). Current practices related to new immigrants involve collection development in the documented native languages, training for citizenship, providing information and referrals to social services, and government agency services geared toward providing survival skills, and employment opportunities. Public libraries in the twenty-first century have to go beyond providing survival skills; they have to implement services to foster the achievement of social capital.

GAY, LESBIAN, BISEXUAL, AND TRANSGENDER POPULATION

Gay, lesbian, bisexual, and transgender (GLBT) refer to an individual's sexual desire for a person of the same sex (*Merriam Webster's Dictionary Online*, 2007), and this group of patrons is made up mostly of homosexuals. Census data from 2000 reported about 1.2 million lesbians and gay men in the United States. The census data alone do not provide a true count of this population because census takers do not ask householders to identify their sexual orientation. The National Health and Social Life Survey (NHSLS), which is the most widely accepted study of sexual practice in the United States, found that 2.8 percent of males and 14 percent of females identify themselves as gay, lesbian, or bisexual (Laumann et al., 2004).

While the GLBT population has the same kinds of information needs as the general population, stigmatization imposed by society at large makes it difficult for this group to be given the full attention needed for effective library service. Most of the literature focuses on the steps of "coming out" (Gough & Greenblatt, 1990). The minimal indexing and cataloging terms found in OPACs hampers access to the materials.

The 1960s brought political and social changes and a greater awareness and acceptance of the gay and lesbian movements; this in turn fostered the growth of gay and lesbian libraries. The Stonewall riots in June 1969 spearheaded the recognition that the GLBT population had the same service and information needs as the rest of the population.

Joyce (2000) found that throughout the 1970s and 1980s, articles were published calling for improved library services for the GLBT population. But it was not until the ALA created the Gay, Lesbian, Bisexual, and Transgender Round Table in the late 1990s that improvements in services took hold. Through their bylaws, approved in 1998, ALA helped legitimize the GLBT group, creating the first openly gay professional organization. Other writers such as Phil Parkinson (in New Zealand) focused on the censorship of materials and their availability. Parkinson pointed out the two other problems: difficulty in finding reviewing sources and lack of specific knowledge specialists. Others named political antagonism as a barrier to effective library services to this group. Rich Ashby in 1978 offered ideas of what public librarians should do to improve services to GLBT users. He addressed staff training, the need for a comprehensive and effective selection policy, helping GLBTs find their way around libraries, and getting suggestions from GLBT users in planning for services.

In the late 1980s, library and information science publishing started focusing on the GLBT populations. The publication of *Gay and Lesbian Library Service* by Cal Gough and Ellen Greenblatt in 1990 provided tools for librarians to use in the development and implementation of GLBT services. The book contains information on how to develop a GLBT collection and how to make the library more user-friendly for GLBTs. It also provides information about planning GLBT library exhibits, and it became the template for improving library services to GLBT patrons. User studies on GLBT information needs examined the coming out information needs of this population and found that the library more than any other source was the major resource for them when they were coming out (Creelman & Harris, 1990).

SERVICES FOR DIVERSE POPULATIONS IN THE TWENTY-FIRST CENTURY

Public libraries have a history of serving everyone. In keeping with the ALA Library Bill of Rights Article VI—which states, "A person's right to use a library should not be denied or abridged because of origin, age, background or views" (ALA, 2010)—they provide access to library resources without regard to any social characteristics. Librarians have developed services designed to serve diverse populations by creating collections, providing educational opportunities, and serving as a location with information referral resources.

In the twenty-first century, librarians will have to adapt these services to suit the diverse populations they serve. A continuing and substantial increase in the diversity of communities may create a rapid change in the complexion of the demographics, particularly in environments having a sizable number of diverse populations. Gomez (2000) observed that public libraries have been socially progressive institutions, and librarians have done their best over the past century to meet the challenges of providing library services to new immigrants.

However, some librarians have been slow to respond to the changing ethno-demographic needs of their communities. For public librarians to effectively address the information and other needs of their diverse populations as well as the community as a whole, they have to know who lives in their community. This brings back the efforts to conduct a needs assessment of their service area to identify who the patrons are and what their needs for information are (Gomez, 2000).

DIVERSE COMMUNITY INFORMATION NEEDS ANALYSIS

Analyzing diverse community needs is one of the most important tools library professionals have at their disposal. Bagdasar (2005) pointed out that a well-formulated plan can help a library gauge the makeup of its community and allow for targeted services. When a library's population is diverse, a community analysis is more critical, as it provides information about the population and its demographic characteristics. The result of the analysis should influence aspects of library operations such as marketing and collection development for the identified special group.

The information is more important when planning services for ethnic minorities in the community (Bagdasar, 2005). For some help with this task, check out the community needs assessment used to determine the information needs of transgender community in Portland, Oregon (Beiriger & Jackson, 2007). Their assessment was used to determine the unique types of material, format, and modes of accessibility used by members of this group. The result of this assessment pointed out a great need for information specific to this group (Beiriger & Jackson, 2007).

According to Worcester and Westbrook (2004), community information analysis (CINA) offers librarians a way to identify the needs of their communities, review their own current services, and use the result to plan library services. They go on to say that a thoughtful CINA explores community characteristics and their significance with a focus on the overall information needs of individuals rather than their use of the library (Worcester & Westbrook, 2004). Some of the tools and accessories for conducting CINA are outlined in Chapter 4 of this book.

CULTURAL AWARENESS

After identifying the different ethnic-cultural groups within the community, librarians should have some cultural awareness about the key communication patterns and information acquisition of the groups within their community, Allard, Mehra, and Qayyum (2007) provide a toolkit for building awareness of the community in order to effectively serve diverse multicultural populations. They emphasize that librarians can more successfully serve diverse populations if they can cross cultural boundaries. The toolkit has five components:

1. Identify cultural dimensions that deal with the individualistic as well as the collective perspective (Hoftede, 1980).
2. Identify cultural communication styles that may be low context or high text (Hall, 1976).
3. Recognize who and what might be marginalized.
4. Recognize mechanisms for supplying information.
5. Recognize who built the information technology. The technology is likely to reflect the creator of the technology's viewpoint.

The toolkit was developed to meet the need for a systematic program to promote intercultural leadership training. An intercultural leadership toolkit symposium was conducted by the authors in October 2006 at the University of Tennessee.

Allard, Mehra, and Qayyum (2007) found "that library and information science graduate students do not have a solid background in intercultural issues, and students and practitioners feel leadership in this area is an important skill for the 21st century information professional." All of this leads to the fact that public libraries will continue to face the challenge of providing services to increasingly diverse and multilingual populations. The profession will benefit from offering librarians the opportunity to develop strong intercultural skills.

PUBLIC SPHERE

The public sphere is where citizens exchange ideas, information, attitudes, and opinions. "It's the virtual space where the citizens of a country exchange ideas and discuss issues, in order to reach agreement about 'matters of general interest' " (Habermas, 1997, p. 105). Nelson and the PLA (2008) articulated 18 discrete components for service response for adult services, and McCook (2011) restructured the 18 components into four categories:

Public Sphere
Cultural Heritage
Education
Information

In the twenty-first century, the focus is on activating aspects of the public sphere and cultural heritage to meet the needs of increasingly multicultural demographics and the baby boomers who will need services tailored to their unique information needs. The contents of information services provided by libraries do not need any change in the twenty-first century; the change will be in the delivery mechanism, from manual to electronic. Social media will play a major role in the delivery of library services in an increasingly digital and network-based resource sharing environment.

The application of technology, especially the Internet, has provided the opportunity for new roles for public libraries (McClure & Jaeger, 2009). This returns to McCook's statement: "The public library's most expansive role is to be the central component of a community's public sphere" (2011, p. 6). In their role in the public sphere, public libraries help foster the democratic and cultural activities that accompany human organizations. McCook goes on to explain how librarians can support communities' links to daily lives and the discourse of their patrons. While explaining the role of the public library as a public sphere, Jaeger and Burnett (2010) offer their theory of information worlds and emphasize that the social elements that interrelate and interact will be central to public library service development for decades to come. They state, "It is through the enhancement of public sphere that the library builds community and encourages authentic dialog" (p. 206).

As stated earlier, the library as a "place" provides a safe and enjoyable space for people to meet, interact, and read (Nelson & Public Library Association, 2008). Buschman (1998) studied the issue of the library as a place and identified the library as a physical entity and a locus of intellectual activity. Public libraries continue to provide meeting rooms for people to meet and conduct their activities without interference. This is in keeping with Article VI of the ALA Library Bill of Rights.

Libraries provide spaces for exhibits and displays of local artists' works. Libraries in the twenty-first century, like bookstores and other entities, have added cafes to their spaces. This will make the library more attractive to patrons. Wise (2005) reviewed this trend of integrating cafes in libraries. Some people describe the inclusion of restrooms and cafes as part of the innovations that will help provide solutions to social problems such as homelessness and other socioeconomic problems that society faces in the twenty-first century.

Public libraries have become outlets. As such, they may emphasize special services to segments of society. According to Lewis and Farris (2002), the National Center for Education Statistics (NCES) conducted a survey of programs offered by public library outlets. They define programs as "planned activities offered by libraries to provide information, instruction or cultural enrichment" (Lewis & Farris, 2002). One of the key findings is that provision of Internet access is a major service and that Internet-enabled services showcase the library as a "connector of friends, families and others" (Lewis & Farris, 2002, p. 10). It provides a means for people to be connected at all times, which creates family and community stability. Patrons use the virtual space to connect to the world and hopefully become informed citizens as connect to local, national, and world affairs.

Public libraries are social meeting places and instruments of social integration. The challenge in the new millennium will be to connect public libraries to broader value systems such as quality of life and social capital (McCook, 2011). Public libraries will not only provide information and instruction, but will also be catalysts for social change. Jaeger and Burnett (2010) identified the public library as the place where people with limited or no access to published and electronic resources can have access to published information in newspapers, movies, books, the Internet, and all other forms of published information.

In the twenty-first century, the public library will be seen as a social and virtual space where all ages and all works of life can mix, exchange views, access materials, and engage in public discourse (Goulding, 2004; Jaeger and Burnett, 2005). Libraries are physical spaces where different community groups with members of diverse populations meet to interact and exchange information. Libraries have also become a virtual public space where Internet and social networking technologies make it possible for members of the community gather in cyberspace, allowing for creation of online communities.

CULTURE

Culture is one of the main influential characteristics of diverse populations. Bennett (1998) observed that librarians need to understand the beliefs that different people hold about the world, the values different cultures share about living in the community, and the way individuals within and among different cultures treat one another. These understandings (known as subjective culture) permit successful communication techniques that honor different cultural perspectives (Bennett, 1998, p. 6).

Culture may be explored from three perspectives. The first is objective, which Bennett (1998) suggests refers to the history and facts about a culture, including the language the culture uses. The second, subjective, refers to beliefs that people hold about the world, the values they share about the community in which they live, and the way they treat one another (Bennett, 1998). Bates and Plog (1990) observed that successful communication requires an understanding of subjective culture. In addition, culture may be learned through music, media, or spiritual teachings and is handed down from one generation to another. This method of handing down culture makes it difficult for librarians to understand other groups' cultures. Librarians must begin to build intercultural competence by understanding their own subjective culture and recognizing others' subjective culture (Allard et al., 2007, p. 3).

Interpretive culture, or lived experience, is an experience that is described in the literature as an ever-changing or hybridized phenomena. This culture influences people's lives continuously. External situational, social, and political issues impact people's lives. Librarians must be cognizant of the three perspectives of culture so that they can develop and design effective processes of knowledge and information management and dissemination for diverse populations (Mehra, Albright, & Rioux, 2006).

CULTURAL HERITAGE

Cultural heritage is the legacy of physical artifacts and intangible attributes of a group or society that are collected and maintained for future generations. Public libraries, by providing a comfortable place for immigrants to meet, provide them not only with access to information they need, but also with opportunities for preserving intangible attributes of their culture as well as the ability to keep in touch with their culture of origin, facilitate communication, and build bridges between the minority and the majority cultures in their new environment. Public libraries have played a role in preserving and activating cultural heritage. In the twenty-first century, the public library continues to play a role in promoting cultural heritage for diverse populations by sponsoring programs such as reading groups, exhibits, and cultural celebrations. Honoring Cinco de Mayo, black heritage, Chinese New Year, and other ethnic celebrations should be done in collaboration with community organizations. Through its Public Programs Office, the ALA will also continue to play a role in promotion these activities.

Libraries in the virtual environment are places of contact for community and culture (Robertson, 2005). Cultural programming consists of "programs and series of programs presented by libraries that seek to entertain, enlighten, educate and involve adult and family audiences, primarily in disciplines of arts, humanities, social sciences, public policy or community issues" (Robertson, 2005, p. 5). Cultural programming is recommended as a service response for adults, and by implementing this programming, libraries will be involved in building audiences as well as in rebuilding and revitalizing the community in which they exist.

Boaden (2005) explored community building through cultural programming and explained that libraries have many communities. Their first is their diverse user community, the second is the corporate or management community, and the third is the community of local service agencies or partners. Each library staff team is another community. She goes on to point out that cultural programming is based on building connections between the libraries and these various communities. Librarians need to encourage creativity, plan to strengthen facilities, and work to develop communities through consultation and partnerships with community organizations.

Implementation of cultural programming by public librarians provides a more holistic approach to supporting the information and other survival needs of diverse populations. Cultural programming has much in common with other disciplines such as environmental and social sciences, and economic planning because it requires the assessment of local trends, and needs, including the conduction of a SWOT analysis of the library environment, which was discussed in Chapter 4. Libraries are the "key cultural institution in their community" (Boaden, 2005), and one of their key roles is to support information access via information technology.

Librarians must develop their skills in building connections to their local communities if they are to be successful in cultural programming. They take an active role in community engagement, consultation, and representation. To serve their diverse populations in the twenty-first century, public libraries must be involved in community librarianship, which is:

> the provision of library and information services of special relevance to a particular community at the community level. Provision focuses particularly on social, domestic, health, or educational facilities, details of local cultural activities, clubs and societies and the range of local authority or governmental services. (Feather and Sturges, 2003, p. 94)

Community librarianship is a mechanism by which librarians can help overcome social exclusion. Public libraries will continue to provide outreach services to all community members who need it. The type of outreach service will depend on the specific needs of the people in the community that the library serves. The ALA, through the Office of Diversity and the Office of Literacy and Outreach Service (OLOS), helps to set guidelines for outreach services and sponsors research in the area of outreach services.

Public library services to diverse populations and other adults have to be tailored to community needs as well as the needs of the individual patrons within the community. This includes ensuring usability for people with disabilities and with linguistic diversity; providing materials and services for people speaking different languages; helping communities overcome economic and technology barriers, including with bandwidth needed to access many web-based aids; helping individuals, including those who are homeless or ex-offenders who face the most serious economic needs. (MacCreaigh, 2010). Public library services to diverse populations will become the norm rather than the exception in an increasingly multilingual, multicultural global environment.

REFERENCES

Alire, C., & Archbique, O. (1998). *Serving Latino communities: A how-to-do-it manual for librarians*. New York: Neal-Schuman.

Alire, C. A., & Ayala, J. (2007). *Serving Latino communities: A how-to-do-it manual for librarians* (2nd ed.). New York: Neal-Schuman.

Allard, S., Mehra, B., & Qayyum, A. (2007). Intercultural leadership toolkit for librarians: Building awareness to effectively serve diverse multicultural populations. *Education Libraries, 30*(1), 5–12.

American Library Association (ALA). (2010). Section two: Positions and public policy statements. Chicago: ALA. Retrieved from: http://www.ala.org/aboutala/governance/policymanual/

American Library Association (ALA), Reference & User Services Association. (2006). *Guidelines for library services for Spanish-speaking library users.* Retrieved April 27, 2013, from http://www.ala.org/rusa/resources/guidelines/guidespanish

Appadurai, A. (1996). *Modernity at large: Cultural dimensions of globalization.* Minneapolis: University of Minnesota Press.

Ashby, R. (1987). Library services to gay and lesbian people. *Assistant Librarian, 80,* 1.

Avila, S. (2008). *Crash course in serving Spanish speakers.* Westport, CT: Libraries Unlimited.

Bagdasar, N. (2005). Community analysis and knowledge management. *Library Journal, 80*(3), 6.

Bates, D. G., & Plog, F. (1990). *Cultural anthropology* (3rd ed.). New York: McGraw-Hill Education.

Bennett, M. (1998). *Basic concepts of intercultural communication.* Yarmouth, ME: Intercultural Press.

Beiriger, A., & Jackson, R. M. (2007). An assessment of the information needs of transgender communities in Portland, Oregon. *Public Library Quarterly, 26*(16), 45–60.

Boaden, S. (2005). Building public library community connections through cultural planning. *Australasian Public Libraries and Information Services (APLIS), 18*(1), 29–36.

Buschman, J. (1998). History and theory of information porvery. In Ventrella (Ed.), *Poor people and library services* (pp. 16–29). Jefferson, NC: MacFarland & Co.

Chatman, E. A. (1991). Life in a small world: Applicability of gratification theory to information seeking behavior. *Journal of American Society of Information Science, 42,* 11.

Clark, S., & MacCreaigh, E. (2006). *Library services to the incarcerated: Applying the public library model in correctional facility libraries.* Westport, CT: Libraries Unlimited.

Creelman, J., & Harris, R. (1990). Coming out: The information needs of lesbians. *Collections Building, 10*(3/4), 5.

Cuban, S. (2007). *Serving new immigrant communities in the library.* Westport, CT: Libraries Unlimited.

Du Mont, R. R., Buttlar, L., & Caynon, W. A. (1994). *Multiculturalism in libraries.* Westport, CT: Greenwood Press.

Feather, J., & Sturges, P. (Eds.). (2003). *International Encyclopedia of Library and Information Science.* London: Routledge.

Gomez, M. (2000). Who is most qualified to serve our ethnic-minority communities? *American Libraries, 31*(11), 39.

Gough, C., & Greenblatt, E. (Eds.). (1990). *Gay and lesbian library service.* Jefferson, NC: McFarland.

Goulding, A. (2004). Libraries and social capital. *Journal of Librarianship and Information Science, 36*(1), 3–6.

Guerena, S., & Erazo, E. (2000). Latinos and librarianship. *Library Trends, 49*(1), 138–181.

Habermas, J. (1997). *A Berlin republic: Writings on Germany.* Lincoln, NE: University of Nebraska Press.

Hall, E. T. (1976). *Beyond culture.* New York: Doubleday.

Hauptman, L. M. (1988). *Formulating American Indian policy in New York State, 1970–1986.* Albany: State University of New York Press.

Heckart, R. J. (1991). The library as a market place of ideas. *College and Research Libraries, 52,* 14.

Hirst, A. (2003). Latino communities and library services: An overview. Retrieved from http://students.washington.edu/aliss/silverfish/archive/april2003/hirst.pdf

Hoftede, G. (1980). *Culture's consequences: International differences in work-related values* (2nd ed.). Beverly Hills, CA: Sage.

Jaeger, P. T., & Burnett, G. (2005). Information access and exchange among small worlds in a democratic society: The role of policy in redefining infomration behavior in the post-9/11 United States. *Library Quarterly, 75*(4), 464–495.

Jaeger, P. T., & Burnett, G. (2010). *Information worlds: Social Context, technology, and information behavior in the age of the Internet.* New York: Routledge.

Jones, C. (1973, June 27). *Reflections on library services to the disadvantaged: A talk delivered at the 92nd annual conference.* Paper presented at the American Library Association, Chicago.

Josey, E. J., & Abdullahi, I. (2002). Why diversity in American libraries. *Library Management, 23*(1/2), 10–16.

Joyce, S. L. (2000). Lesbian, gay and bisexual library service: A review of the literature. *Public Libraries, 39*(5), 270–279.

Keller, S. (Ed.). (1998). *Harmony in diversity: Recommendations for effective library service to Asian language speakers.* Sacramento, CA: California State Library.

Kravits, R., Lines, A., & Sykes, V. (1991). Serving the emerging majority: Documenting their voices. *Library Administration & Management, 5,* 5.

Laumann, E. O., Ellingson, S., Mahay, J., Paik, A., & Youm, Y. (2004). *The sexual organization of the city.* Chicago: University of Chicago Press.

Lewis, L., & Farris, E. (2002, November). Programs for Adults in Public Library Outlets *Statistical Analysis Report*: National Center for Education Statistics. Report # NCES 200310. Retrieved from http://nces.ed.gov/pubsearch/pubsinfo.asp?pubid=2003010.

MacCreaigh, E. (2010). Tough times after hard time: How public libraries can ease the reentry process for ex-offenders. *ASCLA Interface.* Retrieved from http://ascla.ala.org/interface/2010/03/tough-times-after-hard-time-how-public-libraries-can-ease-the-reentry-process-for-ex-offenders/

McBride, A. (2006). *Plessy v. Ferguson* (1896). *Supreme Court history: The first hundred years: Landmark cases.* Retrieved from http://www.pbs.org/wnet/supremecourt/antebellum/landmark_plessy.html

McClure, C. R., & Jaeger, P. T. (2009). *Public libraries and Internet service roles: Measuring and maximizing Internet services.* Chicago: American Library Association.

McCook, K. de la Peña. (2011). *Introduction to Public Librarianship* (2nd ed.). New York: Neal-Schuman.

Mehra, B., Albright, K. S., & Rioux, K. (2006). A practical framework for social justice research in the information professions. *Proceedings of the American Society for Information Science and Technology, 43*(1), 1–10.

Nelson, S. S., & Public Library Association (2008). *Strategic planning for results.* Chicago: American Library Association.

Patterson, L. (1995). Information needs and services of Native Americans. *Rural Libraries, 15*(2), 37–44.

Pew Research Center (2013). Immigration trends. Retrieved April 27, 2013, from http://www.pewhispanic.org/topics/immigration-trends/

Public Library Association (PLA). (1985). The public library: Democracy's resource; A draft statement of principles. *Public Libraries, 24,* 153.

Quezada, E. (1992, February). Multicultural library services (special issue). *Wilson Library Bulletin.*

Rios Balderrama, S. (2000). This trend called diversity. *Library Trends, 49*(1), 194–214.

Robbin, A. (2000). We the people: One nation, a multicultual society. *Library Trends, 49*(1), 6–48.

Robertson, D. A. (2005). *Cultural programming for libraries: Linking libraries, communities and culture.* Public Programs Office. Chicago: American Library Association.

Santa Cruz, N. (2010, June 10). Minority population grows in the United States, census estimates show. *Los Angeles Times.* Retrieved from http://articles.latimes.com/2010/jun/10/nation/la-na-census-20100611

Suarez-Orozco, C., & Suarez-Orozco, M. (2001). *Children of immigration.* Cambridge, MA: Harvard University Press.

U.S. Census Bureau. (2006). *We the people: American Indians and Alaska Natives in the United States.* Retrieved from http://www.census.gov/prod/2006pubs/censr-28.pdf

U.S. Census Bureau (2010). Census Briefs. Retrieved April 27, 2013, from http://www.census.gov/prod/cen2010/briefs/c2010br-11.pdf

U.S. Citizens and Immigration Services. (2004). *Library services for immigrants: A report on current practices.* Retrieved from http://www.uscis.gov/sites/default/files/USCIS/Office%20of%20Citizenship/Citizenship%20Resource%20Center%20Site/Publications/G-1112.pdf

Virginia Tech (2010). Virginia Tech Diversity Strategic Plan (2010–2013). Retrieved from http://www.diversity.vt.edu/diversity-at-vatech/diversity-strategic-plan/diversity-strategic-plan.html

Wheeler, M., & Johnson-Houston, D. (2004). A brief history of library service to African Americans. *American Libraries, 35*(2), 42–45.

Wise, M. (2005). Books, hot coffee and a comfortable chair. *Aiki. 21*(1), 11–12.

Worcester, L., & Westbrook, L. (2004). Ways of knowing: Community-information needs analysis. *Texas Library Journal,* 102–107.

Zhang, X. (2001). The practice and politics of public library services to Asian immigrants. In S. Luévano-Molina (Ed.), *Immigrant Politics and the Public Library.* Westport, CT: Greenwood Press.

CHAPTER 10

Special Populations

Public librarians provide services to all members of the community. To do this, they need to understand who the members of the community are. In the 1950s and 1960s, the American Library Association (ALA) Community Project pioneered community analysis as a basis for understanding the makeup and information needs of a community and providing appropriate adult programming in public libraries to meet these needs. One of the outcomes of community analysis is the focus on developing outreach and other programs to "special publics." Special publics—or special groups—include the poor, homeless, aging, and the physically handicapped. This chapter reviews the various aspects of public library services to these groups. The characteristics of these groups will be identified using the ALA guidelines for services to determine acceptable service responses, to identify best practices, and to provide information on resources that librarians can use to supplement their resources.

SERVICES FOR SPECIAL POPULATIONS

Libraries are required to provide services to all. Library patrons have a variety of information needs that have to be considered when planning for services. While providing basic reference services for the primary group of users, librarians also need to identify any special populations and adapt services to accommodate those needs. Bopp and Smith (2011) emphasize that provision of services to special populations is an ethical as well as a legal requirement. Libraries supported by public funds have a "legal as well as ethical obligation to provide service without discrimination based on class, race, gender or other defining social or physical characteristics" (p. 279).

Article V of the Library Bill of Rights emphasizes the library's commitment to fair use of resources and equal access to all library users: "A person's right to use a library should not be denied or abridged because of origin, age, background, or views" (ALA, n.d.).

WHO ARE THE SPECIAL POPULATIONS?

A special population is a group of people set apart by some unique characteristic. Their uniqueness may be defined in many terms, for example, socio-economic, disability, lifestyle (which is discussed in another chapter), or age group. The following classifications may also be used:

1. Socioeconomic:
   o Poor
   o Homeless
2. Disabling conditions:
   o Physically handicapped
   o Blindness and visual impairment
   o Deafness and hearing impairment
3. Age groups:
   o Baby boomers
   o Young elderly (70–85)
   o Elderly (over 85)

These are special publics, and each special public has subgroups with information needs. Most members of those special publics have major differences from the general population and belong in the category of "underserved library patrons." Each section of this chapter defines the special population, describes their needs, and then makes suggestions for services.

PEOPLE WITH PHYSICAL DISABILITIES

Making available library and information resources as well as other needed information for living to all people regardless of their life situation is both an ethical and a legal obligation for all public institutions. Section 504 of the Rehabilitation Act of 1973 requires that equitable access to library facilities and services be provided for persons with disabilities. In 1990, the Americans with Disabilities Act (ADA) was passed as part of civil rights legislation.

Who Are People with Disabilities?

The ADA defines a person with disabilities as someone who has "a physical or mental impairment that substantially limits one or more major life activities" (ADA, n.d.). Title II, Public Service, refers to the exclusion of people with disabilities from services provided by state and local governments, which covers services provided by public and academic libraries. The ADA, as it relates to libraries, seeks to ensure equal access to information for people with disabilities (Freeman & Mabry, 1991).

"One of the hallmarks of a civilized, humane society is the extent to which it cares for its people who have disabilities" (Cylke, Moodie, & Fistick, 2007, par. 2). In the United States, nearly one person in five (19 percent) is estimated to have disabilities, with one in 10 having a severe disability, making this group the country's largest minority. Someone with a disability has difficulty seeing, hearing, speaking, moving, or performing daily activities or certain social roles such as working or attending school. An individual with a severe disability is unable to perform one or more activities of daily living, uses an assistive device to perform these activities, or needs assistance from another person to perform basic activities (U.S. Census Bureau, 2007). With the aging population, this percentage is expected to increase.

Kaufman-Scarborough and Baker (2005) state that not all people with disabilities choose to disclose their disabilities to library staff or other professionals. The impact of a disability has more far-reaching effects on a person's life than the direct aspects of the disability, for example, people with severe disabilities are more likely to live with reduced incomes, are less likely to be employed, and are less likely to be high school or college graduates than people with no or less severe disabilities (Steinmetz, 2006). In a survey conducted between October 1994 and January 1995, Meyer (2001) found that 82 percent of people in their prime employable years (21–64) without a disability had a job compared to 77 percent of those with a nonsevere disability and 26 percent of those with a severe disability.

In 2001, the ALA council approved a policy on services to people with disabilities that translated the ADA legal requirements relevant to library environments. The policy states that libraries must provide equitable access for people with disabilities through modified services "such as extended loan periods, waived late fees, extended reserve periods, library cards for proxies, books by mail, reference services by fax or email, home delivery service, remote access to resources, volunteers to help patrons and various measures to help hearing impaired patrons" (ASCLA, 2001, par. 6). In addition, "Libraries should include persons with disabilities as participants in planning, implementing, and evaluating of library services, programs and facilities" (ALA/ASCLA, 2001, par. 7). Librarians must remove physical and communication barriers that are within the ability of the library's resources to accomplish, such as modifying parking lots and curbs, entrances, doors, tables, desks, and public conveniences. In addition, assistive technologies, for example, screen readers, speech recognition, and braille readers, should be integrated into library services and facilities (ALA, 2007).

Other barriers to library services include web accessibility, staff attitudes, and lack of staff training about accommodations for people with disabilities. The ALA policy suggests that print materials in alternative formats such as large type, audio recording, braille, and electronic formats be provided. Collections should have materials on a variety of topics in alternative formats as well as current materials on the spectrum of issues that affect people with disabilities (ALA, 2007).

ADA and Libraries

Public libraries are subentities of state and local governments and so must comply with ADA requirements. Libraries are covered by Title I (employment), Title II (government programs and services), and Title III (public accommodations). Libraries are required to make their facilities accessible to employees with disabilities. The problem with compliance with ADA requirements is that there is no checklist of ADA requirements that each library must implement. Gunde (1992) points out that each library must provide services that allow each patron with a disability to benefit from the services. He goes on to say that because the needs of each individual with a disability differ and that the range of disabilities is infinite, it is not possible to categorically state which specific measures a library will need to take. ADA regulations are guidelines for making decisions about ADA compliance and must be made on a case-by-case basis, taking into consideration the specific conditions in the library and the resources it has to make achievable modifications.

The ALA, through the Association of Specialized and Cooperative Library Agencies (ASCLA), has produced a toolkit called "Library Accessibility: What You Need to Know" (DeLatte, 2008). This toolkit contains a series of 15 tip sheets to help librarians understand and address access issues. Alexander (2005) identified numerous issues that must be addressed by the development of a carefully thought out disabilities services policy for the target population. Some of these policy issues relate to access, staff awareness, and expanded services. An example of such a policy statement can be found at the website for the Emerson College Adaptive Technology Workstation (http://www.emerson.edu/policy/adaptive-technology-workstation). Some of the questions and issues to address in creating a disabilities service policy can be found at the White House's disability website (http://www.whitehouse.gov/issues/disabilities/).

The Need for Information for Disabled Citizens

Because the needs of different groups of disabled citizens vary, each will be discussed separately.

Blind and Visually Impaired

Reading provides people with access to knowledge and a world of information. Individuals with any sensory impairment such as low vision or blindness are not capable of accessing reading materials that are in printed format. Epp (2006) estimates that only 5 percent of the world's publishing in English is ever made accessible in alternative formats for people who cannot read print.

As people age, they are likely to become visually impaired. Visual impairment represents the greatest disability group and the group that most needs alternatives to traditional print (Parry, 2008). The World Health Organization (WHO) estimates that in 2012 there were 285 million people worldwide with visual impairment, of which 39 million were blind. By 2020 the number will have increased to 76 million (WHO, 2012). In the United States, it is estimated that 10 million people have low vision or blindness, and every seven minutes an individual becomes visually impaired or blind. Of the 10 million individuals, approximately 1.3 million are legally blind (American Foundation for the Blind, n.d.).

Over the years, many private and public efforts have been made to help people with visual impairments read. Born in 1809, Louis Braille, who himself was blinded at the age of three, was sent to a school for the blind in Paris, where he developed Braille. Basing his efforts on military code—which was based on a 12-dot cell, two dots wide by six dots high—he used a more simplified method based on a six-dot cell that could be detected by a single fingertip and allow for more rapid reading.

In 1829, the Massachusetts government founded the Perkins Institute for the Blind, which taught people to read Braille. The New York Institute for the Blind was founded in 1831.

In the mid-nineteenth century, William Moon developed a raised alphabet for people who are blind that consisted of curves, lines, and angles. Books using the Moon alphabet are available for children in the United Kingdom through the ClearVision Project and the Royal National Institute for Blind People (RNIB) National Library Service. The Library of Congress established services for the visually impaired in 1897 when a reading room with Braille books was opened. The room also contained Braille typewriters and other devices. By the end of the nineteenth century, most states had established similar institutions. In 1904, Congress authorized mailing books for people who are visually impaired. By 1925, the reading room that was fully staffed with professionals became known as the Library of Congress Service for the Blind and is now called the National Library Service for the Blind and Physically Handicapped (NLS).

The NLS is a comprehensive resource sharing network for public libraries. The NLS administers the free program that loans recorded and Braille books and magazines, music scores in Braille, and large print and specially designed playback equipment to residents of the United States who are unable to read or use standard print materials because of visual or physical impairments (http://www.loc.gov/nls/aboutnls.html). Founded in 1931 by the Library of Congress, NLS has a central library, 57 regional libraries, nine subregional libraries, and four other public and private libraries, making a total of 71. NLS circulates recorded books, Braille magazines, and other forms of information sources. Information on NLS activities can be found at their website (http://www.loc.gov/nls/).

Library services for people who are visually impaired can easily be implemented by participating in NLS activities. The network offers services similar to those of public libraries, summer reading programs, and book clubs. It is estimated that more than 811,000 individuals and organizations receive reading materials in Braille and audio formats (NLS, 2007). NLS serves as a clearinghouse for all types of materials relating to blindness and physical disabilities. In 1997, NLS was also instrumental in the development of the Web-Braille system, which offers Braille materials through the Internet. Users can search the NLS online catalog for downloadable Braille books for immediate, 24-hour access. These books can be used on portable, refreshable Braille devices that allow patrons to carry dozens of Braille volumes at once (http://www.loc.gov/nls/technical/dtbprogress/progress.htm).

Resources alone are not sufficient, though. Offering services for people who are visually impaired requires that the library provide access to the facility as well as its resources. Wade (2003) identifies low-tech and high-tech strategies for addressing access issues. She points out that the first step is for patrons to be able to move around the physical library environment when they go there. This can be addressed by using bold signage with contrasting colors and color trails. For these to be effective, library staff must guide and provide orientation to first-time users. To supplement the color trails, tactile signs in Braille can also be used for patrons who have no sight perception.

Once access to the library has been addressed, access to the resources can be addressed. For low-vision users, large print books are available. The larger fonts make the text easy to read. Wade (2003) points out some of the drawbacks to large print books such as the low number of available large print titles, not enough titles for the serious reader, and the bulky nature of the books that may not work for people who are not able to hold the books. Braille texts provide access to print materials, and Braille printers should be provided so that patrons can print out Braille copies of information they need.

Technology has impacted services for people who are visually impaired. According to the American Foundation for the Blind, "Technology has removed many barriers to education and employment for visually impaired individuals" (American Foundation for the Blind, n.d.). This group identifies three categories of assistive technology for helping people who are visually impaired:

- The ones that run on the off-the-shelf computers. These can speak the text on a screen and magnify the text in a word processor, web processor, email program, or other application.
- Standalone products designed specifically for people who are blind or visually impaired, including personal assistive devices and electronic book players that provide access to books, phone numbers, and other information.
- Optical character recognition (OCR) systems that can scan printed material and speak the text and Braille embossers that can turn text files into hard-copy Braille documents.

Tank and Frederiksen (2007) observed that libraries providing services to people with print disabilities recognized the challenges and opportunities created by the change from information to knowledge society and are acting to make a difference in the changing environment. They point out that digitization created the impetus for the formation in 1996 of the Digital Accessible Information System (DAISY) Consortium, a global initiative to manage the transition from analog to digital library services for people who are visually impaired. "Digital formats provide new possibilities to counter the risks [of] social exclusion of print disabled people and promote equality in access to information and knowledge" (Tank & Frederiksen, 2007, p. 940).

The DAISY Consortium was formed by talking book libraries in collaboration with the Libraries for the Blind section of the International Federation of Library Associations and Institutions (IFLA) to promote a new digital talking book standard. The DAISY Consortium also worked with Microsoft to develop plug-ins for the DAISY standard. This collaboration resulted in the Save as DAISY project, which converts Open XLM-based Word document to DAISY XML, which is compatible with the Web. DAISY Digital Talking books allow the synchronization of audio with external content and images, providing an accessible and enriched multimedia reading experience. Currently, more than 500,000 people use the DAISY program internationally (Gargano, 2008).

Librarians providing services to people with print disabilities recognized one of the ways of meeting the challenge is through digitization and the creation of the DAISY standard by the National Information Standards Organization (NISO). The DAISY standard for the development of the Digital Talking Books (DTB) system helps individuals unable to read print sources to access print materials on the computer and provides direct access to specific points, enabling readers to move from heading to heading, from page to page, and from word to word (Gargano, 2008). It is an internationally recognizable multimedia system that is compatible with the Internet.

Technology has impacted services to people who are visually impaired in other ways. The NLS Braille program moved into the digital age with the development of Web Braille in 1997. Now using refreshable Braille, patrons can have immediate access to browse the catalog, and download books and magazines without waiting for printed Braille versions to arrive in the mail. Bell and Peters (2005) noted that talking book libraries and mainstream libraries are teaming up to use technological innovations to deliver cutting-edge services and programs with a wide variety of reading technologies and electronic books to ensure that patrons who are print impaired have the same access to library materials and services as their sighted counterparts.

OCLC is working with OverDrive, Talking Communities, and other partners to develop and test digital collections and services that will be accessible to all. Collaboration between libraries has resulted in the creation of Online Programming for All Libraries (OPAL) at http://www.opal-online.org/. OPAL is administered by the Alliance Library System, the Mid-Illinois Talking Book Center, and the Illinois State Library Talking Book and Braille Services. OPAL provides many programs, including online discussions, children's programming, and training sessions.

Magnifying devices can also be provided. For near vision, they may be in the form of glasses, handheld, or on a stand. For looking at far-off objects, they may be in the form of a telescope. Magnifying devices work only for people with some vision; for people with no vision, text readers need to be provided in the form of human volunteers or software that can translate text into sounds. An example is Open Book software that reads scanned material aloud.

Assistive technologies (AT), or adaptive technologies, have been providing new methods of access that are used in different ways to improve or provide access to print as well as electronic resources. AT are said to increase independence in accessing printed information (Ethridge, 2005). Assistive devices can be either computer based or non–computer based. Computer-based AT for visual disabilities include screen magnifiers, screen reading software, and scanning and reading software. Screen magnification software allows magnification of everything on the computer screen, which makes it possible for people who are visually impaired to use an Online Public Access Catalog (OPAC) as well as any electronic document. Magnification can be added to keyboards by adding large print stickers such as ZoomCaps for people with some vision.

Screen reading software can provide auditory feedback by reading menus, dialog boxes, and text. The patron uses the function keys instead of tactile devices such as a mouse to navigate the screen. Scanning and reading software is another variation of screen reading technology. Librarians can use this software to convert printed material into a computer-readable file that can be converted to an audio file. Examples of such devices include Kurzwell, Open Book, and Cicero.

Access to electronic resources provides some challenges. Many library resources are in electronic form, and people with disabilities must be able to access them. Materials in the library catalog need to be made accessible to people who are visually impaired. Patrons have to know what is available in the library, which can be accomplished by including cataloging information that will identify the items. Cataloging rules such as MARC 21 are available for Braille. Web accessibility is a big part of making electronic resources accessible to patrons who are visually impaired. In addition, because of the visual nature of the Internet, it is necessary to create web pages that can be read by text readers. A consortium of universities created a set of guidelines for their web designers that can be used to create better web pages, "The College and University Guidelines, Policies, Processes, and Web Accessibility" (http://webaccessibility.jhu.edu/cofhe.html).

For librarians not familiar with ways to make library automation available to their patrons, *Checklists for Making Library Automation Accessible to Patrons with Disabilities* was created by Berliss (1992). While these checklists are now more than 20 years old, much of the content remains helpful when dealing with problems of print handicapped library patrons as well as other patrons with physical disabilities. The first checklist deals with staffing, and the other three discuss equipment adaptations that are inexpensive and easy to implement. The documents include appendixes of vendors and resources. Berliss states that adaptions intended to be used by people with disabilities may be used by other patrons because there is no standard library patron or standard equipment user.

For the services to be effective, staff should be sensitized to the problems facing persons with physical challenges. Wade wrote, "The single most important aspect of creating an accessible environment is staff attitude" (2003, p. 113). Library staff and the public must be educated about the library needs of people with print disabilities if this special group is to receive the same level of service as other patrons. This also applies to services for people with hearing impairments.

Deafness and People Who Are Hearing Impaired

The World Health Organization (WHO) estimated in 2005 that 278 million people worldwide have moderate to profound hearing loss in both ears, and that 80 percent of these people reside in low- or moderate-income countries. In the United States, between 20 million and 30 million people have some degree of hearing loss, and 1 million of these are children (National Technical Institute for the Deaf, n.d.). According to the Hearing Loss Institute of America, that number is expected to double by 2030 as the population ages. One in three people over the age of 65 have some hearing loss.

Statistics show that deafness is the most "chronic disability in the United States" (Goddard, 1996, p. 3). Librarians must therefore make serving people who are hearing impaired a priority.

Hearing is critical to speech and language development, communication, and learning. How and when a person loses hearing—at birth, in childhood, or in adulthood—directly impacts how the hearing loss will affect the individual (National Technical Institute for the Deaf, n.d.). Rodriguez and Reed (2003) noted that 90 percent of deaf children are born to hearing parents, few of whom know sign language. Many of these parents choose not to learn, which results in the loss of acquisition of language by their children at a vital age.

The early years of language learning is critical in the development of social, psychological, and educational foundations later in life. "Adults who become deaf or hearing impaired later in life may have some residual hearing which may be amplified with hearing devices" (Rodriguez & Reed, 2003, p. 39). They found that three out of four 18-year-olds who are deaf are considered functionally illiterate. In fact, "the average reading level of deaf high school graduates in the United States is roughly third or fourth grade" (Rodriguez & Reed, 2003, p. 39).

Librarians in public libraries can help solve some of these problems by providing opportunities for education and literacy. The Association for Specialized and Cooperative Library Associations (ASCLA) notes that "... most libraries have not considered focusing particular attention on the provision of services to persons who are deaf ... [who therefore] often have ... a tendency not to use libraries" (2004).

Services are determined by the type of a patron's hearing impairment. Noland (2003) explains that not all people who are deaf can be placed into one category; some may read lips, sign or make gestures, or employ a combination of these methods of communication. Librarians serving people who are deaf must not expect the same programs to serve all categories of people who are deaf. Individuals who are deaf may have lost their hearing at birth prior to acquiring spoken language (prelingual deafness), through progressive hearing loss, or through disease or trauma after the acquisition of speech and language (postlingual deafness). People who are postlingually deaf rely on hearing aids and lip reading, while people who are prelingually deaf learn sign language as their first language.

Jeal (1996) contends that adapting a few areas of traditional library services for people who are hearing impaired can improve overall services to people who are deaf. *The Guidelines for Services for the Deaf and Hearing Impaired*, published by IFLA, covers major issues related to library personnel, communication, building appropriate collections, and developing services and marketing programs for people who are deaf (IFLA, 2000). In 1996, the ASCLA adapted the guidelines for the American Deaf Community (Goddard, 1996). In 2001, a tip sheet for communicating with patrons who are deaf or hard of hearing was included in the ASCLA publication *Planning for Library Services for People with Disabilities* (Rubin, 2001).

Vavrek (1995) outlines three service functions typically provided by public libraries: educating, entertaining, and providing information. Instruction in library use helps patrons become aware of all the services and resources the library can offer. Not all libraries have the resources that are needed to serve people who are deaf, and one way to better serve this population is by using resources outside the library through resource-sharing activities and implementation of technological solutions. Among these are text/telephone systems, captioning of spoken information, and speech recognition technology to translate speech into text.

The Internet can also be used to improve services to people who are deaf. Many resources for people who are deaf are available on the Internet and can be accessed by the deaf community and the professionals serving them. Day (1999) found that as a source of information, a graphic interface is an effective medium of visual communication and that the Internet is particularly beneficial to people who are deaf. Another suggestion for this group includes a bilingual video library, a database conducted in sign language and videophony.

Older Adults

Librarians are cognizant of the change in the demographics related to aging, and the world at large is now gaining an additional 1 million older adults each month (Butler, 2008). The U.S. population of those 65 and older is projected to grow to 81 million by 2050 from 37 million in 2005. Due to baby boomers now reaching the age of 65 and above, older adults as a demographic group will grow in numbers more than other ages. The tail end of the baby boomers will turn 65 in 2029, which means that libraries will have a greater number of older patrons for whom they will have to provide relevant and necessary services.

Marshall and Marshall (2010) discuss new patterns of aging related to baby boomers and their impact on services offered by libraries and social service agencies. They say that boomers are expected to make their influence felt on issues such as health care, lifelong learning, and civic engagement. They go on to say that boomers are active, healthy, and more educated than older adults were in previous years. "The sheer numbers of aging baby boomers is expected to increase the members of disadvantaged older adults who have low incomes, low literacy and various sorts of limitations" (Marshall & Marshall, 2010, p. 3). When planning services, librarians must consider the needs of the active older adults, that is, people over the age of 50 who remain active. Marshall and Marshall point out that the demographic shift will affect libraries and museums because patrons will be aging, as will the library workforce. All of these issues have implications for serving older adults.

Information Needs of Older Adults

Older adults do not make up a homogenous entity, and they have different needs based on socioeconomic status. The ALA identifies two groups of older adults, active and frail. Active older adults live in their own homes or retirement communities, are involved in community activities, and manage their own transportation. They are one of the fastest-growing groups of older adults. Frail older adults are the oldest adults, and this category often includes persons living in residential facilities; they usually have serious disabling conditions, and therefore are considered to have physical disabilities.

Services for Older Adults

The public library has a long history of providing services to older adults in keeping with its objective of providing services to all members of the community. The history of library services to older adults can be traced to the establishment of the Adult Education Department of the Cleveland Public Library in 1941. In 1943, the department cooperated with the Benjamin Rose Foundation to plan recreational programs for older adults in settlement houses and churches. In November 1946, the Cleveland Public Library subsequently established its Live Long and Like It Library Club for men and women over the age of 60. Initially, its programs focused on problems of aging, but they were broadened to include a variety of subjects (Long, 1968). The club is said to have pioneered programs that met the interests of its members and encouraged them to keep mentally alert, be active by being avid information seekers, and participate in the programs (Potts, 1958). This was the first informal educational program organized specifically for older adults, and it inspired other librarians to plan programs for older adults. Other libraries became involved, including the Boston Public Library with its Never Too Late Group, which was organized by Muriel Javelin in 1950. The Brooklyn Public Library followed by organizing Senior Citizens in its Flatbush Branch in 1952. Other programs were implemented in Chicago, Detroit, and Milwaukee. These programs collaborated with community agencies to set up their programs. The programs prospered in the 1950s and 1960s with funding from the Fund for Adult Education from the ALA's American Heritage Project.

The ALA formalized its commitment to services for adults by changing the name of the Adult Education Division to the Adult Services Division in 1957, with Eleanor Phinney as the secretary. The Adult Services Division included indirect guidance, reader guidance, library-sponsored group programs, and services for organizations and the community (Lee, 1966). The Committee on Library Services to an Aging Population was established in the same year within the Adult Services Division.

At the request of the U.S. Office of Education, the ALA Office of Adult Education conducted a study that identified four leading services for the aging: supplying books, publicizing materials, Shut-In Service, and work with other agencies. Other services included providing a place to meet, supplying audiovisual materials, serving people with disabilities, providing talking and Braille books, and sponsoring workshops (Phinney, 1957). Based on this survey, a statement on services for older adults was developed by the Committee on Library Services to an Aging Population and was officially adopted by the Adult Services Division in 1964. The statement was revised in 1971 and is the officially adopted statement of responsibility.

The statements were published, revised, and approved in 1987, 1999, and 2008, respectively, and are now known as the "Guidelines for Library and Information Services to Older Adults" (http://www.ala.org/rusa/resources/guidelines/libraryservices). The guidelines were expanded to address increased levels of literacy, people living longer, and the increased application of new technologies by libraries and the passage of the ADA in 1990.

The ALA guidelines for services to older adults address seven major aspects of library activities: (1) acquiring and incorporating current data into planning and budgets for older adults (those 55 years of age or older); (2) representing the needs and interests of older citizens in the library's collections, programs, and services; (3) designing collections and facilities to ensure safety, comfort, and attractability for older patrons; (4) creating a community information center geared toward older patrons; (5) targeting programming to the needs of older patrons; (6) designing outreach for non-mobile (nonvisiting) patrons; and (7) training staff in best practices of service to older adults. The guidelines, which were revised in 1999 and 2005, were approved in 2008 (RUSA, 2008).

As in all planning for service responses by librarians, the first step is to conduct a community analysis to determine the number of older adults in the community and a needs assessment for desired services. The demographic information can be gathered using American Factfinder, which has the latest information from the American Community Survey (ACS) and the U.S. Census Bureau. Depending on the outcome of the analysis, services can be planned using the guidelines for services for older adults. Tips and tools for assisting older adults are articulated in "Keys to Engaging Older Adults @ Your Library," a toolkit published by the ALA Office for Literacy and Outreach Services (OLOS). The toolkit addresses accessibility factors that deal with disabling conditions such as auditory, visual, and mobility issues and how to deal with them, some of which were addressed in earlier sections of this chapter on services for people with physical disabilities. It also highlights services for patrons who are homebound via mail, bookmobiles, volunteers, and electronic access when possible. The toolkit advocates partnering with community agencies and local organizations interested in services to older adults, such as local agencies on aging, senior centers, health-care centers, and associations of retired persons, the best known of which is the American Association of Retired Persons (AARP).

This growth in the number of older adults requires librarians to give serious consideration to the needs of this group, which is more educated and more active than previous generations. Women make up a higher proportion of this group, so when planning programs and collection development, topics of interest primarily to women versus to primarily to men must be given balanced consideration. Hildreth (2006) projected that baby boomers are likely to be more healthy and more mobile, be more likely to age in place, want more meaningful engagement in their communities (either paid or unpaid), expect to design and manage activities for themselves and others, view retirement not as an end, but as a new chapter in which to begin new activities and set new goals. She further explains that these older adults tend to seek welcoming places, meaningful activities, opportunities to learn, social and civic connections, and information options.

Programming is an integral component of services for older adults. Programs should be educational, cultural, and fun. Programming may involve readers' advisory activities such as book discussion groups, author visits, cultural shows, and movies. Hobby programs are popular with older adults. Marketing programs to older adults is important if the programs are to be successful. Information about library programs should be publicized using all communication modes and media as well as good as old-fashioned word of mouth. Publicity and promotion are important in bringing older people into the library.

Implementing technology related to services to older adults is necessary and critical. Librarians can implement technology in two ways—by using technology to provide access and by using it in the form of AT to enhance the life of older adults. Computers and the Internet help older adults to communicate and increase their learning opportunities through lifelong learning. Providing computer training is an important service that libraries can offer older adults. A SeniorNet survey (cited in Prasad, 2009) estimates that 94 percent of seniors stay in touch with family and friends using email, 70 percent research health information, 72 percent access news, 52 percent make online purchases, and 38 percent play games and spend 12 hours or more per week on the computer, more than any other group (Prasad, 2009, pp. 105–106). Older adults can benefit from other Internet resources for travel, entertainment, and research. The library must provide special computer and Internet training for older adults. SeniorNet (http://seniornet.org/), which provides computer education and access to older adults, may provide inspiration and resources that public libraries can utilize.

Collaboration, cooperation, and partnering are key for successful implementation of library services for older adults. Networking is necessary for coalition building. The library has to be involved in community activities, participating or providing information to support community-building programs.

In terms of reference services for older adults, just as with the library community in general, one size does not fit all. Each library should plan its services based on the demographics of the service area and the resources it has available to provide the services. Many resources and tools are available to help libraries provide services for older adults, some of which are listed at the end of this chapter.

The Homeless and Poor People

Providing services to the poor and the homeless presents one of the greatest challenges U.S. public librarians have ever faced (Ayers, 2006), because the number of the poor and homeless increases every year. The number of homeless people saw a 53 percent increase from 2005 to 2010. According to the National Alliance to End Homelessness (2012), on any given night, 643,007 people are homeless.

The literature identifies some problems librarians face when trying to plan services for the poor. Identifying the number of poor and defining who is poor is problematic. In her article "Why Librarians Matter to Poor People," Gieskes (2009) presented findings from a 2007 survey designed to assess and collect data on library services to the poor. The response by librarians to the survey was low, but the findings are pertinent to this discourse. Identifying the poor in a community was problematic, as most respondents did not know who the poor were or how to recognize them. They also did not know if their library had any official policy related to services to the poor. One of the findings was their perception of a lack of official ALA policy on services to the poor, apart from policies scattered among committees and divisions. ALA policy on services to the poor is described later in this chapter. They perceived that there is a gap in focused professional guidance on what library services or level of services should be provided to poor people. In seeking assistance and information to serve the poor, many of the respondents were not aware of the existence of ALA resources. The respondents suggested that ALA publish a guide, provide programs and resources, and take a leadership role in deciding what services librarians should or should not offer for poor people. Eighty-five percent of respondents advocated training to sensitize library staff to issues affecting the poor.

The literature revealed few empirical studies on library services to the poor (Gieskes, 2009). Gehner (2005) found that documentation of poverty-focused service remains anecdotal and that only one book explicitly treats library services in the context of poverty, *Poor People and Library Services* (Venturella, 1998). Another book, *Public Library Services for the Poor* (Holt & Holt, 2010), also discusses poverty-focused service. E. J. Josey's (1986) words resonate today:

These people are not problem patrons. They are patrons in need of your help, because you are a civilized agency. The library has the power to help them and as librarians you have the power to forge conditions that serve not only the homeless but also the best interest of your city and library. (p. 33)

Who Are the Homeless and the Poor?

People are homeless if they lack a fixed, regular, and adequate nighttime residency, that is:

- A supervised publicly or privately operated shelter designed to provide temporary living accommodations
- An institution that provides temporary residence for individuals intended to be institutionalized
- A public or private place not designated for, or ordinarily used as, a regular sleeping accommodation for human beings (Stewart B. McKinney Act, 42, USC 11301, 1994)

Homeless people come from all walks of life. They are members of our society, and they are men, women, and children from all backgrounds. The newly homeless can be families with children that were yesterday families living in your community with children attending school with your children. Homeless is an artifact of the economy. Two trends are largely responsible for homelessness over the past 20–25 years: a growing shortage of affordable housing and a simultaneous increase in poverty. The National Coalition for the Homeless (NCH) states that persons living in poverty are at highest risk of becoming homeless, and demographic groups who are likely to experience poverty are also more likely to experience homelessness.

Being homeless involves more than lacking stable and appropriate housing. Homeless individuals often lack adequate services to overcome contributing factors in their lives such as unemployment, domestic abuse, mental illness, or addiction disorders. In 2007, NCH estimated that men comprise 51 percent of the homeless, families with children 31 percent, single women 17 percent, and unaccompanied youth 2 percent. The homeless population is estimated to be 42 percent African American, 39 percent white, 13 percent Hispanic, 4 percent Native American, and 2 percent Asian. Sixteen percent of homeless people are considered to be mentally ill, 26 percent substance abusers, and 13 percent unemployed.

The poor live below the poverty line. In 2012, the threshold for poverty was $23,050 annual household income for a family of four in the 48 contiguous states and District of Columbia ($26,510 for Hawaii and $28,820 for Alaska), according to *Federal Register* (2012), as reported by the U.S.

Department Health and Human Services. During this time, the federal minimum wage was $7.25 per hour; meaning an individual working 40 hours per week for 52 weeks per year would have a gross annual income of $15,080. To remain above the poverty line, a single parent with three children in 2012 would need to earn more than $11.08 per hour and work 40 hours per week, 52 weeks of the year. According to the Bureau of Labor Statistics, the Occupational Employment Statistics for May 2012, 35 percent of office and administrative support workers have an annual income below $22,500. Ten percent of library support staff earn less than $18,500 a year, and 25 percent earn less than $100 more than the poverty threshold for a family of four (U.S. Department of Labor, Bureau of Labor Statistics, 2012). It is possible to look around at your colleagues and see individuals who are classified as poor.

Libraries can play an important role in the lives of the poor and homeless. Public libraries provide information in a variety of formats and on all subjects, and they are in a position to open doors to opportunities that can change the lives of the poor. Librarians, as keepers of the keys of knowledge, have an obligation to spread information like a balm over those scarred by poverty. The knowledge contained in public libraries can heal the poor in body, mind, and spirit. This same knowledge can also empower the poor to change their lives (Ayers, 2006).

The ALA has been involved in addressing issues that involve services to the poor. In June 1990, a policy with 15 objectives related to library services for the poor was approved. The ALA stated that "it is crucial that libraries recognize their role in enabling poor people to participate fully in a democratic society, by utilizing a wide variety of available resources and strategies" (ALA, 1990). In 1990, the ALA approved Policy 61 (now Policy B.8.10), concerning library services for the poor. This policy was intended to ensure that low-income citizens had access to libraries and library services useful to the poor. Six years later, in 1996, the Social Responsibilities Round Table (SRRT) of ALA created the Hunger, Homelessness and Poverty Task Force (HHPTF), to implement Policy B.8.10 and to increase awareness of the dimensions of, causes of, and ways to end hunger, homelessness, and poverty as well as to better recognize the connections between the library, information access, and overcoming poverty. (HHPTF, n.d.)

The OLOS subcommittee on Library Services to the Poor and Homeless also develops and recommends initiatives to OLOS on how to achieve implementation of ALA policies. OLOS was established to foster the implementation of the tenets of Policy B.8.10 and to articulate the role for citizens as well as library professionals in addressing the problems of poverty. Policy B.8.10 articulates actions for library professionals that relate to library services and policies, staff training for services to the poor, budgeting and funding, outreach services, public awareness, and professional associations and activities.

The Need for Information

Library patrons come to the library with different needs, and the homeless are no different—they have both general and specific needs. Some come to rest and socialize because there is no place to go except the public library (Grace, 2000). Some needs are information related, and others are not. A lot of the homeless come to the library with genuine everyday information needs. Grace (2000) noted that homeless people think of the library as a place where they feel safe and can be warm and dry, chat with their friends, read, and watch movies. She adds that the library is a mechanism of sustaining survival for them. Hersberger (2005) identified the following everyday information needs of the homeless: finances, relationships, childcare, housing, health and health care, employment, education for themselves and for others, transportation, and public assistance for themselves and for others. She noted that public librarians are sometimes not able to provide the best answers to all of these information needs. Librarians must therefore collaborate and network with social services and other relevant agencies to tackle the gargantuan task of helping the homeless obtain the information they need.

While the basic need for information is the same for all poor and homeless people, for the urban poor it is more critical. The fact that library services are different for poor people than for middle-class or affluent people has been stated in the literature (Auld, 2005; Bernardi, 2005). Library services have to be fitted into the lives of the poor if they are expected to benefit from the services that can help them change their lives. Holt and Holt (2010) point out that poverty is an economic condition that is related to national economic growth, unemployment rates, and workers' skill levels. Poor people—just like homeless people—can be unemployed, single parents, physically ill, addicted to drugs and alcohol, or lacking interpersonal and work skills. Holt and Holt say that because Americans place such high value on wealth, they tend to see poor people as inherently problematic (Holt & Holt, 2010).

Living in poverty brings with it a number of conditions that impact a poor person's use of libraries. Libraries in poor neighborhoods are usually in high-crime areas where it is not safe to be outside, and the library becomes a safe haven for children. These children most likely do not have enough to eat, and programs that provide food become a necessary component of successful children's programming (Holt, 2006). Librarians must understand the obstacles faced by the poor, be involved in all aspects of the community, and work with social services and other agencies to provide needed services and opportunities to the poor in their community.

Librarians analyze their communities and plan service responses to meet the needs. They offer traditional services to patrons, and special services are designed to serve the needs of some segments of the community.

These services are evaluated and adjusted to meet changing demographics. Special services for the poor should be offered in place of or in addition to other library services so that they reach the disadvantaged population in the service area. In developing library services for the poor, the librarian should conduct a needs assessment, plan programs to meet the needs, deliver innovative services, and evaluate the impact of these services on assessed needs (Holt & Holt, 2010). Some special services that help the poor include:

- Computer training labs with formal instruction on how to use the computers. Because some people who are poor cannot afford to buy computers or pay for Internet access, the library's computers provide access they would not otherwise have. The entire family gains access to Internet-based communication to conduct job searches and communicate with friends and family. They also are able to learn basic computer skills.
- Family literacy programs combined with children's programs help families become literate. These programs help parents become "first teachers" of their children (Abif, 1998).
- Housing referral provides timely information on housing authority programs.
- Jobs and career information assists with job searching skills, resume writing workshops, access to job listings, and online job applications. The centers should be staffed by librarians who provide instruction on how to use the resources provided in the job centers.
- Branch libraries located in poor neighborhoods, sometimes called equity branches, have modified library policies to suit the needs of the patrons in those neighborhoods.
- Community information and referral services help patrons learn about state agencies and nonprofit entities that provide support for the poor.
- Cultural and ethnic programming is related to the culture of the members of the neighborhood.
- Space is available for youth and children to hold performances such as talent shows and spelling bees.
- Humanities programming provides exposure to all aspects of the arts and relevant life issues as they relate to life experiences with which the poor can identify.
- Meeting places in the library provide less fortunate patrons with spaces where they can feel safe, feel welcome, and get help with life situations they may be facing.

Homeless people may have unique needs. Most are seeking food and shelter, and the library should have information on shelters and soup kitchens in the area. Having no fixed address prevents the homeless from taking advantage of some library programs, and librarians can help them get an address from a shelter so that they can get library cards. Thus, the library provides, at all times, essential information needed by the homeless.

Librarians serving the poor and homeless should be prepared to take services to where their patrons are. Outreach is an integral component of services to these groups and is vital to connecting with people in low-income communities, where patrons may not visit the library but do visit many social service agencies and churches. As part of this outreach, library resources should be placed in agencies or shelters where the poor and home-less are likely to go. Library programs such as literacy and GED services can be provided in the locations and perhaps in collaboration with these agen-cies. Outreach to these populations is not just about the library serving the citizens in its service area, it is also about the library being a proactive part-ner to increase the economic and educational security of its community (Brown & Neerman, 1988).

Smith (2005) suggests that librarians must be proactive in seeking oppor-tunities in low-income areas such as providing free reading materials in doc-tors' offices, day care centers, and malls. Outreach can take many forms, including bookmobiles, home delivery of library resources, and delivery of off-site programs. With the expansion of remote library services, it is recom-mended that public libraries implement online outreach. Houghton (2007) observed, "Our users, all of them, not just the kids are increasingly wired and libraries need to meet them on their own turf." Some of the strategies she recommends are listing your library in a variety of directories, listing your library events and services on local community websites and calendars, creating a profile for your library on social networking sites such as MySpace and Facebook, and offering assistance using instant messaging (IM). Audio and video content should be made accessible by making sure that podcasts are listed in podcast directories and audio content is transcribed using Dragon Software or MacSpeech (for Mac Users) (Houghton, 2007).

Holt (2006) outlines some strategies for attracting staff and continuing services for the poor:

- Solicit information from patrons about what their information needs are
- Deliver services at times that are convenient to patrons and at the right locations
- Make partnerships with agencies that know their neighborhoods and constituencies
- Publicize services in neighborhood venues such as churches and supermarkets
- Recognize that children lead their parents to things that they want, and plan family events that will bring both children and parents to the library

Holt (2006) also recommends cross-service use of library resources such as meeting rooms that can double as parent waiting rooms in which there are resources for parents to look at while they wait for their children.

Bullard (2005) outlines four guiding principles for implementing library services in urban areas:

- Empowerment
- Programs
- Partnerships (collaboration)
- Community

Empowerment is provided through services that directly solve immediate problems, which usually requires labor-intensive staff interactions with patrons. The programs are used to support empowerment and also carry out the library's mission. Reliance on partnerships and collaboration enables the library to join with community agencies in grant-in-aid funding, private fund-raising, program design, public relations, and marketing. Collaboration is both necessary and desirable because the urban environment has many overlapping clienteles, which dictates collaboration between groups if not actual participation. Bullard (2005) provides two outstanding examples of how collaboration works. The first, Ready to Learn Providence, is a collaboration between early childhood educators and the Providence After School Alliance to form a coalition of afterschool providers in which the library offers early childhood literacy programs and is involved in planning a neighborhood-based afterschool hub. The second is called AfterZones.

The third guiding principle involves the community setting: the library should provide a meeting place for neighborhood groups and a safe haven for the many latchkey children in these environments. A sense of place is said to contribute to the role of the library in fostering civic participation and developing social capital (Bullard, 2005).

CONCLUSION

This chapter has provided a review of services for special populations—people who are poor and homeless, people with physical disabilities, people with visual and hearing impairments, and older adults. These groups taken together make up a majority of prospective public library patrons. Libraries are already serving most of the patrons in their community using service responses recommended by the library profession. By modifying traditional services to fit the needs of the special populations in their community, they are living up to the Library Bill of Rights and also meeting ADA requirements to ensure that people with disabilities have equal access to information. Public libraries are serving traditional patrons, but also nonusers, who account for the prospective patrons that a public library is expected to serve.

ADDITIONAL READINGS

Holt, L. E., & Holt, G. E. (2010). *Public library services for the poor: Doing all we can.* Chicago: American Library Association.

Rothstein, P., & Schull, D. D. (Eds.). (2010). *Boomers and beyond: Reconsidering the role of libraries.* Chicago: American Library Association.

RESOURCES

ASCLA, http://www.ala.org/ascla/

Deaf Resource Library, http://www.deaflibrary.org/

Gallaudet University, http://vl2.gallaudet.edu/

Key resources for engagement of baby boomers in volunteerism, https://infopeople.org/sites/default/files/webinar/2012/02-23-2012/bibliography.pdf

Keys to engaging older adults, http://www.ala.org/offices/olos/toolkits/olderadults

National Association for the Deaf, http://www.nad.org/

National Coalition for the Homeless, http://www.nationalhomeless.org/

National Council for Aging, http://www.ncoa.org/

REFERENCES

Abif, K. (1998). At work in the children's room. In K. Venturella (Ed.), *Poor people and library services* (pp. 44–61). Jefferson, NC: McFarland.

Alexander, L. B. (2005). ADA resources for library and information professions. *Journal for Education for Library and Information Science, 46*(3), 10.

Alliance for Technology Access. (2002). Starting points: Eliminating barriers to people with disabilities. Retrieved from http://www.atacess.org/resources/acaw/documents/Starting_Points_v2.1_accessible.pdf

American Foundation for the Blind. Assistive technololgy. Retrieved May 8, 2013, from http://www.afb.org/section.aspx?FolderID=2&SectionID=4&TopicID=31

American Library Association (ALA). (n.d.). Library Bill of Rights. http://www.ala.org/advocacy/intfreedom/librarybill

American Library Association (ALA). (1990). Policy B.8.10: Library services to the poor. Retrieved from http://www.ala.org/aboutala/governance/policymanual/

American Library Association (ALA). (1996). Extending our reach: Reducing Homelessness through library engagement. Retrieved from http://www.ala.org/offices/extending-our-reach-reducing-homelessness-through-library-engagement-7

American Library Association (ALA). (2007). Library services for people with disabilities policy. Retrieved from http://www.ala.org/ala/mgrps/divs/ascla/asclaissues/libraryservices.cfm

American Library Association (ALA), Association of Specialized and Cooperative Library Agencies (ASCLA). (2001). Library services for people with disabilities policy. http://www.ala.org/ascla/asclaissues/libraryservices

American Library Association (ALA), Association of Specialized and Cooperative Library Agencies (ASCLA). (2004). Library service for people with disabilities policy. Retrieved September 16, 2010, from http://ala.org/ascla/asclaissues/libraryservices/

American Library Association (ALA), Reference and User Services Association (RUSA). (2013) *Library services to an aging population: 21 ideas for the 21st Century.* Retrieved April 30, 2013, from http://www.ala.org/rusa/sections/rss/rsssection/rsscomm/libraryservage/ideas21stcentury.

Americans with Dissabilities Act (ADA). (n.d.). http://www.ada.gov/pubs/ada.htm.

Auld, H. (2005). Library services in low-income urban communities. *Public Libraries, 44*(6), 320–320.

Ayers, S. (2006). The poor and homeless: An opportunity for libraries to serve. *Southeastern Librarian, 54*(1), 66–74.

Bell, L., & Peters, T. (2005). Digital library services for all. *American Libraries, 36*(8), 46–49.

Berliss, J. R. (1992). *Checklists for making library automation accessible to patrons with disabilities.* Madison, WI: Trace Research & Development Center.

Bernardi, J. (2005). The poor and the public library. *Public Libraries, 44*(6), 321–323.

Bopp, R. E., & Smith, L. C. (2011). *Reference and information services: An introduction* (4th ed.). Santa Barbara, CA: Libraries Unlimited.

Brown, M. E., & Neerman, J. (1988). Application of dissipative structures: Understanding the security of West Philadelphia. Unpublished manuscript, Wharton School, University of Pennsylvania.

Bullard, K. (2005). Four guiding principles. *Public Libraries, 44*(6), 9.

Butler R. N. (2008). Q&A Robert N. Butler. *Library Journal, 133*(2), 90.

Cylke, F., Moodie, M., & Fistick, R. (2007). Serving the blind and the physically handicapped in the United States of America. *Library Trends, 55*(4), 12.

Day, J. M. (1999). Online deafness and deaf culture information resources. *Web Sites 23*(1), 5–8.

DeLatte, M. (Ed.). (2008, September 16). Library accessibility: What you need to know. Retrieved from http://www.ala.org/ala/mgrps/divs/ascla/asclaprootools/accessibiltytipsheets/default.cfm

Epp, M. A. (2006). Closing the 95 percent gap: Library resource sharing for people with print disabilities. *Library Trends, 54*(3), 18.

Ethridge, J. (2005). Removing barriers for visually impaired users through assistive technology solutions. *Mississippi Libraries, 69*(4), 82–84.

Federal Register (2012). Annual update of poverty guidelines. Retrieved from http://www.gpo.gov/fdsys/pkg/FR-2012-01-26/html/2012-1603.htm

Freeman, S. A., & Mabry, M. G. (1991). The Americans with Disabilities Act (ADA). *Public Libraries, 31,* 112–114.

Gargano, C. (2008). Visually impaired gain greater access to digital information with the DAISY digital talking book. *EContent, 31*(6), 16–17.

Gehner, J. (2005). Poverty, poor people, and our priorities. *Reference and User Services Quarterly, 45*(2), 117–121.

Gehner, J. (2005). Libraries, low-income people, and social exclusion. *Public Library Quarterly, 29*(1), 39–47.

Gibson, M. (1977). Preparing librarians to serve handicapped individuals. *Journal of Education for Librarianship, 18*(2), 9.

Gieskes, L. (2009). Why librarians matter to poor people. *Public Library Quarterly, 28*(1), 49–57.

Goddard, M. L. (Ed.). (1996). *Guidelines for library and information services for the American deaf community.* Chicago: American Library Association.

Grace, P. (2000, May). No place to go (except the library). *American Libraries,* p. 3.

Gunde, M. G. (1992). Working with the Americans with Disabilities Act. *Library Journal, 117*(8), 41.

Hannah, K. (2003). Developing accessible library services. *Library & Information Update, 2*(11), 50.

Hersberger, J. (2005). The homeless and information needs and services. *Reference and User Services Quarterly, 44*(3), 199–202.

Hildreth, S. (2006). When baby boomers retire: Institute on services for baby boomers. Retrieved from http://www.library.ca.gov/newsletter/2006/2006fall/institute.html

Holt, G. E. (2006). Fitting library services into the lives of the poor. *Bottom Line: Managing Library Finances, 19*(4), 179–186.

Holt, L. E., & Holt, G. E. (2010). *Public library services for the poor: Doing all we can.* Chicago: American Library Association.

Homelessness and Poverty Task Force (HHTPF). (n.d.). http://www.hhptf.org/about

Houghton, J. S. (2007). Twenty steps to marketing your library online. *Journal of Web Librarianship, 1*(4), 89–90.

International Federation of Library Associations (IFLA). (2000). *Guidelines for Services for the Deaf and Hearing Impaired* (2nd ed., J. M. Day, Ed.). IFLA Professional Reports: 62.

Jeal, Y. (1996, June). Taking steps to ensure service for all. *Library Association Record, 98.*

Jeal, Y., Roper, V., & Ansell, E. (1996). Deaf people and libraries: Should there be special considerations? Part 2: material and technological developments. *New Library World, 97*(2), 13–18.

Josey, E. J. (1986). *Libraries, Coalitions and the Homeless.* Paper presented at the Annual conference of the American Library Association, New York City.

Kaufman-Scarborough, C., & Baker, S. M. (2005). Do people with disabilities believe the ADA has served their consumer interets? *Journal of Consumer Affairs, 39*(1), 1–26.

Lee, R. E. (1966). *Continuing education for adults through the American public library, 1833–1964.* Chicago: American Library Association.

Lilienthal, S. M. (2011, June 15). The problem is not the homeless: People living with substandard housing are in need of innovative library service. *Library Journal, 136*(11), 30–34.

Long, F. (1968, July). The Live Long and Like It Library Club: The Cleveland Public Library. *Library Trends, 17*(4), 68–71.

Marks, K. S. (2005). Deaf patrons in the rural library: The benefits of community networks. *Bookmobiles & Outreach Services, 8*(2), 7–19.

Marshall, J., & Marshall, V. (2010). New patterns of aging: Implications for libraries and cultural institutions. In P. Rothstein & D. D. Schull (Eds.), *Boomers and beyond: Reconsidering the role of libraries*. Chicago: American Library Association.

Meyer, J. (2001). *Age: 2000. Census 2000 Brief* (Vol. C2KBR/01-12). Washington, D.C.: U.S. Department of Commerce, U.S. Census Bureau.

National Alliance to End Homelessness. (2012). *The state of homelessness in America*, 2012. Retrieved October 4, 2012, from http://www.endhomelessness.org/library/entry/the-state-of-homelessness-in-america-2012.

National Library Service (NLS). (2007). NLS Factsheets: Books for the blind and physically handicapped individuals. Retrieved from http://www.loc.gov/nls/reference/factsheets/annual2007.html

National Technical Institute for the Deaf. (n.d.). http://www.rit.edu/overview/ntid

Noland, A. (2003). How Cleveland serves the deaf community. *Public Libraries*, 42(1), 2.

Parry, F. (2008). Improving library services to people with disabilities. *Electronic Library*, 26(1), 134–135.

Phinney, E. (1957). Library services to an aging population: Results of a post card survey. *ALA Bulletin*, 51(8), 607–609.

Potts, E. (1958, September). Senior citizens read and talk. *Wilson Library Bulletin*, 33(2), 42–43.

Prasad, P. (2009). Reference services to senior groups in the San Antonio Public Library. *Reference Librarian*, 50(1), 99–108.

Rodriguez, R., & Reed, M. (2003). Our family needs to read, too. *Public Libraries*, 42(1), 4.

Reference and User Services Association (RUSA). (2008). Guidelines for library and information services to older adults. Retrieved from http://www.ala.org/rusa/resources/guidelines/libraryservices

Rubin, R. J. (2001). *Planning for Library Services for People with Disabilities*. ASCLA Changing Horizon Series No. 5. Chicago: ASCLA.

Schmetzke, A. (2002). Web accessibility at university libraries and library schools. *Library Hi-Tech*, 19(1), 14.

SeniorNet. (2002). SeniorNetSurvey on Internet use. Retrieved from http://www.seniornet.org/php/default.php?PageID=6880&Version=0&Font=0.

Smith, S. (2005). Serving differently. *Public Libraries*, 44(6), 1.

Steinmetz, E. (2006). *Americans with disability: 2002* (Current Population Reports. ed., pp. 37).

Stewart B. McKinney Homeless Assistance Act. (1994). http://www.huduser.org/publications/homeless/mckin/intro.html

Tank, E., & Frederiksen, C. (2007). The DAISY standard: Entering the global virtual library. *Library Trends*, 55(4), 932–949.

U.S. Census Bureau. (2007). Census brief. Retrieved from http://www.census.gov/prod/3/97pubs/cenbr975.pdf.

U.S. Census Bureau. (2012). Nearly 1 in 5 people have a disability in the U.S. Retrieved April 27, 2013, from http://www.census.gov/newsroom/releases/archives/miscellaneous/cb12-134.html

U.S. Department of Labor, Bureau of Labor Statistics. (2012). Occupational employment statistics. Retrieved from http://www.bls.gov/oes/.

Vavrek, B. (1995). *Rural and small libraries: Providers for lifelong learning.* Washington, D.C.: U.S. Department of Education, Office of Educational Research and Improvement, Educational Resources Information Center.

Venturella, K. M. (1998). *Poor people and library services.* Jefferson, NC: McFarland.

Wade, G. L. (2003, April). Serving the visually impaired. *Portal: Libraries and the Academy, 3*(2), 7. Retrieved from Project Muse website, doi:10.1353/pla.2003.0048

Walling, L. L. (2004). Educating students to serve information seekers with disabilities. *Journal of Education for Library and Information Science, 45*(2), 9.

World Health Organization (WHO). (2012). Visual impairment and blindness. Retrieved from http://www.who.int/mediacentre/factsheets/fs282/en/

APPENDIX

Guidelines for Library and Information Services to Older Adults

1. Acquire current data about the older population and incorporate it into planning and budgeting.[1]

   1.1. Conduct surveys on a regular basis of the older population and the aging service providers in the community, including their numbers, demographic characteristics, and other information, such as their location and housing; educational, socioeconomic and ethnic background; religious organizations and other groups to which they belong; agencies that serve them; and the local media that targets older adults in the community.

   1.2. Supplement surveys with focus groups and user studies among the community's older population to determine their needs and interests and to gauge how services, collections and programs might be made more appropriate and relevant to this population.

   1.3. Collect data on the specific and varied information needs of older adults due to language, culture, education, income, Internet skills and access, gender identity/expression, sexual orientation, and age.

   1.4. Utilize the above data in combination with the more general informational needs basic to older adults in their everyday lives. Such subjects include: health, health care, social security, financial planning, housing, independent living, elder law, caregiving (including grandparenting), lifelong learning (including adult literacy and computer skills), community service, civic engagement, and volunteering. The library's collections, programs, and informational services should reflect the diverse interests and needs of older adults.

   1.5. Ensure that any services that target older adults are an integral and ongoing part of the library's operations and budget. Additional funding may be required for collections, accessibility equipment/software, and the time expended by library staff in services to older adults and community. If a special grant or external funding is sought to support a pilot or demonstration program, consider how the program will be integrated into the library's regular budget and services at the end of the grant.

Source: From *Library Services to an Aging Population Committee, Reference Services Section, Reference and User Services Association of the American Library Association* (1987; revised 1999; approved 2008). Used with permission from the American Library Association.

1.6. Involve older adults in the library's planning process by establishing an advisory committee. This committee might include older adults who are regular library users; library volunteers, staff, board members, or members of the library's Friends group; and leaders of organizations of older adults and other community organizations.

2. **Ensure that the special needs and interests of older adults in your community are reflected in the library's collections, programs, and services.**

   2.1 Appoint a librarian to act as a coordinator of services to older adults, ensuring that there is at least one designated staff member monitoring and developing the library's collections and services with older adults in mind.

   2.2 Consider how the library can be made more visible, more welcoming, and more relevant to older adult users.

   2.3 Advertise the library's services and website in local newspapers, magazines, radio or television programs that target older adults, and in senior centers, nutrition programs, and residential housing.

   2.4 Offer to speak to organizations of older adults about the library's services on a regular basis.

   2.5 Establish an ongoing liaison with agencies that serve older adults (especially senior centers that employ activity coordinators) to explore cooperative programming, recruit volunteers or friends of the library, and seek suggestions for programs or services that would encourage library use.

   2.6 Work with state library agencies that may provide staff training and development and information resources for older adults.

3. **Make the library's collections and physical facilities safe, comfortable and inviting for all older adults.**

   3.1 Evaluate your library's accessibility by older adults with physical, visual, aural, reading and other disabilities, according to the Accessibility Guidelines for Buildings and Facilities of the Americans with Disabilities Act.

   3.2 Consider providing at least one wheelchair in the library for public use.

   3.3 Accommodate users for whom prolonged standing is difficult by placing chairs or stools near stacks, information desks, checkout areas, computer terminals, and other areas. If possible, create a "Senior Space," using easy chairs gathered in an area adjacent to books and magazines of interest to older adults.

3.4 Consider placing materials frequently used by older adults on easily accessible shelves.

3.5 Place paperbacks, clearly labeled and well spaced, in areas of the library that are especially well lit, accommodating older adults who prefer paperbacks over heavier and more cumbersome hardback books.

3.6 Assure that spacing between shelving accommodates users in wheelchairs.

3.7 Ensure that signage is clear, Brailled (where appropriate), and readily visible to all, including users in wheelchairs. Library brochures should be in at least 14-point font type.

3.8 Provide at least one computer station prominently labeled and installed with large type software for older adults with low-vision. If needs warrant and resources are available, acquire other assistive technology such as a stand-alone Reading Machine which speaks the book's text to a blind reader; speech synthesizer and related software; low-tech magnification and other devices.

3.9 Provide TTY access, closed-captioned videotapes, and assistive listening systems to older adults with hearing disabilities.

3.10 Acquire and make available books and periodicals in large print.

4. **Make the library a focal point for information services to older adults.**

4.1 Cooperate with local Area Agencies on Aging, senior nutrition programs, senior volunteer programs, and others in the aging service provider network by advertising their service and making their publications and other information more readily accessible. The library can provide an invaluable service by organizing and consolidating information about government and community programs and services available to older adults.

4.2 Consider developing or expanding the library's Web site to provide links to the sites of organizations of older adults, government departments and agencies serving older adults, newspapers and other Web sites whose focus is older adults.

4.3 Ensure that the library's collection includes materials that are pertinent for caregivers of older adults, for their children or other family members, and for professional caregivers in the community.

5. Target the older population in library programming.

5.1 Incorporate adequate funding for programs, materials, and services for older adults in the library's operating budget, and actively seek supplemental funding through partnerships with other agencies, organizations, and foundations interested in serving older adults.

5.2 Plan programs each year that specifically target older adults and enhance their ability to remain independent and skillful library users. Publicizing such programs can heighten the library's visibility among the older population.

5.3 Select themes for programs that deal with specific interests of older adults identified through user surveys, focus groups, or circulation statistics reflecting borrowing patterns by older adults.

5.4 Plan programs for specific age groups or generations within the older population, being aware that interests and information needs vary greatly.

5.5 Include intergenerational programs and participate in intergenerational projects sponsored by others in the community. Consider partnerships with local schools, daycare facilities or community organizations.

5.6 Pursue other opportunities for cooperative programming with partners such as community and senior centers; Area Agencies on Aging and other community agencies; and educational institutions offering continuing educational programs for older adults. Cooperative efforts might involve active participation in planning and delivering programs, assistance in advertising programs, or providing book displays and booklists in conjunction with the library's programs.

5.7 Consider providing computer and Internet courses specifically designed for older adults to accommodate a slower pace of instruction, provide sufficient time to develop "mousing skills," and allow for the possibility that some older adults may have visual, physical, or hearing disabilities. If possible, include individual tutoring provided by peers or others.

5.8 Explore opportunities to provide library services and programming to older adults outside the library, such as in senior or community centers, nursing homes, and senior housing units. Consider offering computer and Internet training in these locations.

5.9 Use library displays to combat ageism or the stereotypes in our society about older adults.

5.10 Provide opportunities for older adults to volunteer in the library.

5.11 Create opportunities for lifelong learning programs.

6. **Reach out to older adults in the community who are unable to travel to the library.**

6.1 Survey community needs and consider library budget planning to accommodate possible increases in demand for outreach services such as delivery of library materials by mail and mobile library services. Analyze community demographics, population forecasts, and housing trends to plan to meet this need effectively.

6.2 Offer the library's services to assistive living, alternative housing, senior day care, congregate meals sites, senior community centers, nursing homes and senior residential or care homes in the community. Also offer assistance to older adults who are confined to private residences or who are unable to carry library materials home.

6.3 Advertise the library's services through local media, public health agencies, and other agencies that work with older adults.

6.4 Eliminate waiting lists for library services through innovative approaches to delivery of materials, a redistribution of personnel, or establishment of a volunteer delivery system. Partner with Regional Libraries for the Blind and Physically Handicapped to expand available services.

7. **Train the library's staff to serve older adults with courtesy and respect.**

7.1 Provide sensitivity training to staff at all levels to make them aware of difficulties older adults may have in using the library, and how to make the library a more welcoming and comfortable place for older adults.

7.2 Train staff to recognize and combat ageism and stereotypes about older adults.

7.3 Ensure that all staff are aware of any special services the library offers that may be of interest to older adults, such as home delivery service, a talking books collection, a service to retrieve materials from the stacks, reading aids, or waiving of fines or fees.

7.4 Promote the employment of older adults as professional and support staff members.

8. Bibliography

Architectural and Transportation Barriers Compliance Board, (2002). *ADA Accessibility Guidelines for Buildings and Facilities (ADAAG)*. Retrieved June 6, 2008, from http://www.access -board.gov/adaag/html/adaag.htm

Association for Library Service to Children, American Library Association, (2004). "Books for Children Portraying Aging and Older Characters in a Positive Light." Retrieved June 6, 2008, from http://www.gwumc.edu/cahh/booklist/booklist_2004 1110.pdf

International Longevity Center–USA, New York, NY, (2006). *Ageism in America*. Retrieved June 6, 2008, from http://www .ilcusa.org/pages/publications/ageism-caregiving-sleep/ageism-in-america.php

Mates, Barbara T. (2003). *5-Star Programming and Services for Your 55+ Library Customers*. American Library Association, (ALA Programming Guides). Paperback.

Missouri State Library, Jefferson City, MO, (2002). *Serving Seniors: A Resource Manual for Missouri Libraries*. Retrieved June 6, 2008, from http://www.sos.mo.gov/library/development/ services/seniors/manual/

Rubin, Rhea. (1993). *Intergenerational Programming, a How-To-Do-It Manual for Librarians*. Neal-Schuman Publishers, Inc.

PART IV

Developing the Adult Services Librarian

"Education is not filling a pail but the lighting of a fire."
—William Butler Yeats

CHAPTER 11

Competence and Professional Development for the Adult Services Librarian

This chapter reviews competencies needed by the adult services librarian and outlines the need for professional development.

Competencies for librarians begin with *Core Competencies of Librarianship*, which outlines the knowledge and skills that each person graduating from an American Library Association (ALA)-accredited master's program should have. They also form a benchmark for skills and knowledge needed by any individual taking on or aspiring to gain employment in a professional position in a library. The *Core Competencies of Librarianship* were developed over almost a decade of work by various groups around the country. The first Congress on Professional Education was held in 1999 in Washington, D.C. The Presidential Task Force on Library Education presented the final draft of the *Core Competencies of Librarianship* was presented to the ALA Executive Board, and the draft was approved at their fall 2008 meeting. The final statement was approved and adopted as policy by the ALA Council on January 27, 2009, during the 2009 Midwinter Meeting in Denver, Colorado (ALA, 2009). The ALA's core competencies of librarianship are grouped into eight categories: (1) foundations of the profession, (2) information resources, (3) organization of recorded knowledge and information, (4) technical knowledge and skills, (5) reference and user services, (6) research, (7) continuing education and lifelong learning, and (8) administration and management. These core skills and knowledge form the foundation upon which more focused knowledge and skills of adult services librarianship are built (ALA, 2009). All of the ALA core competencies come into play when providing quality services and programming for adults in the public library.

Adult services librarians require additional specialized knowledge bases to be able to provide quality adult services and programming. These include (1) services to diverse population, including cultural competence; (2) services to special population, including older adults, people with disabilities, and the homeless; and (3) knowledge of the resources and government social services agencies that can help provide support for these groups. Because adult services librarianship overlaps with reference librarianship, competencies outlined by the Reference and User Services Association (RUSA) are also critical components of the necessary knowledge and skills for adult services librarians. By gathering the various competency lists, a librarian will be able to complete a through self-assessment of his or her current knowledge and skills, which will aid the individual in prioritizing new competencies to be gained as well in constructing a personal plan for acquiring the needed knowledge and skills over a doable timeline.

The emergence of technology has changed the role of adult services librarians from making information accessible to patrons to training patrons to use technology to access resources. Gottesman (2002) explained that this paradigm shift means that librarians are now expected to assist patrons as they integrate materials into their research process at the time they are conducting research. With the development of the web and especially Web 2.0, Mathews and Pardue (2009) observe that "librarians continue to look like IT (information technology) professionals" (p. 257) and that as technology continues to change, so do the skill sets required by librarians. They challenge library and information science (LIS) professions to examine what skills are necessary in the age of information (Mathews & Pardue, 2009).

Library 2.0 is the Web 2.0 application used to design and deliver library services. Various library and information science professionals have tried to identify competencies that librarians in the twenty-first century must have. Partridge, Lee, and Munro (2010) explain that the lists of competencies tend to be tailored to the unique context of a particular library situation and to focus more on interpersonal skills and less on technological skills.

Peltier-Davis (2009) produced a 14-point checklist with which librarians can implement Library 2.0 in their libraries. The list includes having the ability to take risks and work under pressure, being skilled at enabling and fostering change, having a sense of humor, and becoming an advocate for the profession. Saint-Onge (2009) articulated a list of "must have" competencies for law librarians who are using Library 2.0, including being able to see the big picture; establishing closer connection to information available through the library, and not to the library itself, as a physical entity; embracing the role of teacher; adopting a market approach to service design and delivery; and having the confidence to take up the challenge and embrace the future.

The shift in focus from attitudinal skills to information technology (IT) skills was provided by King (2007), who created a list of over a dozen IT competencies for Library 2.0, including being able to post a blog; create, upload, and edit photos; and edit videos, podcasts, and screencasts. He also identified related large-scale IT skills that include understanding how basic IT functions work within a library setting and how they complement a traditional physical library.

King also thinks that librarians 2.0 should understand the concept of creative commons and the basics of copyright. Other researchers, such as Huwe (2004), insist that librarians must be current with web content creation skills using HTML, CSS, and XML as well as website administration to support a library's development and information content creation requirements. Because library and information science programs cannot provide instruction on all of these competencies within their curriculum, some are demanding that students entering their programs have computer-based competencies (Kluegel, 2003).

A more focused and comprehensive discussion of the competencies for librarians in the twenty-first century is articulated in the publication "Competency Index for the Library Field" by WebJunction and published by OCLC. The publication identifies 12 competency sets for different library environments and includes competencies for personal and interpersonal as well as public services. For the adult services librarian the relevant competencies include (1) personal and interpersonal competencies, (2) public service competencies, (3) library management competencies, and (4) core technology competencies (WebJunction, 2009).

PERSONAL AND INTERPERSONAL COMPETENCIES FOR ADULT SERVICES LIBRARIES

According to WebJunction (2009), clear and effective communication is the basis for success in one's relationship with co-workers, managers, users, and all stakeholders, and communication competencies are integral to customer services. Librarians are therefore expected to communicate effectively verbally and in writing. They should demonstrate good public speaking skills and good customer service behavior.

GENERAL ADULT PROGRAMMING COMPETENCIES

For this category, the librarian is able to design, implement, and sponsor library programs that offer information, special skills, or entertainment. The librarian promotes library programs in the community, coordinating with marketing efforts and developing programs that acknowledge and celebrate the community's culture. Further, the librarian identifies program venues outside of the library and uses appropriate evaluation strategies that have been described in previous chapters to evaluate programs. Adult service librarians use these results to provide future programming efforts.

COMMUNITY RELATIONS COMPETENCIES

As stated throughout this book, to design effective services, adult services librarians have to know what their communities need. They should conduct needs analysis and user surveys. They must to be able to demonstrate the library's impact on and value to the community. They build support for the library using the most appropriate methods among different community entities. Librarians maintain positive public relations though communicating and promoting the library's values, service accomplishments, and needs of stakeholders. They must be able to devise strategies and initiate strategic partnerships with community organizations (WebJunction, 2009).

PUBLIC SERVICES COMPETENCIES

Most adult services librarians are expected to provide services to diverse populations and special populations such as older adults and other underserved groups. As stated earlier, librarians analyze demographic and other data collected about the community and develop services to meet the needs and interests of community members. Adult services include outreach programming that librarians have identified through relevant methods to determine the interests of adults in the community.

ADULT SERVICES AND OUTREACH

Adult services librarians should be able to define and implement outreach services to patrons who are unable to come to the library. They also try to use Internet tools and social networking media to engage and provide services to users. Gutsche (2010) provides public service competencies related to social networking and adult services. She lists skills and knowledge associated with social networking:

- Understands and articulates the importance of engaging with users in nontraditional ways that extend beyond the physical library
- Instigates and evaluates tools and identifies those most applicable to the library services and community needs (blogs, wikis, widget/toolbars, social network, and other engaging online tools)
- Explores the potential of social networking to interact with users and meet their information needs
- Assists users with setting up and using web tools and participating in social networking communities

- Understands the unique opportunities, norms, and limitations of online engagement with users
- Devises strategies to keep up with emerging tools and techniques, and connects with professional communities to seek and share best practices

OLDER ADULT PROGRAMMING AND SERVICE COMPETENCIES

Adult services librarians design and implement library services to meet the needs and interest of older adults in the community. Specifically, librarians analyze demographic and other data collected about older adults in the community and develop a wide variety of services to meet their needs and interests. Librarians understand the range of ages of older adults (baby boomers to the elderly) and identify their particular needs and interests, acknowledging the range of skills, knowledge, strengths, and limitations they bring to the library. Librarians identify agencies, institutions, and organizations serving older adults and maintain regular communication with each agency, institution, and organization for the purpose of maintaining up-to-date information on the services they offer to older adults. When appropriate, librarians partner with organizations within the community that have compatible purposes with the library related to serving older adults. Developing cooperative services and programs extends and enhances services to older adults.

READERS' ADVISORY (RA) COMPETENCY

Core competencies, while at times viewed as individual capabilities, also encompass the knowledge, skills, and attitudes that characterize a group or unit, such as RA. They can be used as a tool to develop and continually provide superior services to library patrons (Naylor, 2000). Core competencies help create a vision for RA and allow for better human resource planning and more effective training programs (Naylor, 2000).

The Ontario Public Library Association (OPLA) (2010) constructed core competencies for RA around collection knowledge, reader service skills, RA conversations, and reader development. OPLA's adds to the competencies of a background understanding of why people read and how diverse interests, needs, and backgrounds affect reading choices. This expands RA from working with sources and readers to working with the reading theories to better understand both (OPLA, 2010).

Others make providing RA a competency itself (New Jersey Library Association, 2002, http://www.njlibrarytrustees.org/; King County Library System, http://www.kcls.org/). The question then becomes, how does one develop RA competencies? Van Fleet (2008) looked at library and information science programs and the place of RA in their curricula, noting that as an area of study, its marginalization continues to persist, through to a lesser extent than in the past. She notes that most RA courses address three levels of student learning: (1) knowledge of the RA literature base as well as a variety of genres; (2) basic skills and techniques of RA services, including hands-on practice, and (3) an attitude toward readers and reading. Van Fleet reported that about half of the master's programs in library and information science offer courses that cover RA. While some formal training is available, personal professional development planning may be the more accessible route for a specialization in readers' advisory.

Minnesota has developed a career renewal program to assist library employees as they work to develop individual personal development plans to improve their skills and broaden their knowledge in areas relevant to their current jobs as well as areas of interest related to possible future responsibilities. One of the competency areas identified and developed is RA service. Minnesota groups competencies into eight areas: background in fiction and nonfiction; people as readers and readers as people; appeal of books; RA transaction; managing; teaching; professional knowledge and attitudes; and general competencies. Within each area are not only skills and knowledge competencies, but also attitudinal disposition and personal plans for reading.

Competency in RA can be viewed as an individual quality or as quality collectively maintained by a group or unit within the library. As RA appears to be developing into an important and growing service area (Van Fleet, 2008), librarians may want to incorporate RA competencies into their mission and goals.

RA is a mainstay service in public libraries in the United States, Canada, and Europe. Moyer (2007) tells us that the most consistent use of a library by patrons is to borrow leisure reading, usually fiction. It is imperative that adult services librarians be trained to provide RA services to patrons. The competencies needed for RA, according to WebJunction (2009), are related to assisting users with choosing popular and recreational reading, viewing, and listening materials. The knowledge and skills needed include:

- Demonstrating a broad knowledge of the library's collections and a wide range of materials of interest to library readers
- Demonstrating the ability to read widely, formulate connections between resources, and converse with users about the resources
- Understanding the theory of appeal, listening carefully to information elicited from users, and basing recommendations on an interpretation of what appeals to the users
- Identifying and recommending a selection of materials that aligns with what appeals to the users

- Creating booklists, read alikes, read around, book talks, displays, electronic documents, and special tools to increase access to library resources and promote their use
- Using web tools (blog, wikis, and social networks) to encourage participation and contributions from readers
- Seeking feedback from readers on recommended materials and adjusting future recommendations accordingly

Adult services librarians need to develop strategies and sources to stay well informed as a readers' adviser. The skills and knowledge required for these include:

- Identifying and using a variety of online and print RA resources to identify material
- Maintaining an ongoing knowledge of major new authors, and of fiction genres to nonfiction subjects and current releases
- Keeping current with popular culture through various channels
- Connecting with professional communities to seek and share best practice for reading advisory (WebJunction, 2009)

MULTICULTURALISM AND DIVERSITY

The need to have diversity training within the library school curricula has been discussed in the literature, and the issue has been discussed in this book under other headings such as "diversity awareness" and "multicultural librarianship." The ALA *Standards for Accreditation of Masters' Programs in Library and Information Studies* in 1992 added multiculturalism to the mission, curriculum, and student's standards, and these were reconfirmed in the *2008 Standards for Accreditation of Master's Programs in Library and Information Studies.*

Even though most of the literature on diversity focuses on issues of underrepresentation and the importance of recruiting and retaining minority faculty and students, some researchers have recommended items to be addressed in the development of a course on cultural diversity. In the absence of a coherent way of including diversity in the curriculum, some researchers recommend linking diversity to real-life situations. Jeng (1997) suggests that a "good pedagogy is to establish the missing link in the classroom between lectures and LIS life is the scenario approach: to present specific scenarios that can happen to individual librarians in real libraries" (p. 335). "To achieve diversity in substance as well as in form, libraries have to open their arms to all perspectives and experiences. This requires competency in matters of cultural pluralism that are not intuitive and must be learned like any other essential skill" (Smith, 2008, p. 143). Directors of public libraries must therefore require cultural awareness as a skill for librarians who serve diverse populations.

CULTURAL COMPETENCE

Cultural competence is an integral part of diversity awareness. Librarians need to have cultural competence in order to have the skills to serve diverse populations. The concept has become so important that the Association of College and Research Libraries' (ACRL) Diversity Standards created cultural competencies for academic libraries. The standards are intended to emphasize the need to serve and advocate for diverse constituencies. "Cultural competency" is defined by the Michigan Education Association (2010) as:

- Having a congruent set of behaviors, attitudes, and policies that enables effective working relationships in cross-cultural situations
- Responding respectfully and effectively to people of all cultures, languages, classes, races, ethnic backgrounds, and religions
- Recognizing, affirming, and valuing the worth of individuals, families, and communities
- Protecting and preserving the dignity of each person

"Cultural competency goes beyond diversity awareness. It denotes an individual's ability to effectively interact with and among others whose values, behaviors and environments are different from one's own" (Michigan Education Association, 2010, par. 2).

Mestre (2010) explained that gaining cultural competency is a developmental process that evolves over an extended period and involves an ability to understand the needs of diverse populations and interact effectively with people from other cultures. She points out that while diversity training aims to make individuals culturally aware and sensitive, training for cultural competency is geared toward training individuals to recognize the various learning and communication styles of others, and also to be able to adjust one's habits based on those style differences in order to best interact with cultures other than one's own.

According to Rios Balderrama (2006), to achieve cultural competency, we must (1) be interested in learning from and with people from other cultures (2) self-assess our own cultural values and consider how we obtained them, and (3) grow our competency levels from awareness to knowledge and experience. Cultural competency has implications for library patrons seeking to use information. Patrons need to be able to articulate their information needs beyond generating language. Patrons who are both native and non-native speakers may have difficulty recalling the exact or correct terms needed to express their ideas. Personal beliefs might prevent patrons from requesting certain information they need (Helton, 2010).

Josey and Abdullahi (2002) proposed that library schools should plan for systematic inclusion of intercultural issues within the curriculum. They identify four characteristics that students can develop with this change in curriculum:

- Sociocultural consciousness
- An affirming attitude toward students from diverse backgrounds
- Commitment and skills to act as agents of change
- Culturally responsive teaching practice (Josey & Abdullahi, 2002 p.12)

Each library and information science program must strive to continuously update its curriculum to include cultural competency as one of the skills needed for serving patrons in our increasingly diverse populations.

Adapting from the health literature, Press and Diggs-Hobson (2005) suggest that it is time for librarians to codify cultural competencies. They name attitude, knowledge, and skills as the three broad competency areas. Attitude implies multicultural awareness and sensitivity that lead to a comfortable working relationship with patrons when differences exist. Culturally competent librarians should also routinely self-assess their own cultural beliefs and values and how they might impact patrons and colleagues.

CONTINUING EDUCATION AND PROFESSIONAL DEVELOPMENT

Librarians in the twenty-first century must stay current with the technology that is the dominant feature in the delivery of library services. According to the ALA, "continuous learning is critical to renewing the expertise and skills needed to assist patrons in the information age. Library workers must continually expand their knowledge in order to keep up with the rate of change" (ALA, n.d.). The technological competencies in the twenty-first century, according to Mathews and Pardue, are needed if librarians are going to continue to look like information technology communication professionals. They point out that as "technology continues to change, so, too, do the skill sets required by librarians" (Mathews & Pardue, 2009, p. 256). Gutsche (2010) also said that "an increasing number of positions in libraries are moving closer to the technical end of the scale and consequently technology competencies are starting to comprise an ever growing piece of the performance pie, impacting every job in the library" (p. 30).

Participating in professional development and continuing education activities is an integral component of the competencies of adult services librarians. As stated earlier, the skills and education needed by librarians in the

Library 2.0 environment cannot be acquired through formal education. To stay current after leaving library and information service programs, other professional and continuing education activities are needed. Professional associations—including the ALA, the Public Library Association (PLA), and other library and information science associations such as the American Society for Information Science and Technology (ASIST)—provide continuing education workshops during their annual conferences, and they conduct specialized training activities between conferences.

Conferences

Woolls (2007) considers conference attendance to be one of the essential components of keeping current with trends and developments in the library field. Researchers document some of the values of conferences as educational opportunities for librarians and opportunities for socializing and networking (Harrison, 2010). In a study by Vega and Connell (2007), respondents indicated that conferences provided opportunities for "professional rejuvenation." Conferences are also said to give new life to a career that can sometimes get old (Vega & Connell, 2007). Librarians should try to attend one or two conferences a year if they have the funding to do so. Conferences should be considered a strong weapon in their professional arsenal of professional development options.

Workplace Training

On-the-job training, or workplace training, is another avenue through which librarians can receive training. Workplace learning is recognized as a valid approach for newly employed librarians. Workplace training plays an important role in the acquisition of the knowledge and skills required to keep abreast of the ever-changing technological landscape. Davis and Davis (1998) contend that library workplace training is one of the primary methods of investing in human capital and increasing the library personnel's competence. Diversity training and cultural competency are competencies that have been documented as being acquired on the job by librarians who did not get such training in their library science education (Mestre, 2010).

Training for RA Services

As stated earlier, RA services are the mainstay of services in public libraries. Moyer (2007) observed that most of the literature on RA is about continuing education for professionals and that there are few articles about RA education at the graduate level (Moyer & Weech, 2005). A review of the literature, according to Shearer and Burgin (2001), indicates that few graduates of ALA-accredited library science master's degree programs have been prepared to provide RA services.

In discussing the education of the public librarian, Moyer (2007) noted that "it became clear that librarians get as much, if not significantly more of their training for RA from continuing education events" (p. 71). RA events are featured at PLA conferences as well as ALA conferences. Moyer (2007) concluded that the literature presents little evidence that professional library science education is preparing future librarians to provide RA services.

Professional Development through the Virtual World

Online education has grown tremendously, and librarians are major participants. They are involved in developing all types of services and library resources to support online education. It is therefore not surprising that they have become involved in using the virtual environment as means of sustainable learning and collaboration. Second Life (SL) is an example of such an environment. It is a three-dimensional virtual world in which librarians have taught or co-taught classes and created interactive learning resources to support distance education.

Some researchers have documented the different ways in which librarians have been active in SL (Bell and Truemen, 2008; Mon, 2009; Ostrander, 2008). The Community Virtual Library (http://www.info island.org/) provides the forum for some of the SL activities. It provides free library resources to the residents of SL. Librarians have formed professional relationships, and hosted professional activities and meetings. Webber and Nahl (2011) articulate the values of such virtual worlds for professional interaction; they draw from expertise around the world as there is no travel cost or travel time, making it easy for people to participate. They conclude that the "social presence" in the virtual space makes it possible for people to chat and get to know each other. Examples of professional development in SL include Virtual World Best Practices in Education (2010), which was a 48-hour continuous event that enabled people from different time zones to participate, and there were formal presentations, demonstrations, and workshops.

The University of Illinois offered a series of workshops between 2007 and 2009 on virtual world librarianship by establishing a library presence in SL. They used the Community Virtual Library to offer classes for librarians and students. Other activities in SL include tours, exhibits, and special events such as Webber and Nahl's series on information literacy. Upcoming events are listed on the SL educator's calendar. There is also a long-running Virtual World Educators' Roundtable that meets every Tuesday at 2:30 p.m.

Blakiston (2011) contends that one way to obtain, develop, and sustain new knowledge is to transform the library into a learning organization, that is, attending conferences is no longer sufficient for staying current in the field. Rather, continual learning needs to become part of the working environment in the library. Senge (2006) first articulated the concept of learning communities in his book *The Fifth Discipline: The Art and Practice of Learning Organizations*. He defines a learning organization as a place where "people continually expand their capacity to create the results they truly desire, where new and expansive patterns of thinking are nurtured, collective aspiration is set free, and where people continually learn how to learn together" (p. 3). He states that by transforming into learning organizations, libraries will move beyond traditional approaches to development by weaving ongoing learning into the organization (library) as a whole.

Continuing professional education has flourished through the creation of learning communities. Librarians are participating in learning communities through organizations such as WebJunction, which have facilitated Learning 2.0 communities, including the "23 things" created by Charlotte Mecklenburg Public Library. In this program, the staff is encouraged to go through an online program where they are presented with 23 things that they needed to know. Participants are linked together through an official 23 Things site, and they were required to create their own blogs through which they interacted and learned from each other. Signorelli and Reed (2011) maintain that learning communities are dynamic and sustainable over time. Continuing education and professional education of librarians will continue to be needed, and directors of public libraries should endeavor to use all available techniques—physical as well as virtual—to make sure that librarians stay engaged and involved in the ongoing lifelong learning that the profession requires.

EDUCATING STUDENTS TO SERVE PEOPLE WITH DISABILITIES

Research emphasizes the importance of training librarians (Hannah, 2003). Epp (2006) found that "many librarians lack the necessary training in the use of technology, tools and sources of alternate formats and adaptive or assistive technology." She went on to say that users need expert trainers with pedagogical backgrounds who not only utilize the technology, but also know how to assess learning styles, teach, and overcome barriers to effective use of the new technology (Epp, 2006 p. 423). Many opportunities for the needed training are provided through workshops and staff development activities. Library science programs should include more training in dealing with underserved and special populations in their curriculum.

Studies on how library schools are preparing students to serve people with disabilities have been reported in the literature (Gibson, 1977; Schmetzke, 2002). The role of trained staff in the delivery of services to people who are poor, are homeless, or who have disabilities is emphasized in the literature. Jeal, Roper, and Ansell (1996) recommend deaf awareness training (DAT) for people working with those who are hearing impaired and also training in basic sign language (BSL). They say, "We need to train staff in very general terms in how to react to persons with disabilities" (Jeal, Roper, & Ansell, 1996, p. 14). Library staff must be trained to identify and locate materials in their own libraries, on the Internet, and also through interlibrary loan. They need to develop more accessible library websites, catalogs, and online databases (Schmetzke, 2002). Walling (2004) recommends that adaptive or assistive technology (AT) be a major component of the training. An increased understanding of the benefits of AT can help to improve services to people with disabilities, and library and information science programs should provide more information about AT. Regardless of their area of specialization, students must be made aware of the requirements of the Americans with Disabilities Act (ADA) and the barriers to information that people with disabilities face. Course content often includes examples of information needs and information seeking, and some of the examples should include people with disabilities. Walling (2004) also says that whenever course content includes discussion of service provision, collections development, or resources, there should be some discussion of alternative methods for service delivery, alternative formats, and resources for identifying and accessing them.

The programs and services of the National Library Service for the Blind and Physically Handicapped (NLS) should be discussed. Faculty should be involved in the ALA sections that deal with services to people with disabilities or underserved (e.g., ASCLA, LSSP) and any agencies involved with services to these groups of patrons.

REFERENCES

Abram, S. (2005). Web 2.0, huh?! Library 2.0, librarian 2.0. *Information Outlook, 9* (12), 3.

American Library Association (ALA). (n.d.) Continuing education. Retrieved from http://www.ala.org/educationcareers/archive/ce/continuingeducation

American Library Association (ALA). (2009). Core competences. Retrieved from http://www.ala.org/educationcareers/careers/corecomp/corecompetences

Association of College & Research Libraries (ACRL). (2011). ACRL diversity standards: Cultural competency for academic libraries. Retrieved from http://www.ala.org/ala/mgrps/divs/acrl/standards/diversity_draft.pdf

Bell, L., & Truemen, R. B. (2008). *Virtual worlds, real libraries: Librarians and educators in Second Life and other multi-user virtual environments.* Medford, NJ: Information Today.

Berry, J. (2000). Educating for library jobs. *Library Journal, 125*(17), 1.

Blakiston, R. (2011). Building knowledge, skills, and abilities: Continual learning in the new information landscape. *Journal of Library Administration, 51*(7/8), 728–743.

Davis, J. R., & Davis, A. B. (1998). *Effective training strategies: A comprehensive guide to maximizing learning in organizations.* San Francisco: Berret-Koehler.

Eltruk. (2002). Diversity and cultural competency. *Library Management, 23,* 5–7.

Epp, M. A. (2006). Closing the 95 percent gap: Library resource sharing for people with print disabilities. *Library Trends, 54*(3), 18.

Feng, A. (n.d.). Corporate librarian 2.0: New core competencies. Retrieved August 23, 2010, from http://units.sla.org/division/dpht/division_info/travel -presentations/feng_essay.pdf

Ghosh, M. (2009). Information professionals in the open access era: The competencies, challenges and new roles. *Information Development, 25*(1), 33–42.

Gibson, M. (1977). Preparing librarians to serve handicapped individuals. *Journal of Education for Librarianship, 18*(2), 9.

Gottesman, L. (2002). Digital reference: Bringing the reference desk to cyberspace. *Library of Congress Information Bulletin, 61*(3/4), 4.

Gutsche, B. (2010, March 1). Coping with continual motion: A focus on competencies can help librarians stick to values while absorbing future shock. *Library Journal*, p. 4.

Hannah, K. (2003). Developing accessible library services. *Library & Information Update, 2*(11), 50.

Harrison, R. (2010). Unique benefits of conference attendance as a method of professional development for LIS professionals. *Serials Librarian, 59*(3/4), 263–270.

Helton, R. (2010). Diversity dispatch: Increasing diversity awareness with cultural competency. *Kentucky Libraries, 74*(4), 22–24.

Holmberg, K., Huvila, I., Kronqvist-Berg, M., & Widen-Wulff, G. (2009). What is library 2.0? *Journal of Documentation, 65*(4), 13.

Huwe, T. K. (2004). Keep those web skills current. *Computers in Libraries, 24*(8), 3.

Jeal, Y. (1996, June). Taking steps to ensure service for all. *Library Association Record, 98.* p. 322–322.

Jeal, Y., Roper, V., & Ansell, E. (1996). Deaf people and libraries—should there be special considerations? Part 1: Traditional library service. *New Library World, 97*(1) 12–21.

Jeng, L. H. (1997). Facilitating classroom discussion on diversity. *Journal of Education for Library and Information Science. 38*(4), 334–339.

Josey, E. J., & Abdullahi, I. (2002). Why diversity in American libraries. *Library Management, 23,* 10–16.

King, D. L. (2007). Basic competencies of a 2.0 librarian, take 2. Davidleeking.com. Retrieved from http://www.davidleeking.com/2007/07/11/basic-competencies -of-a-20-librarian-take-2

Kluegel, K. (2003). Professional competencies for reference and user services librarians: RUSA Task Force on Professional Competencies. *Reference & User Services Quarterly, 42,* 290–295.

Mathews, J. M., & Pardue, H. (2009). The presence of IT skill sets in librarian position announcements. *College and Research Libraries, 70*(3) 250–257.

Mestre, L. (2010). Librarians working with diverse populations: What impact does cultural competency training have on their efforts? *Journal of Academic Librarianship, 36*(6), 479–488.

Michigan Education Association (MEA) (2010). Cultural competence. Retrieved from http://www.mea.org/diversity/

Mon, L. (2009). Questions and answers in a virtual world: Educators and librarians as information providers in Second Life. *Journal of Virtual Worlds Research*, 2(1), 17.

Montiel-Overrail. P. (2009). A conceptual framework for library and information science professionals. *Library Quarterly*, 79, 29.

Moyer, J. E. (2007). Learning from leisure reading: A study of adult public library patrons. *Reference & User Services Quarterly*, 46(4), 66–79.

Moyer, J. E., & Weech, T. L. (2005). The education of public librarians to serve leisure readers in the United States, Canada and Europe. *New Library World*, 106, 14.

Naylor, R. J. (2000, March/April). Core competencies: What they are and how to use them. *Public Libraries*, 39(2), 108–114.

Ontario Public Library Association (OPLA). (2010). Readers' advisory core competencies. Retrieved from https://www.accessola.org/web/OLAWEB/OPLA/RA_Core_Competencies.aspx

Ostrander, M. (2008). Talking, looking, flying, searching: Information seeking behavior in Second Life. *Library Hi-Tech*, 26(4), 13.

Partridge, H., Lee, J., & Munro, C. (2010). Becoming "Librarian 2.0": The skills, knowledge, and attributes required by library and information science professionals in a Web 2.0 world (and beyond). *Library Trends*, 59, 315–335. Retrieved April 28, 2013, from http://eprints.qut.edu.au/39553/1/39553.pdf

Peltier-Davis, C. (2009). Web 2.0, library 2.0, library user 2.0, librarian 2.0: Innovative services for sustainable libraries. *Computer in Libraries*, 29(10), 16–21.

Peterson, L. (1999). The definition of diversity: Two views; A more specific definition. *Journal of Library Adminstration*, 27(1/2), 1.

Press, N. O., & Diggs-Hobson, M. (2005). Providing health information to community members where they are: Characteristics of the culturally competent librarian. *Library Trends*, 53(3), 397–410.

Professional Competencies for Reference and User Services Librarians. (2003). *Reference & User Services Quarterly*, 42(4), 290.

Rios Balderrama, S. (2006). The role of cultural competence in creating a new mainstream. *Colorado Libraries*, 32(4), 3.

Saint-Onge, M. (2009, January). Law librarian 2.0: Building the law librarian of the future. *Library Relations Group Monthly Column*. Retrieved from http://law.lexisnexis.com/infopro/Librarian-Relations-Group/Monthly-Column/archive1-2009

Schmetzke, A. (2002). Web accessibility at university libraries and library schools. *Library Hi-Tech*, 19(1), 14.

Senge, P. M. (2006). *The fifth discipline: The art and practice of the learning organization* (Rev. ed.). New York: Doubleday.

Shearer, D. K., & Burgin, R. (2001). *The readers' advisory's companion*. Englewood, CO: Libraries Unlimited.

Signorelli, P., & Reed, L. (2011, May/June). Professional growth though learning communities. *Americanlibraries.org*, p. 4.

Smith, P. (2008). Culturally conscious organizations: A conceptual framework. http://www.academia.edu/202920/Culturally_Conscious_Organizations_A_Conceptual_Framework

Van Fleet, C. (2008). Education for readers' advisory service in library and information science programs: Challenges and opportunities. *Reference & User Services Quarterly, 47,* 224–229.

Vega, R., & Connell, R. (2007). Librarians' attitudes toward conferences: A study. *College & Research Libraries, 68*(6), 503–516.

Virtual World Best Practices in Education. (2010). Video at http://www .secondlifeupdate.com/news-and-stuff/virtual-worlds-best-practices-in -education-conference-march-12-13-video/

Walling, L. L. (2004). Educating students to serve information seekers with disabilities. *Journal of Education for Library and Information Science, 45*(2), 9.

Watson, D., & RUSA CODES Readers' Advisory Committee. (2000). Time to turn the page: Library education for readers' advisory services. *Reference & User Services Quarterly, 40*(2), 143–146.

Webber, S., & Nahl, D. (2011). Sustaining learning for LIS through use of a virtual world. *IFLA Journal, 37*(1), 5–15. doi: 10.1177/0340035210397137

WebJunction. (2009). Competency index for the library field. Retrieved from http:// www.georgialibraries.org/lib/training/ComptencyIndexLibraryField.pdf

Welburn, W. (1994). Do we really need cultural diversity in library and information science curriculum? *Journal for Education for Library and Information Science, 35*(4), 4.

Woolls, B. (2007). Keeping up: Your personal staff development. *School Library Media Activities Monthly, 23*(8), 56–58.

URLs FOR ORGANIZATIONS MENTIONED IN THIS CHAPTER

King County Library System, http://www.kcls.org/
Michigan Education Association, http://www.mea.org/
New Jersey Library Association, http://njla.org/
Ohio Library Council, http://www.olc.org
Reference and User Services Association (RUSA), http://www.ala.org/rusa/

USEFUL WEB RESOURCES

Designing a 21st Century Road Map for Public Libraries: Tapping Our Inner Futurist. http://lybrarian.wordpress.com/2013/04/26/designing-a-21st-century -roadmap-for-public-libraries/

Levien, R. E. (2011). *Confronting the future: Strategic visions for the 21st Century Public Library.* ALA Office of Information Technology. http://www.ala.org/ offices/sites/ala.org.offices/files/content/oitp/publications/policybriefs/ confronting_the_futu.pdf

PLA Libraries and 21st Century Literacies: Leveraging the People's University. https://www.palibraries.org/?PAF_TaskForce

INDEX

About the Author

Professor ELSIE A. ROGERS HALLIDAY OKOBI, an alumna of the University of Pittsburgh's Library and Information Science and Interdisciplinary Program in Information Science (IDIS) programs, has been teaching graduate courses in the Department of Information and Library Science at Southern Connecticut State University since 1990. Her primary responsibilities are reference, technology and automation, services for adults, and services for underserved groups. Dr. Okobi is a member of the graduate faculty and has served as graduate program coordinator for the department since 2000.

In recent years, Professor Okobi made invited presentations at the Special Libraries Association Annual Conference (1999, 2001, 2003); African Telemedicine Conference, University of Nigeria School of Medicine, Nsukka, Nigeria (2000); Center for African Studies, The Ohio State University (2000); Tropical Disease Research, World Health Organization, Dar es Salam, Tanzania (2001–2002); Connecticut Distance Library Consortium (2001); Hamden Public Schools Conversations on Education (2001); skills training for reference librarians, National Library of Nigeria, Abuja (2006); Bridging the Digital Divide with free Internet Resources, Durban, South Africa (2007); Expanding Library Education to the United Arab Emirates, Abu Dhabi (2008); Skills training for reference librarians, American University of Nigeria (2008); International Conference on Education, Gender & Sustainable Development in the Age of Globalization, Abuja, Nigeria (2009); Quantitative and Qualitative Methods in Libraries (QQML2010) Conference, Chania, Greece (2010); and Introduction to

Internet and E-Resources, Kenya National Library Staff, Nairobi, Theka, Kisumu (2012). She was also appointed to the Connecticut State Library Task Force on Library Services to Older Adults (2003). Dr. Okobi conducted research and interviews for seven entries in the *Dictionary of African Biography* (2011), which was edited by E. K. Akyeampong and H. L. Gates Jr. (Oxford University Press). She is currently conducting research on Ben Enwonwu, a Nigerian sculptor and artist. Dr. Okobi was honored with the Diversity Leadership Development Award from the Special Libraries Association (1999).

43981507R00144

Made in the USA
Middletown, DE
24 May 2017